WITHDRAWN

HARVARD LIBRARY

WITHDRAWN

SEARCHING FOR CULTURAL FOUNDATIONS

Edited by
Philip McShane

UNIVERSITY
PRESS OF
AMERICA

LANHAM • NEW YORK • LONDON

Copyright © 1984 by

University Press of America,™ Inc.

4720 Boston Way
Lanham, MD 20706

3 Henrietta Street
London WC2E 8LU England

All rights reserved

Printed in the United States of America

Library of Congress Cataloging in Publication Data

Main entry under title:

Searching for cultural foundations.

    Includes bibliographical references.
    1. Knowledge, Theory of—Addresses, essays, lectures.
2. Philosophy—Addresses, essays, lectures. 3. Lonergan,
Bernard J. F.—Addresses, essays, lectures. I. McShane,
Philip.
BD161.S38 1984   110   83-23594
ISBN 0-8191-3727-8 (alk. paper)
ISBN 0-8191-3728-6 (pbk. : alk. paper)

CONTENTS

Preface   Distant Probabilities of Persons Presently Going Home Together in Transcendental Process

                     Philip McShane   i

Chapter 1   Middle Kingdom: Middle Man

                     Philip McShane   1

Chapter 2   Report on a Work in Progress

                     Robert Doran   44

Chapter 3   Dialectically-Opposed Phenomenologies of Knowing: A Pedagogical Elaboration of Basic Ideal-Types

                     Michael Vertin   65

Chapter 4   The Human Good and Christian Conversation

                     Frederick Lawrence   86

Chapter 5   Lonergan's Search for Foundations: The Early Years, 1940-1959

                     Frederick E. Crowe   113

Notes: Preface   140
              Chapter 1   148
              Chapter 2   168
              Chapter 3   171
              Chapter 4   185
              Chapter 5   187

PREFACE

Distant Probabilities of Persons Presently[1] Going Home Together in Transcendental Process

Philip McShane

"I thought I saw the fallen flower
Returning to its branch
Only to find it was a butterfly".[2]

To envisage with foundational adequacy that butterfly, the remote third stage of meaning to be called forth slowly by emergent probability, is quite beyond present communal talent. The transposed academy, mediating enriched patterns of commonsense kindness and sincerity through the incarnation of the tandemness of its sufficient differentiations,[3] can be at present only the object of concrete fantasy and religious hope. So it is that the key word and mood of our present title is Searching.

The volume represents, incompletely, the sharing of personal searching by the five authors, and to indicate, in particular, the incompleteness in question is, I think, important, if others are to benefit from our efforts in their own attempts at creative collaboration.

The possibility of collaborating on the issue of foundations was envisaged by us in the summer of 1981. Beginning in that autumn, our group came together at different locations, each time focusing attention on the published work and the personal search of a member of the group. Preliminary to each meeting was the task of entering into another person's search through his published expression. That task was doubly difficult. There was the more evident difficulty of finding time and energy, through an ordinary academic year, to work through material that might seem to be unrelated to the day-to-day struggle to teach and survive the various hindrances to teaching and survival that make up present university life. But the deeper difficulty relates to a meaning of the challenge of searching. That meaning has its ground in what I may call our foundational immaturity.

There is, in fact, no such thing as specialist foundations. Certainly, there are special categories and general categories: but even these can be only delicately distinguished and only mistakenly separated.[4] Specialized categories are no more viable than the engine or the front half of a ship.[5] Now the demands of this position are too much for present theological and philosophical culture. In the first, unpublished, preface to *Insight*, Lonergan defends the work against possible reproach for excessive ambition: "if I may borrow a phrase from Ortega y Gasset, one has to strive to mount to the level of one's time". He goes on to indicate the urgency, complexity and difficulty of that strife, and moves to a stand on the central nucleus of creative collaboration:

> If the extent and complexity of modern knowledge preclude the possibility in our time both of the *uomo universale* of the Renaissance and of the medieval writer of a *Summa*, at least the collaboration of many contains a promise of success, where the unaided individual would have to despair.
>
> Still a collaboration has its conditions. It supposes a common vision of a common goal. It supposes at least a tentative idea that would unify and coordinate separate efforts in different fields. It supposes a central nucleus that somehow could retain its identity yet undergo all the modifications and enrichments that could be poured into its capacious frame from specialized investigations.

The reaching of that central nucleus with its capacious frame, identifiable in its maturity as the *Praxis*, the ongoing use, of the general categories in all functional specialties, is the terrible solitary beauty of Lonergan's achievement. His achievement is a peak; our task is a climb beyond present muscles.

Lest the plain truth of that metaphor be missed it may be well to ponder, by way of illustration, that metaphysics is sublated by foundations, and that an adequate contemporary metaphysics contains an explicitation of the cultural invariants of economic dynamics. In this respect, of course, Lonergan stands uniquely "with it" in this century, and I may recall here at length (since it is unpublished) Lonergan's interesting comment on two of the experts who were scheduled to have essays in the third volume of the Florida Papers:

> Both .... complain that I am not with it. The former would have me align myself more with Marx and Freud and Norman Brown. The latter would want me to think with Marx and Sartre. Neither seems to be aware that I am a child of the depression of the thirties and that I have an as yet unpublished paper on economic analysis as the premise for moral precepts. I agree with Marx inasmuch as I find intrinsic to the developing economy a surplus; I disagree inasmuch as I have no doubt that it is a blunder to conceive this surplus as surplus value; it is to be understood and conceived, not in terms of marginal analysis, but in terms of macroeconomics. Again, I agree with Marx inasmuch as he finds the fact of surplus a source for moral indignation, but I disagree with him on his interpretation of the fact of surplus and on the moral conclusions he draws. Further, I agree with Marx inasmuch as he wants philosophers not only to know but also to make history, but I feel he made a very incomplete rejection of the mistaken efforts of Fichte, Schelling, and Hegel to restore the hegemony of speculative reason that had been attacked by Kant. After all, Marx is only a left-wing Hegelian. He does not really belong to the company of a Kierkegaard who took his stand on faith, of a Newman who took his stand on conscience, of a Dilthy who wanted a philosophy of action, of the personalists and many existentialists of the present century, and of Paul Ricoeur's still unfinished philosophie de la volonte. With such men I am more easily in sympathy than with Jean-Paul Sartre or Norman Brown.

I have digressed on the question of the large difficulty of foundational immaturity, because it was a difficulty that was communicated continually to the group through our collaboration, and so it is a fruit of our search that cannot be sufficiently emphasized, especially in an academy which is endlessly tempted towards the Joycean norm, "sufficient for the day is the newspaper thereof".[7] The first and lesser difficulty, that of the concrete circumstances of our work, remained unchanged after our meetings so that, while glimpses of enlarged foundations were reached through our dialogue, building such glimpses into each of our contributions was beyond immediate time and energy. The five chapters, then, represent substantially what each of us brought to our effort at collaboration. However, I had the advantage, as organizer and editor, and through the circumstances of sabbatical leave, of more prolonged personal effort towards enlargement and integration, and I am venturing in this preface to give what hints I can regarding further personal and collaborative searchings for the foundational implementation of the eightfold <u>Wendung Zür Idee</u> adequate to the initiation of a culture of the third stage of meaning. Here it is appropriate to include an indication of the direction taken by each of us in his contribution.

The order in which the essays appear represents the order of our meetings. My own first chapter was an effort to supply a large heuristic context. It is in open continuity with my previous reachings for a fuller foundational perspective,[8] its central novelty being a conception of modernity as the long phylogenetic period of problematic fragmentation - which has an ontogenetic counterpart significant for an adequate view and achievement of adult growth - between the first and second time of the temporal subject.[9] This heuristic conception resolves the issue of axiality discussed by people like Jaspers, Toynbee, Mumford and Voegelin, in a manner that throws light on Lonergan's composite treatment of the second and third stages of meaning.[10] There is an incidental focus on China in this chapter, related to Voegelin's interest in the Chinese Ecumene: Voegelin's <u>The Ecumenic Age</u>,[11] as will be seen, was inspirational in moving me towards the fuller heuristics of history contained in the chapter.

The fact that the heuristics of the chapter, and indeed of the volume, seem to centre on the northern hemisphere is, of course, merely an accident of focus and of interests. So, for instance, the ancient Roman view, "<u>semper aliquid novi ex Africa</u>", is more profoundly true in our times. Davidson Nicol writes of "...a continent intensely personal, filled with wonderful things, larger than life, only dimly and partially grasped".[12] Moreover, that dim grasp in its depth is closely related to Robert Doran's search in chapter two, and we may enlarge the context of the searchings of our first two chapters by adverting to the vigorous challenge of Leonard Barnes' Africa in Eclipse:

> Because African communities suffer from underdevelopment, the contemporary type-African is a proto-human whose psycho-social evolution has been arrested at a preliminary stage. Because NATO communities are denatured by overdevelopment, the contemporary type-European is an ex-human who, by overshooting his mark, has regressed into sub-humanity. Having squandered his civilized inheritance, he has lost both motive and aptitude for conducting Africans on to the higher ground he has himself deserted.[13]

Regarding African freedom, Barnes remarks:

> There is not much of Locke or Rousseau in it; it owes little to French Revolution or Italian Risorgimento ... They instinctively apprehend that one does not enter society from the outside ... Hence Africans are untouched by the shallow cant of liberal individualism. Formulations such as freedom = absence of restraint, or freedom = presence of opportunity, astonish them by their empty abstraction. They perceive by the light of nature, without having to be told, that human freedom can exist only as a co-operative phenomenon, a group product of a special kind of social order.[14]

Our concern throughout is with a mediating cooperative foundational phenomenon, grounding a transposed and novel kind of social order, and the second chapter focuses on a key feature of what Mumford calls world-cultural humanity. Fr. Doran's concern is to develop a depth psychology integral with Lonergan's intentionality analysis which would make possible an appropriation of religious and moral conversion within the third stage of meaning. His work points towards a humility that is reflectively and psychically possessive of its own nescience, thus grounding the foundational dynamic of an authentic post-modern culture, a central mediation of the search for direction in the movement of life, be that life in the African bush or in Boston. Fr. Doran's invitation is to a difficult integral search for refined personal genuineness constitutive of foundational post-modern adequacy. Both the invitation and the genuineness rest within the "startling strangeness"[15] of critical realism, the primary achievement of which is already no mean task.

Michael Vertin's contribution centres on that primary achievement of intellectual conversion, articulating that conversion in such a thorough fashion as to provide a comprehensive schema of sets of basic suppositions about cognition. He thus articulates not only the fundamental components of the critical realist position but also the varieties of the absence of such components. The essay is an uncompromising acceptance of Lonergan's invitation to "make conversion a topic",[16] spelling out with discomforting precision the possibilities of falling short of the learning, identification and orientation[17] involved in luminous control of the meanings of cognition.

While Lonergan writes explicitly of only three conversions and five generic differentiations of consciousness it is plausible to suppose that there are five generic types of conversion and of differentiation that can be put in loose correspondence. By happy coincidence the five chapters of the volume can also be put into loose correspondence with these generic types of foundational personality development. Michael Vertin, clearly, focuses on intellectual conversion. Fr. Doran's energies have been devoted to thematizing the conversion of the psyche. My own stress is on that shift to authentic nescience that relates to the second level of consciousness which I call theoretic conversion. Frederick Lawrence's essay can be seen as centering on religious conversion. Finally, Fr. Crowe's chapter calls for, and points to, authentic scholarship, and it has occurred to me that such scholarship can be related to refinements of moral conversion. For, authentic scholarship would seem to be a sympathetic openness to the village strangeness of a universe of differentiated persons cradled in sin yet rocked[18] by Divine Love.

Such scholarship is called forth by the pain of <u>oratio obliqua</u> in the presence, however opaque, of infinite conversation. Finally, I would note an asymmetry. Moral conversion and religious conversion are prior to their related refinements. Carmelite mysticism, for instance, presupposes Christian conversion. On the three lower levels of consciousness, however, differentiation is prior to basic conversion: so, for example, one has to devote oneself with lengthy seriousness to understanding electrons, or stones - whatever - before one is moved to theoretic conversion.

Lawrence's chapter seeks a perspective on the mediation by Christian conversion of the reality and the foundational thematic of the human good. He uses Lonergan's structuring of the ongoing dynamics of community as heuristic structure and as newly naming what we are looking for when we ask, "What's the right way to live?". Within that heuristic he locates the contribution and disorientation both of ancient philosophy and of the waves of modern political thought identified by Leo Strauss, to reveal how these orientations have engendered pervasive languages subtly reductive of meaning and value. He sees entry into the conversation that is third-stage repentant Christian conversion as central to the dynamic of appropriating a new foundational language and thus generating a new life-story redemptively beyond the distorting success stories of modernity. Under the dynamic of the Spirit of the Risen Jesus a shift in probabilities is called forth to displace the dominant liberal languages of achievement in favour of the story of one who suffers, dies, rises, befriends. This shift in probabilities is mediated by a third-stage self-luminous Christian foundational framework revelatory of divinity and community as intrinsically conversational.

There is a biographic dimension to these essays which deserves attention in relation to elderhood and the incarnation of general categories in the third stage of meaning. It was a dimension to which we adverted early in our discussions. The basic issue is the dialectic genesis and incarnation of a luminosity of anamnesis and prolepsis in one's odyssey within the Iliad of history. A closely related issue is the nature of discipleship, and we spent some time on the varieties of resentments, biases, neuroses, which exclude open critical discipleship.

One moves towards serious foundational interest, and one reaches a positional ship-shaped adequacy of personal foundations only through discomforting adult growth. That movement is not the call[19] of many: one of our twentieth century difficulties is the assumption of a well-populated democracy of first-rate thinkers; there are, in fact, few Beethovens, and there is nothing wrong with being a second-rate fiddler. But in so far as the movement occurs, that reach and reaching can be expected to take on the character of a multiply-differentiated sensitized search for direction in the movement of biography and history that, in third stage realization, is integrally open, incarnate, poetic. Harold Bloom notes of Yeats: "Yeats most characteristic kind of poem could be called the dramatic lyric of internalized quest ... as though the poet himself as quest-hero undertook continually an odyssey of the spirit".[20] Yeats himself remarked: "why should we honor those who die upon the field of battle; a man can show as reckless a courage entering into the abyss of himself".[21]

Foundations persons, and through their mediation all functional specialists, are called towards, into, and beyond positional authentic subjectivity: the calling is a central life-story, paradoxically both personal biography and total history, and the luminous ingestion of both. So, though it is deeply solitary, it is not the solitariness of "the state of being Blake named Ulro, the hell of the selfhood-communer. The Solitary is in negative quest, in vain flight away from his own creative potential".[22]

In Lonergan one may come to recognize a profound converse of Blake's Ulro, and it is as an aid to this recognition of fidelity to the inner creative potential that Fr. Crowe's essay fittingly concludes our volume. Fr. Crowe does not enter into personal biography, a story of unique dedication to discovering and promoting the discovery of Lonergan and his enterprise.[23] He seeks rather to signpost Lonergan's own slow climb to cognitional foundations. Beginning with Lonergan's studies within the Thomist context, he indicates the manner in which Lonergan moved beyond the language of that context to refine the Thomist solution and move fully into a contemporary context. Fr. Crowe identifies *Insight* as an invitation to exercises, a pragmatic engagement, calculated to yield the core of foundations, and he notes, with Lonergan, that "the foundation to be reached will be no more secure or solid than the inquiry utilized to reach it".[24] He goes on to indicate the emergence both of a deeper interest in the existential subject and of foundations as a theme after the completion of *Insight*, and the manner in which Lonergan envisaged foundations in the late fifties. The foundations of 1959 are not those of 1972 or later, but Lonergan had reached a plateau, a high base camp, which contains his secure cognitional foundations.

At the beginning of his chapter, Fr. Crowe notes that work in this volume "is an effort in a sense to go beyond a point we have not yet reached", and, as I have indicated, his view was a common ground of our collaboration. But I do not think that it is a common assumption among readers of Lonergan's works, and so I am led to prolong this preface first with some reflections on the slow personal growth in foundational meaning, then with some considerations of the remote and massive transformation of science and commonsense[25] that can be mediated only by academic commitment to such slow growth. The first reflections will, I hope, encourage younger people towards a patient critical heartfelt nescience in their search for wholesome meaning, but the reflections will also, I suspect, call forth resentment from some of those belonging to what might be called the Lonergan establishment who may feel that they are in essential control of Lonergan's meaning. What is at stake is a deep discontinuity in the meaning of philosophic growth mediative of cultural discontinuity, and in such a cultural crisis there is, to use Fr. Crowe's words, "need for a measure of bluntness".[26] The brief considerations of transformation with which I conclude aim at giving some concrete impressions of the rich remote discontinuity: hopefully, they will serve as encouragement in the refusal of half-measures. "What will count is a perhaps not numerous center, big enough to be at home in both the old and the new, painstaking enough to work out one by one the transitions to be made, strong enough to refuse half-measures and insist on complete solutions even though it has to wait".[27]

Let me begin by reflecting on the lecture just quoted.

I can still recall the shock of hearing Lonergan deliver it in the summer of 1965. It intimated a massive shift in the meaning of the man. Later, in the early seventies, my wife and I undertook to make typescripts of lectures given earlier in the sixties relating to meaning. One could hear, sense, from the tapes over those years, a change of tone, of embodiment, in Lonergan's expression of his meaning of meaning. Later came the various versions of chapter three of Method in Theology. It is a chapter on which I have lectured for some weeks in perhaps twenty courses during the past decade. I still find its meaning elusive: but then, after twenty-five years of reaching for the meaning of Insight, I find it also elusive.

Now in this discovery and self-discovery I seem to be an oddity. I recall meeting a scholar, after I had grappled with Insight for nearly a decade, and in the course of conversation he claimed that after a year with the book he felt he had a comfortable grasp of its essentials. Again, I was once both amused and surprised at a leading "Lonergan specialist" when I found him disconcerted at my efforts to disclose the meaning of "a flexible circle of ranges of schemes of recurrence"[28] in terms of the descriptive zoology of rabbits in burrows and fields, eating, mating, fleeing etc., within various patterns of sensibility. He had, it seemed, settled for "the plain meaning of the text". Then there was the learned fellow who reacted to my claim that I found metaphysics altogether more difficult than quantum electrodynamics or relativity by asserting that, on the contrary, metaphysics was much easier than physics. And there was the solemn comedian at the Florida conference who asked Lonergan whether he had discovered feelings by reading Scheler: to which Lonergan replied, "I've got feelings too". And so on: anecdotes could be multiplied, for I fear that I write not of exceptions but of a rule. So that I have wondered regularly, in these past decades, what can be going on in these minds, these bones, these lives?[29]

A first level of answer to the question is in terms of nominalisms, fragmentations and sub-differentiations of consciousness, scotomae, anxieties, resentments, biases. A deeper level locates these in genetico-dialectic system as a central feature of the second stage of meaning: primitive and post-modern linguistic meaning have discontinuously better schemes and schedules of probability than the axial millenia of forked tongues. And, of course, that system must be a praxis: the solution to the problem is not a treatise on its expression but a therapy of its roots. Such a praxis is remote. Doran's work pushes forward in one major direction, but gradually a larger enterprise will call on orthomolecular medecine,[30] transcultural reflexology, biorhythmic analysis - including the larger rhythms of water, walkabout, space-poetics - the redemptive transposition of dream and fantasy, sexuality and friendship,[31] the admission of the centrality of theoretic conversion and the mediative thematization of existential metaxic plausibility.

Let us turn from envisaging such remote possibilities of the epiphany and discouragement of nominalism in history to some lighter comments that may help us to discourage the nominalist in ourselves.

Besides anecdotes of tragic individuals there are anecdotes of conference comedy. I resist the anecdotal urge regarding the latter, however, preferring to make one discomforting suggestion. It seems to me that, of those who attend Lonergan conferences, much fewer than 10% have been moved to theoretic conversion and to the strangeness of the contemporary intellectual conversion that it providentially[32] may mediate. The peculiarity of such gatherings, however, is that there lurks in the group the unexpressed assumption that somehow not a few have seen the light of a contemporary critical realism. This, of course, may well be an unwelcome observation: but at least it makes conversion a topic! And I may further decrease my popularity by suggesting that there is a fruitful parallel to be made between The Finnegans Wake Experience[33] and what I would call the Lonergans Wake experience, that there is a lesson to be learned from Roland McHugh.

McHugh's book describes his odyssey with Joyce, and includes some delightfully relevant satirical asides on the rocks and sirens of Joycean studies. So, writing from his background as a specialist in grasshopper acoustics, he remarks, "grasshopper sexuality is primarily acoustic: a female will walk away from a silent male towards a loudspeaker emitting male song.

So each male surrounds itself with a fluid territory which it keeps saturated with its own song. I eventually discovered that professors at James Joyce Symposia behaved similarly".[34] Of a week-long conference in Trinity College, Dublin, consisting largely of papers by American professors with roots in "the early Joycean industry", McHugh writes: "I could smell ignorance of the text ... It was impossible to get down to intelligent discussion of FW at any point during the week".[35]

McHugh later tried a different strategy: the examination of particularly difficult passages by a competent study group. Certainly it is a strategy that those who come together with serious interest in Lonergan's writings might take up: what, for instance, is the praxis called for by the lines and paragraphs of Insight, page 464 or Method in Theology, page 250?

In writing thus about the reading of, or failure to read, Lonergan or Joyce, I am not putting the men and their achievements on a par. For one thing, they operate in different fields of meaning and expression. More important, however, for my present points regarding Lonergan's Wake is Lonergan's heuristic containment, in lagging expression, not only of Joyce but of meaning and expression in its second stage. To Lonergan's writings, Walter Benjamin's law of history, "there is no document of civilization which is not at the same time a document of barbarism",[36] applies in a unique fashion. For Benjamin's law applies with particularly high schedules of probability to the second stage of meaning, and Lonergan's documents are documents of a transition of civilization, a leap forward beyond those schedules. If professors, then, can maul a literary genius of the second stage of meaning, one can expect a massive industry of shrunken linguistic meaning when a genius points to a stage of meaning the glimpse of which requires the discomforting leaps named conversions and the dialectical growth of refining differentiations and feelings.

I would conclude these cautionary notes with two reflections: the first on Lonergan's lagging expression, already mentioned; the second on what I may call Lonergan's Way.

I have noted that Lonergan's writings are documents of cultural, indeed axial, transition. I would further

note, however, that his astonishingly cared-for and
controlled expression is not the language of that later
origination of meaning. Plato's glimpse of the
problematic mediated by theoretic conversion led Plato
only to "a highly literate dialogue".[37]   As Lonergan's
Verbum articles show, in their subtle turn to the
subject, "neither Aristotle nor Aquinas handled the
matter in a triumphantly definitive fashion".[38]   By
the 1970's, Lonergan could write: "at a higher level
of linguistic development, the possibility of insight
is achieved by linguistic feedback, by expressing the
subjective experience in words and as subjective".[39]
But the language of Lonergan's writings was not mediated
by an enlargement of such insight into possibilities of
expression.   It suffers the normal lags of abnormally
creative intelligence.   It lacks the sting of a linguistic envelopment and confinement[40] in a clearer statistics of authentic or inauthentic subjectivities.   It
is merciful to, and at the mercy of, the second stage
of meaning.

Finally, there is the issue of Lonergan's Way.   "Does
Lonergan offer a theory or a way?" was a regular topic
at the Florida conference in 1970.   Perhaps the problem
may be better focused by noting that the issue centres
on the fact that "it is quite difficult to be at home"[41]
in one's odyssey in history.   If it is possible to
illuminate the home and the homegoing, then "that is
something that each one, ultimately, has to do in
himself and for himself".[42]   Lonergan established the
possibility by incarnating its actuality and detach-
edly documenting its dynamics.   Both the incarnation
and the documentation called for the thematic of the
fully contemporary operative integral heuristic structure
of being at home[43] that is a metaphysics sublated by
foundations.   The thematic certainly can be called a
theory if one stretches the meaning of theory.   But the
thematic can be possessed only by going the way "to
discover oneself in oneself".[44]

Lonergan's Way is not Lonergan's nor is it for everyone.
It would seem, however, that it is normative for authentic academic living in the third stage of meaning.
The later stages of modernity are an epiphany of its
need.   It is a "vast undertaking ... that calls for
years in which one's living is more or less constantly
absorbed in the effort to understand"[45] understanding

and meaning. At the centre of that lifestyle is the
darkness of mystery, focused by inverse insight,[46] and
the way remains a climb, so that "late in life, with
indomitable courage, we continue to say that we are
going to do what we have not yet done: we are going to
build a house".[47]

From these few remarks on adult academic growth we move
to some illustrative considerations of the transposition of science and commonsense to be mediated by that
community's growth in the next millenium and beyond.
It is a matter of history moving dialectically forward
out of a fragmented and neurotic adolescence. We will
consider in turn the transposition of journalism, management, education and logic. The considerations, and
their sequence, are not arbitrary, but draw attention
to what may be called the vacuum of the functional
specialties of oratio recta.[48] Up to this point in
the preface I have stressed the remote foundational
achievement of Lonergan as expressed particularly in
the oratio recta of Insight and Method in Theology.
My illustrations intimate, I hope, the wider gap between personal foundational achievement, great or small,
and the richness of the implementation essential to
metaphysics.[49] Thus, journalism's entrapment helps to
lend distant perspective to the heuristics of the specialty of communications; theories and activities of
management draw forth the vacuum for a new systematics;
massive doctrinal alienation in education helps call
us out of a simpler age's view of doctrines. Finally,
logic and its still undiscovered foundations in the
subject may lift us to a suspicion of the fragmented
and truncated logics of foundations operative not only
in every other field of human endeavour but tragically
in that Queen of Science where self's luminous ultimacy
is central.

In my pursuit of some grasp of schemes and patterns of
government, education, oppression in present mainland
China, it was inevitable that I should rely heavily on
varieties of journalism. But the reliance can be
sufficiently tutored to lead one to suspect that there
is a need for a Chinese Chesterton or Kraus.

In its broadest sense, journalism has genera and species
that owe their distinctiveness to different realms of
meaning, different art forms, different cultures and
sub-cultures. Here I wish only to make some few points

regarding printed linguistic meaning informedly oriented to relatively undifferentiated consciousness. The Gutenberg galaxy includes, of course, a massive flow of uninformedly oriented print: even Einstein had the uninformed urge to communicate a mythic essential of relativity that seemed to by-pass the burden of theory, and present theology is regularly doubly uninformed in taking Aquinas less seriously than Einstein did: "<u>cum volo concipere rationem lapidis, oportet quod ad ipsam ratiocinando perveniam: et sic in omnibus aliis quae a nobis intelliguntur</u>".[50]

Present journalism in its usual limited sense, however highly regarded, cannot fall within the third-stage meaning requirement of informedness. So, John Fraser can write, "I do not take the orthodox approach to journalism in China. By instinct and training, I had a predisposition to push beyond observable facts: to me, as a theatre and dance critic, the creative wellspring of any action seemed as important to understand and report as the manifestation of the action itself".[51] But such an interest and a predisposition are a far cry from a painful reaching towards an epochal shift to "the profounder meaning of the name, intelligible"[52] which would call forth slowly the new twists, turns, and tensions of expression that would lift the community into its own mysterious presence.

The difficulty is fortunately[53] deeper. Fr. Crowe has remarked that the twenty-fifth century will look back on our newspapers as we look back now on fifteenth-century slavery. Roger Poole calls, in our philosophic darkness, for new "hierogryphs" to manifest "counter-objectivity" and deep subjectivity.[54] Karl Kraus, the Austrian Chesterton,[55] gave life-witness to his epiphany that "the shouts of newspaper-boys announcing in mysterious vowels latest editions, became monstrous threats to man's spiritual safety or shrieks of anguish from the lowest deep",[56] and his <u>Last Days of Mankind</u>[57] bears massive testimony to the "black magic" of our times:

> Its heroes are troglodytes living in the skyscrapers of history, barbarians having at their disposal all the amenities and high explosives of technical progress, fishmongers acting the role of Nelson, ammunition

salesmen crossing Rubicons, and hired
scribblers tapping out the heroic phrases
of the bards. And there are, on the more
passive and pathetic side, their victims
on active service: farm laborers with a
few weeks of battle training, honest-to-
goodness little people with pensionable
salaries and paid holidays, decent folk
whose imagination is unable to grasp even
a fragment of the horror which they are
commanded to inflict upon the world by
faithfully serving machines, pulling levers
and pressing buttons. And the effects
are registered by men whose imagination
is blunted and whose moral judgment is
corrupted by the insidious poison of jour-
nalistic language which has emptied the
word of all its reality and meaning.[58]

So it is that "never has adequately differentiated consciousness been more difficult to achieve. Never has the need to speak effectively to undifferentiated consciousness been greater".[59]

My task here, however, is the modest one of calling attention to the dimensions of the journey of labour towards the slow emergence in later centuries of a new journalism, mediated by the complex executive reflection of Communications under the eightfold dynamic of method. That labour and dynamic will reach for and promote a quite new literary presence[60] of transposed originating meanings,[61] a carefilled luminous presence speaking biography to biography within history in a language beyond "Oxen of the Sun".[62]

The second illustration of transposition focuses on management. Since the early days of founding father Drucker it has blossomed into a host of specialized fields and journals. Yet there is a sense in which Drucker, almost unknowingly, specifies its study as essentially flawed: "a man who knows only the skills and techniques, without understanding the fundamentals of management is not a manager; he is, at best, a technician".[63] As in journalism, so in management, there is need for the mediation of luminous interiority if it is to escape from being a nominalist technique, a technique moreover at the mercy of the complex of disorientations of modern culture. "As long as one is content to be guided by one's commonsense, to disregard the pundits of every class whether scientific or cultural or religious, one need not learn what goes on in one's black box. But when one moves beyond the limits of commonsense competence, when one wishes to have an opinion of one's own on larger issues, then one had best know just what one is doing. Otherwise one too easily will be duped and too readily be exploited. Then explicit intellectual self-transcendence becomes a real need".[64]

Certain directions of Japanese management, looking to a principle of vagueness,[65] and grounding a "7 - S framework"[66] for reflection on management, may seem to open new doors. But what is needed is the quite different implementation of the transpositional possibilities of what I have elsewhere called the 7 Pillars of Wisdom,[67] and the transformation of the principle of vagueness into a perspective on subsidiarity and authority.[68] Again, the authors of In Search of Excellence: Lessons from America's Best Run Companies have it right when they say "treating people - not money, machines, or minds - as the natural resource, may be the key to it all".[69] And they locate the basic clash involved in apparent optimization: "it is in essence the co-existence of firm central direction and maximum individual autonomy".[70] The issue is luminous personal control: "The necessity of rational control has ceased to be a question, and the one issue is the locus of that control. Is it to be absolutist from above downwards? Is it to be democratic from below upwards? ...".[71] Where Adolf Lowe would speak of capitalized Control[72] I would focus on microautonomy, and the need for an epochal shift in the subtlety of personal control. "Changes in the control of meaning mark off the great epochs in human history".[73]

Yet the above comments are indicative only of the transposition of management from the elementary perspective of Insight. There is the deeper perspective of Method in Theology and functional specialization. Despite a growing awareness in the literature of management as culture-specific, and an increasing problematic of specialized studies much as has emerged in other fields,[74] there is little ground for optimism regarding the early adoption of that deeper perspective. Management is as ancient as building a pyramid or a phalanx, and the late modern period has left it narrowed into a web of conceptualisms, welfarisms, centralisms, illegitimate authoritarianisms. What is needed is not some single contemporary systematics grounding management technique, but a genetico-dialectic Pragmatics between which and actual management in any culture there would lie the mediating specialty of executive reflection. This creative symbiosis of Pragmatics and Communications would concretely contextualize future management within a perspective of third-stage culture that would relativize management structures to particular cultures and stages of development in cultures. Such Pragmatics and Communications have very low schedules of probability of emergence in this century.

From the comments on the transposition of journalism and management it should be evident that the more fundamental shift in education to be envisaged cannot be in simple continuity either with traditional humanist, scientific and technical educational structures or with anti-traditional perspectives that stress ecstasy, openness, non-oppression, crap-detection, deschooling, whatever. Nor are the educational structures of the third stage of meaning manifest from the viewpoint of Lonergan's remote foundations. In a seminar on education, Lonergan, in speaking of art, remarked: "What I want to communicate in this talk on art is the notion that art is relevant to concrete living, that it is extremely important in our age when philosophers for at least two centuries, through doctrines on economics, politics and education, have been trying to remake man, and have done not a little to make human life unlivable".[75] But what might be the methodological doctrines of educational transposition that would mediate the specialties of planning and executive reflection, grounding novel schemes for different cultures and different age-levels in structures of open livabilities? One is made deeply aware of tasks still to be envisaged and undertaken when one pauses, with such questions, over the vacuum that is the <u>oratio recta</u> of the last three functional specialties.

But one may pause helpfully over descriptions of present established counterpositional schemes of education in

China, Canada, Chile: marxist exclusion of the concrete quest of child and adult is matched in the so-called free world by the systematic truncation of educator and educated. Indeed I may usefully recount my experience and short-term strategy in my own small university, no exception to free-world truncation. The university has various departments with child studies as a basic interest that have also in common a far-from-subtle systematic disinterest in the question as datum. Recently I managed to introduce a one-semester course having as title <u>The Child as Quest</u>. Its content conflicts directly, needless to say, with that of the departments mentioned - which at least says something for academic freedom. Early in that course I invite my students - as I invite my readers now - to do an elementary exercise: a "descriptive noticing" of the absence, in the indices of bulky textbooks on Child Psychology etc., of any entry under "Q" (some textbooks do have entries under <u>questionnaire</u>!). Such a descriptive noting is scarcely a beginning, and my strategy is only a thumb in a dyke against the waters of truncation. How does one break the established schemes of recurrence of the self-neglecting educators of educators?

The distant goal is an ongoing genesis of schemes of education with focus not on content in the educated but on quest in all, so that the central educational achievement is a felt epiphany of odyssean grounds in history.

We turn, fourthly, to the transposition of logic: for what locks academics, educators, out from themselves is a massively fragmenting logic of self-neglect.

Lonergan, in his lectures on mathematical logic, notes that Hellmut Stoffer distinguishes six types of logic needed to classify expressed forms of thinking: (1) Plane, (2) Dialectical, (3) Existential, (4) Magical, (5) Mystical, (6) Hermeneutical.[76] Elsewhere, Lonergan draws on Susanne Langer to speak of a logic of aesthetics which would seem to deserve a separate classification.[77] What Lonergan aims at in his lectures on mathematical logic is a foundation of that logic which, as one might expect, grounds logic in the subject luminous to self. But that foundation, Lonergan goes on to say, "is sufficient not only for traditional and mathematical logic, but also for considerations of dialectical, existential, magical, mystical and hermeneutical logic".

Here I wish only to make some concluding comments on what might be called culture-relative eclectic confining logics. An adequate heuristic of such logics would call for the heuristic of the full transposition of logics that Lonergan points to in his notes and lectures on logic, and one may suspect that the corresponding transposition of all logics is remote. The remoteness perhaps becomes more plausible and acceptable through some reflection, both on Lonergan's interest in and discussion of logic, and on logic in relation to the stages of meaning.

Lonergan's interest in logic developed in the late twenties, and I suspect that the article "The Form of Inference",[78] published much later, was a product of this period. It represents a remarkable foundational shift, revealing "the quite different basis of valid inference"[79] which, grasped by the subject in his own performance, can initiate the transposition of plane logic. There is little evidence in the literature that such a beginning is occurring: incompleteness theorems and decision problems in modern logic relate more to mechanization than to mind.[80]

The refinements of Lonergan's view on logic through the decades to follow have still to be traced, but one main point may be made that is centrally relevant to our topic. There occurs a deepening appreciation of the pressure, even within plane logic itself, towards the shift from logic to method: what the history and the metahistory of human searching bring forth is the partially luminous ongoing genesis of methods. Being reflectively at home in transcendental method is simply the integral effort to render that ongoing genesis of procedure luminous, in existential degrees, to proceeding subjects.

Lonergan's fuller perspective makes possible a new contextualization of the development of plane logic in the West. In the conclusion of their standard treatise on that subject, Kneale and Kneale note the necessity in our time "to strive for greater precision in the characterization of logic".[81] But the striving is blocked by truncation. What is needed is the larger perspective, possible only through procedural analysis, of stages of meaning in which the development of logic as it is described by Kneale and Kneale becomes a phenomenon of the second stage of meaning calling for its contextualization by, and characterization in, method.

From the envisagement of such a remote task let us come to a closing comment on eclectic logics, relating them not to the present and future of commonsense, but to present theological and philosophical commonsense, thus closing this preface on the issue of academic searching with which it began.

Commonsense, with its incomplete set of insights and its variety of likely disorientations, operates within a framework of overlapping logics. Insights added to its set are contained by the operative logics and involve no basic horizon shift even when there is manifest cultural shifting: driving a Cadillac instead of a cow is not a leap into theory or interiority. Unless consciousness is compact, it is rarely integral. If it is academic, it cannot be relatively compact without living under subtle mutiny, in anxiety, taking refuge in post-scientific technical literacy or in eclectic scholarship. In theology, despite the less subtle presence as topic of mutinous transcendence, it can settle massively in such refuge in the manner described by Frederick Lawrence: "the paradigm of correlations almost universally adopted by theologians who are not just historians today".[82] So it can generate, with second-stage-meaning obstinacy, "sets of terms and relations that ... do not differ in any fundamental way from the symbol systems that have been characteristic of process theologies within that venerable trajectory that stretches back at least to Pythagoras and comes through the early Christians, gnostics, and Fathers, right down to the speculations of the Kabbalah, Boehme, and Schelling".[83]

We arrive, then, at the scandal of theology's foundational contribution to the inert schemes of opposition to the emergence of the third stage of meaning. What is lacking in the logic of such theological foundations is precisely the foundations of logic. Later transpositions of journalism, business, government, education, logic, will make that lack ever more manifest.

Before concluding, I wish to thank my colleagues in this volume, and those who helped us toward some light on our times. In particular, to the Jesuits of Upper Canada, sponsors of a fund to promote Method Institutes, we send warm thanks for financial support in bringing us together and making this work available.

What I have stressed in this preface is my suspicion that we are only at the beginning of history, that the next million years is on the side of the epiphany of quest and goal. Still, might we not end soon in a nuclear holocaust?

Part of the glory of history is man's envisagement of its schedules of probabilities and possibilities. If the sapling of history is cut down from within, still it can have, within, a vision of the temporal nöosphere that, paradoxically, redeems God. The envisagement is the core of future academic growth: its opposite is an elderhood that is the fraud of being in reality "not old folk but young people of eighteen, very much faded".[84] Our molecules, "our arms and legs filled with sleeping memories",[85] passionately demand that we fly after the butterfly.

> "There the butterfly flew away over the bright water, and the boy flew after it, hovering brightly and easily, flew happily through the blue space. The sun shone on his wings. He flew after the yellow and flew over the lake and over the high mountain, where God stood on a cloud and sang".[86]

CHAPTER ONE

Middle Kingdom: Middle Man

(T'ien-hsia: i jen[1])

Philip McShane

Introduction

> "Your Lord Jesus was na Chinese, heya? Then he is barbarian. And wat for you tell me this Jesus God is na new, when only he was na even born two thousand years ago, heya? This is plenty werry new. Ayee yah, our gods are five, ten thousand years old".[2]

Our topic is "Mind and the Mystery of Christ". From an adequate categorical perspective the topic is equivalently the ongoing discovery of mind and Mind and the Mystery of the Trinity in history. For, the heuristics of Foundations are concrete, providing the inner word of a worldview[3] by which one thinks of the realities of mind and grace[4] within the fullness of the emergent probability of meaning. Nor is the normative demand for such thinking solely an issue of Foundations. "The use of the general categories occurs in any of the eight functional specialties".[5] So, for instance, one is not contemporary in research and interpretation if levels and sequences of expression are not reached for heuristically within the universal viewpoint,[6] itself sublated by the subleties of functional specialization. The dodging of that heuristic reaching constitutes "a sin of backwardness"[7] in theology.

Backwardness in theology has been my concern since 1960, when I moved, from a contemporary world of teaching such elementary science as relativity theory, into a ghetto of common-sense eclecticism where I began my study of the Queen of the Sciences. Serious thinking was no longer required, nor, indeed, encouraged.

I write with that measure of bluntness which Fr. Crowe allowed himself in 1964, and I feel that his rhetorical question has more bite now: "Is there not room for a measure of bluntness at this stage?".[8] So I would hazard that the discontinuity warranted by Lonergan's shift of theological meaning has not yet occurred in a way that would parallel the shift in physics inaugurated by Galileo or that in chemistry associated with Mendeleev. The common-sense eclecticism has changed: instead of Suarez and St. Thomas we have Schillebeeckx and Schoonenberg,[9] and, of course, Lonergan — or Lonerganism.

Generalized empirical method is no more tied to Lonergan than modern physics is Galileanism. It is a precise method that hopefully will liberate theology in the next three centuries as Galileo's method liberated physics in the past three.[10] In the second part of this paper, some aspects of the Chinese search for meaning will be considered, but I cannot resist inviting the reader, at this stage, to sublate one of Mao Tse-tung's strong statements regarding the search for a Chinese Way: "In the social sciences and in Marxism-Leninism, we must continue to study Stalin diligently wherever he is right. What we must study is all that is universally true, and we must make sure that this study is linked with Chinese reality. It would lead to a mess if every single sentence, even of Marx's were followed. Our theory is an integration of the universal truth of Marxism-Leninism with the concrete practice of the Chinese Revolution. At one time, some people in the Party went in for dogmatism, and this came under our criticism. Nevertheless, dogmatism is still in evidence today. It still exists in academic circles and in economic cricles too.

In the natural sciences, we are rather backward and here we should make a special effort to learn ... We must be ready to learn even ten thousand years from now. Is there anything bad about that?".[11]

The Christian, surely, is ready to listen to the natural sciences, part of the history that is revelation, for ten thousand years or more? Or is theology to settle for a metastatic imagination[12] that liberates it from serious worldliness and prolepsis? There is no doubt that the present century has witnessed a shift in the schedules of probability of global non-survival. But the adequate theologian is committed to envisage possible and probable seriations in his or her collaboration with divine providence.[13]

The title of this two-part paper is multiply ambiguous.

Middle Kingdom traditionally means China, but it also means the horizontal metaxy discussed in Part One. Middle Man means Christ, but it also means the Mandarin, the Sage, the Sargawit,[14] the Foundations person. Related to that meaning of Middle Man as sage there is the notion of the Academy, normatively caring for being,[15] as a Middle Kingdom, with its middle men and women mediating the meaning of life and of history to the masses of New York, Nanking, Nairobi. In that context I recall, and will recall later, William Cobbett and his book <u>Advice to Young Men and (incidentally) to Young Women in the Middle and Higher Ranks of Life.</u>[16]

Cobbett sought to mediate larger life to those without leasure by advising those better placed: and so would I. And my summary advice is to seek, over the next decades, the noetic and incarnate presence in history of the foundational categories; not to be caught in the present cult of scared non-knowers,[17] hurriedly scanning the baggage of every theological journal. Mao Tse-tung makes the point well in a speech entitled "Get Rid of the Baggage and Start up the Machinery": "'To get rid of the baggage' means to free our minds of many encumbrances[18] ... 'To start up the machinery' means to make good use of the organ of thought. Although some people carry no baggage and have the virtue of close contact with the masses, they fail to accomplish anything because they do not know how to think searchingly or are unwilling to use their brains to think much and think hard. Others refuse to use their brains because they are carrying baggage which cramps their intellect".[19]

Finally, the title has a personal and less significant meaning: "middle kingdom" refers to a halfway house in a personal search for foundations, named in 1974, <u>Process: A Paideiad</u>[20] and to be articulated in the late eighties. At this halfway stage it seems, as will appear more fully in the conclusion, that I am playing Mao to Lonergan's Marx.

In a related and curious way the paper also focuses on the century ending in 1964, a period of the genesis of new mandarins both in China and in Christian theology. In 1964 Lonergan reached a personal pinnacle in the understanding and sublation of Aquinas' theology of God and Christ, expressed in the Latin treatises.[21] In January of that year, <u>Jen-min jih-pao</u> (People's

Daily) carried an editorial asserting the existence
of a middle world between Western imperialism and the
Communist bloc, a view revised and matured by Mao
Tse-tung in 1974: "in my view, the United States and
the Soviet Union form the first world. Japan, Europe and Canada, the middle section, belong to the
second world. We are in the third world ... With
the exception of Japan, Asia belongs to the third
world. The whole of Africa belongs to the third
world, and Latin America too".[22]

While the staggered differentiations of consciousness
of the globe are clearly an object of the heuristics
of Praxisweltanschauung, this essay restricts itself
to those components of the dialectic genesis of meaning that concern Eric Voegelin in the fourth volume
of Order and History:[23] the achievements and fragmentations of the West; the undeveloped Chinese Ecumene.
The first part of the paper deals with problems of
the truncated West. The second part enlarges on
these problems with an eye on the East, and moves
to the question, "What have the subtle and sublime
insights into the subjectivity of God, expressed
in Lonergan's 1964 writings, to do with a Great Leap
Forward in third millennial China?". But within
that question is a more precise and uncomfortable
question: "When will theologians take seriously
the challenge to contemporary Elderhood in Lonergan's
Great Leap Forward,[24] which oddly[25] coincided with
the Great Leap Forward (1957-62) in China?

Even from this short introduction it should be evident
that this essay does not move on a steady front.
Rather, it forays, noting spoils to be caught by an
eight-fold theology that would meet later times as
Thomas sought to meet medieval times. It has unity,
however, as a foundational enterprize: by random
dialectic it seeks to enlarge the meaning and challenge of Method in Theology, 286-91.

PART ONE

The Fundamental Disorientation
of Modern Inquiry

Goethe's remark, "He who cannot account for three thousand years lives only from hand to mouth",[26] will hopefully be a recognized norm in the academy of the twenty-first century. Our present century will then be revealed in its horrors, its pettiness, its decay: these, not just in the visibility of Germany in the thirties, or America in the sixties, but in the now-hiddenness and massiveness of what Eric Fromm characterizes as necrophilia, the spirit of which was first expressed in literary form in 1909 by F. T. Marinetti in his Futurist Manifesto.[27] In his last great book, in the thirties, Edmund Husserl argued that all significant ideals had vanished from science to be replaced by the conventions of a clique.[28] Eric Voegelin, whose work we will turn to regularly in this paper, recently remarked: "I knew ten years ago that our universities, not only in America but in Europe, were completely rotten: brothels of opinion, no science, nothing",[29] and elsewhere he has noted that when he enters a department in a university he always takes stock of the number of people in it who would condemn him to death in a totalitarian society.[30] The sickness, clearly, is not just a professorial disease. Voegelin has spoken of "the murderous grotesque of our time",[31] of the "public unconsciousness"[32] of these past centuries, of the universality of contemporary paranoia.[33] Bernard Lonergan writes of "the monster that has stood forth in our time".[34] Karen Horney's early work deals with the genesis of the neurotic personality of our time,[35] a genesis not unrelated to what David Riesman has to say about other-directedness as an American sickness.[36] Laurens van der Post writes of contemporary schizophrenia;[37] the Greek scholar Victorina Tejera considers our times as anaesthetized;[38] Hans-Georg Gadamer speaks of "narcotized receptivity".[39] Furthermore, that necrophilia has not totally numbed either the popular aesthetic or common sense. Paul Simon's lyrics of the sixties raise the issue of the viability of "people talking without speaking, people hearing without listening", in "dangling conversations". And the question written on a wall in Belfast in the seventies could be raised in many a city West, East or South: "Is there a life before death?".

So, it would seem that our busy banal times increasingly invite the emergence of two types noted by the elder Carl Jung: the "emphatically normal".[40] and the "optionally neurotic".[41] The emphatically normal jog their way through a busy busy life, cloaking loneliness and lunacy. Flaubert's last great novel, published just over one hundred years ago, Bouvard et Pecuchet, who "look on themselves as serious persons engaged in useful work",[42] caught them perhaps in an anticipatory stride. As Ezra Pound noted, "messrs. Bouvard and Pecuchet are the basis of democracy".[43]

Deep in each of us there is a Don Quixote or a Madam Bovary reaching, as Joyce would say, "to read the book of himself",[44] or herself. Deeper still is the inner Penelope or Flying Dutchman of adult growth.[45] But these reachings and these depths are layered over by a cultural swamp of self-neglect: the sociologist Peter Berger notes that "we become what we are addressed as by others", and we are addressed by truncated subjects, as truncated subjects. "The neglected subject does not know himself. The truncated subject not only does not know himself but also is unaware of his ignorance and so, in one way or another, concludes that what he does not know, does not exist".[46]

Clearly, we have only named the problem, and furthermore, it is paradoxically only a named problem in so far as one begins to try to come to grips personally with the solution.

The massive contemporary truncation has deep historical roots. The roots are not easy to characterize nor is the sickness something easily cured in coming centuries. Voegelin speaks of ideologies as generally persisting for 250 years[47] and here we have the result of an aggregate of ideologies. Jung speaks of the next six centuries as a period of the sprouting of subjectivity.

My catalogue of dark critical response to our present world undoubtedly sounds strange, and indeed some of my readers may add that it rings hollow. Nor is there any sure remedy for this. Fichte once wrote an article entitled: "Sun-clear statement to the Public at large concerning the true nature of the Newest Philosophy. An attempt to force the reader to an understanding".[49] Fichte's hope expresses a basic illusion of modernity:[50] clear statements no more generate understanding than maps generate mountaineers. The point is of central importance and an analogy may help.

In his biography of Beethoven, George Marek writes of the amazing climb into sublety of musical meaning that was Beethoven's life, and remarks of the last quartets: "The quartets carry music to a summit of exaltation and to the deepest depth of feeling ... To probe their variety of mood, sweetness, power, intensity, humor, compassion, assertion of life, a book by itself is needed, one which it would be beyond my ability to write".[51]

Great beauty is a remote height which is perceived as ordinary to unrefined sensibility. Many may find Mozart tuneful but Gustav Mahler's last word was "Mozart!". It would seem, however, that great ugliness too is remote: doubly so, indeed, if that ugliness - as recent psychology suggests - conventionalizes even our childhood dreams[52] so that we emerge as deeply crippled adults. What, then, does the contemplative elder Voegelin mean when he writes: "The perversion of Reason through its appropriation by the mental cases that had already worried Chrysippus has grown, in the modern period of deculturation, into the murderous grotesque of our time?[53] We may suspect that we have little clue.

We are dealing, then, with a remotely characterizable issue of subjectivity both in its deep aspirations and its modern truncation, meshed into the large weave of historical process. That characterization can be reached only by a quite novel type of reading of history, a reading mediated by heuristic interiority. Here we can only hope for an impression of the novel challenge.

My impressionistic treatment will begin with some comments on what has been named the scientific revolution, moving from there in an enlargement of perspectives to come to some envisagement of the historical process, not, however, in the fullness of escatology, but sufficiently to characterize a period of more than three thousand years conveniently called modernity. Following this I would like to touch briefly on problems of contemporary inquiry, problems emerging more particularly in recent centuries, in relevantly illustrative areas such as economics, musicology, criticism, and, finally, psychology.

First, then, let us recall aspects of the scientific revolution. Herbert Butterfield in his book, <u>The Origin of Modern Science</u>, remarks that "since the rise of Christianity there is no landmark in history that is worthy to be compared with" the seventeenth century revolution in science.[54] Immediately after that remark Butterfield begins a chapter entitled "The Postponed Scientific Revolution in Chemistry".

From an adequate heuristic perspective it is not surprizing that chemistry emerges as scientific in the late eighteenth century - for chemical reality is more difficult to understand than physics. The shift of the biological sciences into explanatory perspective was a nineteenth century achievement, but it is noteworthy - and I am not entirely jesting - that Konrad Lorenz got a Nobel Prize in the seventies for discovering that zoology was about animals.

My point, then, is that the scientific revolution did not happen; it is happening, and it is only beginning. Moreover, the beginnings in our time are locked within fragmentations of consciousness, that leave the lower sciences of physics and chemistry troubled with paradoxes and confusions regarding subjectivity, objectivity, imaginability; the middle sciences of botany and zoology committed to a naive reductionism that, instead of explaining, explains away; and the higher sciences in a positivist eclecticism that gives edge to the remark "sociology is the science where people count". Moreover, the technological output from the hierarchy of sciences adds further distortions. So, for example, the lucrative successfulness of the easier sciences, physics and chemistry, leads to the identification of technology solely with their advance, and to a narrow perspective on the significance of objectifications of future insights in the vital sciences, and these sciences, in turn, are so heavily disoriented in their present objectification by profiteering aggrabusiness that Colin Trudge titles his recent book on the subject, <u>The Famine Business</u>.[55]

These fragmentations and disorientations of the scientific and technological revolutions lead us to enlarge our context. In the wake of the medieval philosophical development which ended with the deaths of Thomas Aquinas and Albert the Great, there emerged sequences of systematizations of truncation which contemporarily blinker the entire academic enterprize. The research of Lonergan led him to the view that Kant's unsuccessful struggle was with the mind as conceived by Scotus,[56] and Rene Wellek notes that the range of modern views on criticism derives from Kant.[57] Again, Leo Strauss has documented the influence of Machiavelli, and

Professor Lawrence of Boston College has commented:
"Isn't it a shock to discover that the trajectory
of political thought stretching in one wave from
Machiavelli through Hobbes, Locke, Smith, and in
a second wave from Rousseau, through Kant, Hegel and
Marx is rooted in the Machiavellian option to develop
'realist' views in which theory is adjusted to practice
and practice means whatever happens to be done?".[58]

Scotus systematically excluded understanding's generative role in concepts and thus distorted both man's
view of the Eternal and man's metaprocedures in these
past centuries. Machiavelli systematically excluded
transcendent values from historical practice and so
set the stage for contemporary political theory and
practice. Modern structurings of education devotedly
merge both oversights.

In the second part of this paper the place of Christianity in the historical process will be considered.
Here, however, I wish to move to the problem of envisaging total history as posed by Karl Jaspers. It is
the much larger context which would envisage 2,000
million more years of our biosphere,[59] a context which
can ground Jasper's remark, "We are just setting out".[60]
It is a context in which the sorry state of modern
economics can be seen in the new light of the inevitable
presence and pedagogy of the economic rhythms of the
next million years.[61]

Jaspers, in his The Origins and Goals of History, places
a basic axis of history in the period between 800 and
200 B.C. when man reached significant differentiation
in Greece, Persia, Israel, India and China.[62] In the
context of a later discussion of contemporary culture,
he raises the question of a second Axial Period.[63]
Toynbee took issue with Jaspers in his last work,
Mankind and Mother Earth: "It would be misleading to
set a chronological limit to the Axis Age that excluded
those two mighty epigoni (i.e., Jesus and Muhammad)
of Zarathustra and 'Deutero-Isaiah'. Thus the Axis
Age expands from a period of about 120 years to one
of about seventeen centuries running from c.1060 B.C.,
down to A.D. 632, which is the date of the Prophet
Muhammad's death".[64]

In the fourth volume of his projected six-volume work,
Order and History, entitled The Ecumenic Age, Eric
Voegelin moves to a fuller view of the historical

process which broadly resembles the one presently proposed. A central feature of Voegelin's view is his emphasis on the "In-betweenness" of human existence, to which he gives a Platonic name, the Metaxy. The emergence into consciousness of that tension of "In-betweenness" he associates primarily with the noetic differentiation of consciousness in the Greek tradition and the pneumatic differentiation of consciousness in the Hebrew tradition. For reasons that will appear shortly, I am led to rename this "In-betweenness" of historical reality, constitutive of its mysteriousness,[65] the Vertical Metaxy.

Clearly, Voegelin would consider this emergence into consciousness as in some sense axial, but it seems to me that the key to the resolution of the debate regarding axiality lies in his recurring questioning of the meaning of modernity. So, in noting the parallel falsifications of history in the Sumerian King List and Hegel's Philosophy of History, Voegelin is led to query: "And what is modern about modern mind, one may ask, if Hegel, Comte, or Marx, in order to create an image of history that will support their ideological imperialism, still use the same techniques for distorting the reality of history as their Sumerian predecessors?".[66] In a later context he remarks: "A 'modern age' in which the thinkers who ought to be philosophers prefer the role of imperial entrepreneurs will have to go through many convulsions before it has got rid of itself, together with the arrogance of its revolt, and found the way back to the dialogue of mankind with its humility".[67]

I might bring his remark nearer our academic home by noting Leo Strauss' related view of contemporary academics as liontamers.[68] The liontamers and imperial entrepreneurs cannot indefinitely dodge the convulsions of adequate differentiation of consciousness.

To give sufficient meaning to the word "modernity" I would recall the meanings of the classical Latin word "modo", "merely", "just", "directly", and the derived medieval word "modernitas", "present-dayness". I would recall, indeed, the extreme presentmindedness quipped at by Joyce in Ulysses: "sufficient for the day is the newspaper thereof".[69] What is going forward, I suspect, in a period of fragmented consciousness that I would call modern, is a transition between what Lonergan calls the two times of the temporal subject:

a prior time dominated by a spontaneity found best in compact consciousness, a later time with at least a dominant authority[70] of the mediation of generalized empirical method.[71] The prior time, too, can be associated with Lonergan's first stage of meaning; the later time with the third stage of meaning. Then one may expect the transition period to be one of fragmentation and specialization of consciousness in opaque forays into the second stage of meaning, with concomitant unenlightened displacements of the control of meaning out of historical compactness. Within such forays and displacements is the problematic that invites a mediating integration of hard-won genuineness in the noosphere.[72]

This middle kingdom of historical reality needs to be mediated to academic subjectivity by something resembling what Jaspers would call Existenz in communication with Existenz.[73] It leads to a psychological presence in what I would name the Horizontal Metaxy. Psychological presence in the Vertical and Horizontal Metaxies would be the modern counterpart of the reaching of the Classic experience of reason, as described by Voegelin, towards man as self-appreciatively social and historical wonderment.[74]

Presently, we will relate these reflections, in an enlarged context, to the future both of China and of Christology. But it seems good at this stage to take stock of some fragmented and opaque academic forays in the recent West, lest it appear that there is nothing more here than a new Sumerian King List.

Alfred Eichner, in the preface to a recent book, introduces the issue in current economics with discomfortingly homely realism: "late in the day, after they have had two or three drinks, many economic professors will begin to admit to their own reservations about the theory which forms the core of the economic curriculum. The Theory, they will acknowledge, is at odds with much that is known about the behaviour of economic institutions. 'But what else is there to teach our students?' they will ask".[75] Nicholas Kaldor looks back in history to locate with remarkable precision where economic theory were wrong. In the Economic Journal of 1972 he writes: "The difficulty with a new start is to pinpoint the critical area where economic theory went astray ... I would put it in the middle of the fourth chapter of Vol. I of The Wealth of Nations ... in (that) chapter, after discussing the need for money in a social economy, Smith suddenly gets fascinated by the distinction between money, price, real price, and exchange value and from then on, hey presto, his interest gets bogged down in the question of how values and prices for products and factors are determined. One can trace a more or less continuous development of price theory from the subsequent chapters of Smith through Ricardo, Walras, Marshall, right up to Debreau and the most sophisticated present-day Americans".[76] Leon Walras' economic statics of the 1870's,[77] influenced by a notion of general equilibrium derived from an engineer,[78] dominates economic thinking in this past century. Whatever was of value in Marshall and Keynes evaporated in the simplification, the IS/LM analysis, proposed by John Hicks in 1937.[79] Hicks' view is the backbone of modern textbooks in economics, especially in Canada and the United States.[80]

There is, indeed, another tradition of economic thinkers interested in economic dynamics: one may recall Clement Juglar,[81] Karl Marx,[82] Wesley Mitchell,[83] Joseph Schumpeter,[84] Michael Kalecki,[85] Adolph Lowe.[86] Currently accepted economic dynamics, however, is not related to this tradition: it is, rather, a complex mathematics of fairyland assumptions that calls not for well-behaved people but for well-behaved functions. It has been solidly critized by Joan Robinson for decades,[87] but such luminaries as Samuelson and Solow still hold the chair of Moses in a way that will eventually make those who clung to the phlogiston theory two hundred years ago appear open-minded.

I have dealt with the needed transformation of economic theory at some length elsewhere.[88] Here I can only note its continuity with the present issue of adequate psychological presence in history. The main body of present economic theory is trapped in a conceptualist systematics not uninfluenced by Scotus and locked within a larger Machiavellian axiomatics of successful procedure and within a still larger neglect of the pedagogy of history and of the possibilities of an innovative human future. Adolph Lowe, preoccupied for fifty years with the problem of economic growth, recently produced <u>The Path of Economic Growth</u>, which contains some elements of a concrete economic dynamics, but with a focus on the need for <u>Control</u>[89] to implement it, a control continuous with <u>the</u> power-structure of the Ecumenic Age. Nor can one foresee

alternate structures of control without the personal
transition to luminous microautonomy[90] to which the
historical process modernly invites. Moreover, the
powerstructures of truncated modernity ground the
practical impossibility of the communal analysis
and implementation of Humanomics[91] with its mesh of
rhythms of creativity, innovations, take-offs, and
dynamic equilibria within the conditioned schemes
of recurrence of an emergent probability of standards
of human meaning. Negatively speaking, only within
the perspective of a subtle appreciation of the self
in history can there emerge a clear-eyed critique and
dismantling of power, centralization, welfarism,
monopolies, paternalism, planning, empire. The total
issue is massive in its challenge to the entire academy to rise out of a present necrophilia which
systematically cultivates truncation. But it is
also massively personal in its elemental invitation
to ask with felt scientific seriousness, "Who am I?".

However, broad neglected features of economic dynamics
need not rest in obscurity even for truncated subjects,
and so I am led to a homely illustration. Envisage,
then, an isolated island community, with a non-horse-
power technology. Envisage some sub-group grasping
the innovative idea of the plough, with horse, oxen,
whatever. Insofar as the sub-group carries the
community towards the realization of a plough culture,
there occur definite fluctuations in the exchange
economy (inclusive of banking, etc.) of the island.
The fluctuations are associated with the fact that,
for a period, energy and money are being devoted to
the carpentry, tannery, horse-training, etc., which
is to make concretely possible the plough culture.
What is evident is that the community is building
towards a period of higher consumption, greater
leisure. Less evident are the fluctuations in the
flow of finance on the island required to make the
innovation possible and eventually to make increased
consumption a reality. But, clearly, one may note
an initial period of reorientation of present resources
preparatory to the emergence of a new aggregate of
capital ventures associated with horse-ploughing;
there is a following period when production of horse-
ploughs is underway, accelerating, gradually levelling
to the demands of maintenance and replacement; there
is the later period when the benefits emerge in consumption goods and better times.

Of course, this rhythm of evolution internal to the productive process calls for human adaptation, ideally human adaptation grounded in microautonomy, educated to an unusual perspective on what constitutes success.[92] The human adaptation can be lacking: the sub-group may want the Linus blanket of extra money mistakenly called profit. They may add woodworms to the plough; they may advertise the myth of the necessity of a new plough every year; they may turn to persuading neighbouring islands of fruit-gatherers that they too need ploughs; they may find ways to benefit from taxes imposed on origin or destination principles; they may eventually have the fruit-gatherers making cheaper ploughs; and so on. More profoundly evil, they may generate an economic theory which gives their mistaken notions of profit and success an axiomatic status.

I have been drawing attention here to rhythms of economic progress within the larger passion of a history governed from below by an emergent probability of complex schemes of meaning and from above by the dynamics of Absolute Transcendence. Let me turn now briefly to human inquiry into other rhythms, those of music. I do not wish to speak directly of music, although I would note in passing its present importance. Especially true of it is what Lonergan once expressed in a talk on art in a seminar on education: "What I want to communicate in this talk on art is the notion that art is relevant to concrete living, that it is extremely important in our age when philosophers for at least two centuries, through doctrines on economics, politics and education have been trying to remake man and have done not a little to make human life unlivable".[93]

I wish here only to indicate summarily a previous treatment of the need to move scientifically from truncation in the field of musicology if that field is to rise out of its present confusion.

Writing in the journal Perspectives of New Music, David Levin remarks: "What is needed to clear the air is first an exposition of the nature of and relations among theory, analysis and criticism, then secondly, an examination of the pertinence of all this to compositional procedure".[94] The journal I have just quoted from is typical of the confused searchings and incomprehensions of contemporary musicology. In another volume, in an article entitled "Some Current Terms", Ernest Krenek writes of his failure to penetrate the meaning of an essay by Babbitt on "Twelve-tone invariants" and says, "I am afraid that the use of this language in Perspective has reached a point of diminishing returns: the possible increment of scholarly prestige (not to speak of snob appeal) is compensated by the loss of communicability".[95]

Again, Alan P. Merriam points to the need, in the field of ethnomusicology, to "revise our own thinking"[96] if the apparent gap between anthropology and musicology is to be bridged, and elsewhere he touches on the deeper question: "It is clear that only through the fusion of these aspects of knowledge, and probably in single individuals, that the problem will be solved. If this is the case, and if the fusion is the goal, are not the problems insurmountable? Is there any hope of putting together the humanities and the social sciences, areas of study which are considered poles apart? Is there any means of treating the social sciences humanistically, or the humanities in terms of social science?".[97]

Illustration of confusion and conflict could be multiplied indefinitely, in compositional theory, in music history, in criticism. But the core issue throughout is the issue of procedure. If one has no foundational appreciation of what it is to compose, to do history, to adequately appreciate, then one is allowing a central opaqueness to persist in one's enterprize. It is the same opaqueness which makes most interdisciplinary work a nominalist endeavour. It is the central opaqueness whose root is truncation. The neglected musical subject does not know himself; the truncated musical subject not only does not know himself but does not know that the musical subject is unknown.

Still, the crises and disorientations here, as in economics, have the positive aspect of inviting the blossoming of music and musicology in the third stage of meaning. Pierre Boulez, in an article in which he asks the Sonata to tell him what it wants from him, draws on the self-reading oddity of Mallarmé and Joyce, and seems to grope towards a glimpse of such a transition when he writes, regarding Finnegans Wake: "It is not only that the way the story is told has been upset, but also that the novel, if one dares to put it this way, observes itself as a novel, reflects on its own image, becomes aware that it is a novel; and this results in a logic and cohesion of this technique that is constantly on the alert, creating new universes. It is in this way that music, as I see it, is not destined solely to 'express' but must become aware of itself, become an object of its own reflection".[98] If art is normatively the objectification of metaxically-released experiential patterning, then third-stage meaning art will reach for metaxic echoes of luminous subjectivity beyond present fantasy. Joyce's episode in <u>Ulysses</u>, entitled "Oxen of the Sun", symbolizes the reality of our immaturity as human in its movement through the history of English to end with a babel and a birth: in some profound sense we have not yet begun to speak.[99]

I have already indicated a grounding in subjectivity of a criticism of economics, and now an apparently quite different field of music criticism has been touched on. But the profoundly discomforting feature of these issues in our times is that they must merge in a total concrete dialectic if any one of them is to be adequate, and that dialectic is integrally theological and philosophical.

Churchmen and theologians find this an inconvenience, for it seems legitimate, and certainly it is easier, to criticise and advise on the basis of vague moral and religious principles. Again, philosophers of science regularly prefer to criticise science in abstraction from science. And so, Margaret Masterman, in a volume entitled <u>Criticism and the Growth of Knowledge</u>, rightly remarks: "the one thing working scientists are not going to do is to change their ways of thinking because they have Popper and Feyerabend pontificating at them like eighteenth century divines; particularly as both Popper and Feyerabend normally pontificate at even more than eighteenth century length".[101] Again, aesthetic criticism tends to be specialist, sometimes moreover with such a degree of detachment as to exclude the relevant aesthetic experience. So, perhaps, it is not without grounds that an Irish playwright remarked when asked what he thought of critics, "does a lamppost like dogs?".

More seriously, in a recent essay entitled "Fear and Trembling at Yale", the Chairman of Northwestern's English Department, took to task the Yale critics with some quotably spicy words: "Most of us do not associate the practice of academic literary criticism with intense suffering. We think of the professor-critic as a man reasonably well paid for a life of teaching ... writing ... going on sabbaticals, drinking Chivas Regal etc., etc ... But we have little idea of the pain and anxiety, the risk and torment that the serious literary critic has to live with. Some of these critics themselves feel that reading ranks in risk and danger with race-car driving or airplane hijacking".[102]

However, I would note that literary criticism in recent decades is rich in drawing attention to a need for fundamental reorientation. So, Crane's Chicago School pushes for methodological reflection, the Geneva School draws attention to the centrality of consciousness, and Paul de Man indicates the basic need in his book Blindness and Insight: "From the start, we have at least four possible and distinct types of self: the self that judges, the self that reads, the self that writes, the self that reads itself. The question of finding the common level on which all these selves meet and thus of establishing the unity of a literary consciousness stands at the beginning of the main methodological difficulties that plague literary studies".[103]

I would like now briefly to illustrate that problem of the self that reads itself by drawing attention to a particular instance of literary study, the study of Flaubert's Emma Bovary.

Eric Auerback in his study of Bovary concentrates on the key paragraph where Emma and Charles are at table and " ... all the bitterness of life seemed to be served to her on her plate". Of this latter phrase Auerback remarks, "Flaubert does nothing but bestow the power of mature expression upon the material which she affords, in its complete subjectivity".[104] But what does Auerback mean by Emma's complete subjectivity? George Poulet finds Auerback "not completely satisfactory", and tackles the same paragraph with a metaphorical notion of consciousness as concentric circles unifying interior distance. Neither critic is adequately reading the self. Neither

critic is taking with sufficient seriousness
Flaubert's statement: La Bovary, c'est moi". Without serious self-attention the structure of Emma's
consciousness remains opaque. Emma's consciousness,
unrevealed to her, but spontaneously operative, was
an immanent structured reach for "her dreams dropping
in the mud",[106] for the fragrance of the eau-de-cologne
that Bovary Senior used up at the Christening,[107] for
the "I understand",[108] however, mistaken, in relation
to Rudolfe, for the twisted truth reached when "She
knew now the littleness of those passions that art
exaggerates",[109] for the clouded value imprinted in
those late words to Charles, "You are a good man".[110]

Finally, however, the challenge of this paper and of
modernity is not to discuss Emma Bovary's consciousness but to discover our own by a slow discomforting
process which might be characterized by Camus'
statement "It takes ten years to get an idea".

Such a slow discomforting process is as remote from
fashionable consciousness-raising, or nominalist
Lonerganism, as turning on a light is from inquiry
into the self-energy of the electron. It is a shift
into a third stage of meaning and authority and control
that is beyond present fantasy.[111] It is a shift
that is especially blocked by an academic culture
which tolerates the systematic exclusion by the human
sciences and their educational offshoots of scientific
interest in the conscious questing self, so that a
substantial academic contribution to present deranged
schemes of living is made by those, to use Voegelin's
words, who "aggressively claim for their mental disease
the status of mental health",[112] and who maintain a
distinction of human studies from physics or chemistry only by smuggling across the borders of their
apparently objective method inadequate descriptions
of their own data of consciousness.

Voegelin is modestly optimistic when he remarks:
"Man cannot live by perversion alone. Parallel with
the culmination of the grotesque in Hitler, Stalin,
and the orgy of the 'liberation rabble' after the
Second World War, there has also grown the awareness
of its pathological character.

In the nineteenth century, it is true, Schelling had
already coined the term 'pneumopathology' when he had
to deal with the Progressivism of his time, but until

quite recently it would have been impractical to treat the 'opinions' which dominate the public scene as psychopathological phenomena ... It would not be surprizing if sooner or later psychologists and social scientists were to find out about the classic analysis of noetic existence as the proper theoretic basis for the psychopathology of the 'age'".[113]

But with a profoundly disoriented political, economic, military and academic establishment short-term optimism is unfounded. What prevails is Maslow's statistic "less that 1% of adults grow",[114] so that we will come into the twenty-first century without Elders of authority to oppose the neurotic elders of Global Reach. Maslow's disciple, A. R. Aresteh, has remarked: "Unless the psychologist has himself experienced the state of quest for final integration in the succession of identities he will hardly acquire an understanding or incentive for doing research on it".[115] The quite different dynamic of personal development needed can only emerge with the shift from the sparkle of public power to the preciousness of private authority, a shift requiring a recklessness so well focussed by W. B. Yeats: "Why should we honor those who die in battle? A man can show as reckless a courage entering into the abyss of himself".[116]

PART TWO

"Let a Hundred Flowers Bloom"[117]

> "He tore the flower gravely from its pinhold smelt its almost no smell and placed it in his heart pocket. Language of flowers. They like it because no-one can hear".[118]

In 1864, Li Hung-chang addressed a memorial to Prince Kung in Peking, of which the central message was "We should create a special branch of the mandarinate".[119] What was at issue was the opening of Chinese traditional education to Western technical, military, legal and political structures. The century since has been, in the main, a dialectic and superficial absorption of European varieties of truncated development. In 1964 the Chinese disciples of Marx could write of the drive towards full Communism: "Success requires anywhere from one to several centuries. On the question of duration, it is better to prepare for a longer rather than a shorter period of time. On the question of effort, it is better to regard the task as difficult rather than easy".[120] In the same year, a quite different manifesto appeared in Rome, <u>De Deo Trino</u> and <u>De Verbo Incarnato</u>, pinpointing the two times of the temporal subject and locating the autonomy of that subject radically beyond the power of the party, the planner, the profit-seeker, in the Vertical Metaxy: "subordinata quidem est autonomia conscientiae humanae, non tamen omnibus et quibuscumque objectis, sed subjecto infinito ad cujus imaginem facto est et quod imitari tenetur".[121] Not Control within transient empire but microautonomy within historical Mystery is the normative reality of humanity.

I have raised the issue of new mandarins, Foundations persons, before, and the present discussion is continuous with those previous searchings.[122] The Foundations person is one who strives to climb the mountain to elderhood named on pages 286-91 of <u>Method in Theology</u>. That striving involves the crossing of bridges.[123] In particular, there is the bridge of Imps, inviting the Sargawit, the Foundations person, and mediately every theologian and academic - since these are normatively committed to the movement of life within the general categories - to an envisagement of Total Process. "Only when and where the higher rational culture emerged did God acknowledge the fullness of time, permitting the Word to become flesh and the mystical body to begin its intussusception of human personalities and its leavening of history".[124] The present concern is to enlarge the challenge of the bridge of Imps, the challenge to envisage with heuristic adequacy the possible, probable and actual seriations of intussception on the global scale. "Theologians, let alone parents, rarely think of the historical process",[125] and so an invitation to so think may be an "unwelcome message. Foundations persons are mischievous, trouble-makers. They 'make conversions a topic': or bridges. But they may also appeal to the archaic meanings of the word 'imp': to implant, graft; to repair; to furnish with wings. This bridge cannot surely be too far if its grafting into the vortex of method could furnish with wings the task of transforming the global network of neurotic aggressions and greeds with larger novel patterns of kindness and success and hope".[126]

One undoubtedly has to flex one's molecules and mind to envisage within emergent probability the disappearance of the dinosaurs 65,000,000 years ago and the demise of the American Empire's centralized business and government.[127] One requires, for instance, a shift in geographical and historical perspective. "The habitable dry land surface of the biosphere consists of a single continent, Asia, together with its peninsulas and off-shore islands ... The three largest of Asia's off-shore islands are Africa and the two Americas".[128] Again, "the temptation to hypostatize historically passing societies into ultimate subjects of history is strongly motivated. At its core lies the tension, emotionally difficult to bear, between the meaning a society has in historical existence and the never quite repressible knowledge that all things that come into being will come to an end. A society, one might say, has always two histories: (I) the history internal to its existence and (II) the history in which it comes into and goes out of existence. History I is greatly cherished by the members of a society; History II encounters emotional resistance and preferably should not be mentioned".[129]

Voegelin's volume, The Ecumenic Age, raises magnificently the issues of History II, and in his concluding chapters he moves through a consideration of the Chinese Ecumene to a reflection on the problem of Universal Humanity. He is at present working on a fifth volume of Order and History. In this short essay I can make no attempt at summary presentation: I can only assume either that the challenge of Voegelin's volumes has been taken, or that the concern for general and special categories expressed here will lead the reader to undertake it. What I seek immediately is to give pointers towards the sublation of Voegelin's work into the larger heuristic of what I have called elsewhere an adequate Praxisweltanschauung. For that Praxisweltanschauung, the skeletal structure of whose eight-fold way is generalized emergent probability, it is not true that "a plurality of ecumenes presents formidable problems to a philosophy of history".[130] The empire of the t'ien-hsia belongs to probable seriations, and is evidently actual.

Voegelin contrasts the completeness of the Hebrew-Christian pneumatic breakthrough and the noetic breakthrough of the Greek tradition with the incompleteness of the Chinese breakthrough into the fundamental tension-in-existence. The contrast is legitimate but refinements are in order. I will first make some points regarding the Western tradition before turning to possibilities and probabilities within the Chinese tradition in the context of a noetic Trinitarian theology.

If Voegelin breathes Lavoisier's oxygen into Hegel's upsidedown phlogiston history, then Lonergan stands as Mendeleev. Recall the issues raised in Part One of this essay: Butterfield's comments on the scientific revolution; the genesis in these early days of science of the problematic of the opaquely proceeding subject invited by science to ask the meaning of "what" and "is" and of the total self proceeding modernly; the pointers in modernity to the grounds in self of an eight-fold "interpretative reconstruction of the constructions of the human spirit";[131] the question of the mediation of the passing of the middle kingdom of modernity through the luminous abyss of neuro-aspirative self-appropriation. Such issues find heuristic system within an open foundational space-time tabulation of differentiations of consciousness. Voegelin does not live noetically within that heuristic system, but manifests his greatness in the shift of elder perspective of his fourth volume, a shift involving a recognition of differentiations of consciousness.

Later I will have something to say about the psychopathology of common-sense eclecticism, drawing on Voegelin and Lonergan. However, prior to further comment on elements of an adequate heuristic, it would be well to raise briefly the question of living noetically and incarnately within that heuristic system.

Just as a first-year chemistry student can learn to name and order the hundred odd elements using Mendeleev's system, so a year's reading of <u>Method in Theology</u> can leave one comfortable in naming four levels of consciousness, thirty-one generic types of differentiation of consciousness, eight more subtle differentiations underpinning functional specialization, and so on. But can the first year chemist present pedagogically the relativistic quantum analysis of the spectrum of hydrogen? Is the budding dialectitian capable of talking with any precision of the ordered aggregate of books anticipated by page 250 of Method in Theology? The parallel is telling but it does not bring out the deeper human and cultural difficulty: a few more years will leave the brighter chemist capable of teaching recent understandings of chemical realities, but "being at home in transcendental method"[132] seems a task for elders of a later age. And even what may appear to be initial steps in that task generally take more than a few years for the brightest.

I wish now to turn to such initial steps of the task in relation to a central topic of Voegelin, the tension-in-existence mediated by noetic and pneumatic differentiations of consciousness. My purpose is to be suggestive rather than exhaustive, though my suggestions, if taken up seriously, will prove exhausting.

Voegelin returns to these illuminating events of the Hebrew-Christian and Greek traditions in his concluding chapter, where he again raises the issue of Absolute Epoch or Axis-time: "The 'absolute epoch', understood as the events in which reality becomes luminous to itself as a process of transfiguration, is indeed the central issue in the philosophy of history".[133] I have already qualified the notion of axial time by introducing the empirically-plausible notion of a horizontal metaxy. Further qualifications are now in order. First of all, the core source of tension-in-existence in material finitude is the presence of the dynamism of mind. Secondly, the central issue in a philosophy of history is the ongoing discovery and incarnation of mind. That ongoing relevation and molecularization of intelligible processions and their source is what underpins the variety of differentiations of consciousness with their mediation of the movement both towards the eccentric emergence of Foundations persons uncomfortably at home in increasingly refined ranges of schemes of modern existential tensions and towards the later genesis of adequately reflective elder communities of third stage meaning grounding integrity in lesser differentiated consciousnesses. The flexible circle of ranges of schemes of recurrence in which the cultured modern lives, can include any or many of a variety of dialectically and genetically related existential tensions relevant to personal and communal growth, and Voegelin's "tension-in-existence" can be considered a generic description calling for a genetico-dialectic systematics of such modern tensions.

A present envisagement of such a systematics would seem to require fantasy, since the systematics would sublate, on the skeleton of the general categorial explanatory structure of emergent probability, both the history of psychology and the psychology of history, and include not only the subject's own growth, but the growth of the subject's own view of personal and historic growth in the measure of the differentiations of the subject and history. The challenge of such a future systematics is towards integral detached personal search into a search for psychic wholeness and for an ever-larger but never adequate psychic presence in history. Never adequate, and perhaps sensed as such: for there is a bridge of Straws; yet ever gently open to surprizing growth in meaning and meaning history: for there is a bridge of Oxen, genetic in fantasy of a grounded Futurist Manifesto which bone-wise but darkly acknowledges that one's molecules resonate in the symphony of history. It results in the enlarged humility within history of which Voegelin writes, and it turns academic power into academic authority, reversing the delusions which Leo Strauss identified: "The facile delusions which conceal from us our true situation all amount to this: that we are, or can be, wiser than the wisest men of our past. We are thus induced to play the part, not of attentive and docile listeners, but of impressarios or lion-tamers".[134] One is invited to a post-modern movement of life in integral heuristic attention to nature, man and God, for "man is nature's priest and nature is God's silent communing with man".[135]

I wish shortly to consider in strategic order four basic tensions-in-existence and three related psychopathologies. Before doing so, however, an enlarged impression of the varieties of tension-in-existence may invite in the reader a more vibrant response to the concreteness of the personal challenge.

So, there is the tension-in-existence, in developed

or incipient form, which may be called mystical. It is normally genetic of other tensions: "There's the effort to say what's happening, to find out what's happening: 'Am I going nuts?'". People with that experience are profoundly disturbed and they can be very apprehensive".[136] The secondary tension can be aesthetic or dramatic, but with a noetic core. That core noetic tension can lead contemporarily to issues of transcultural interiority, as in William Johnston's The Inner Eye of Love.[137] In an earlier culture it reached for a theoretic theology, as in St. Theresa of Avila's preference for a learned rather than a pious director. In a simpler culture, the incarnate noetic drive may blossom in telling metaphor: so, Dame Julian of Norwich could claim, "He shewed me a little thing the size of a hazel nut, in the palm of my hand, and it was round as a ball. It is all that is made. It lasteth for ever and ever shall, because God made it: God loveth it: God keepeth it". But the blossoming may remain, especially in community, in the silence of enlivened repetition, so that They Speak By Silences.[138] It may have the primitive expression of Akhenator (14th century B.C.) or of a communal compact consciousness' magic circle dance.[139]

This tension-in-existence of mysticism is one to which the Sargawit, the Foundations person, must be open and may be invited, for the Sargawit seeks to see, or be shewed "all that is made", "a little thing the size of a hazel nut in the palm of my hand". But it is incommunicably beyond the stuff of Foundations.

While I have already raised the issue of aesthetics in the third stage of meaning with regard to music and literature, it seems worthwhile, in this more complex context, to make some suggestive comments on the tension-in-existence of modern sculpting and modern dance.

Henry Moore's words magnificantly anticipate the challenge of sculpting in the third stage of meaning: the sculptor "gets the solid shape, as it were, inside his head - he thinks of it, whatever its size, as if he were holding it completely enclosed in the hollow of his hand ... he identifies himself with its centre of gravity, its mass, its weight".[140] One may note an echo of Asistotle's "sense in act is the sensible in act",[141] and further add the context of

Insight, chapter 8. For the sculptor of the third stage of meaning, the real statue is not already-out-there. The symbolic presence within subjectivity is appropriated within interiority and mediated by that appropriation. Just as the Foundations persons, Jack and Jill, become differently present to one another, so too does Jill's statue for Jack: or Jill's dance.

Susanne Langer stresses the fundamental nature of dance as an art of movement or power: moreover, "the dance often reaches the zenith of its development in the primitive stage of a culture when other arts are just dawning on its ethnic horizon".[142] Later, in her discussion of primitive dance, she remarks on "the great trauma that Western civilization has of necessity inflicted on all the arts - secularization".[143]

The emergence of a third stage of meaning with its mediation of integral subjectivity places issues concerning Sacred and Profane in a new context, and one may be led to ask in what sense the dance is secular. Of Nijinsky's famous leap in Le Spectre de la Rose Jean Cocteau wrote: "He evaporates through the window in a jump so poignant, so contrary to all the laws of flight and balance, following so high and curved a trajectory, that I shall never again smell a rose without this ineffaceable phantom appearing before me".[144] Dame Marie Rambert expressed herself more simply: "I don't know how far from the ground it was, but I know it was near the stars".[145]

In what sense was Nijinsky's leap a leap in being? Certainly it was not a leap in non-being, and one might say that it was a profane leap only by abstraction. In the conclusion of his work, The Sacred and the Profane: The Nature of Religion, Mircea Eliade noted that "in the presence of any tree, symbol of the world tree and image of cosmic life, a man of the premodern societies can attain to the highest spirituality, for, by understanding the symbol, he succeeds in living the universal".[146] Refined modern sensibility can still echo such premodern response to a tree, dance, sculpting. So, the dance critic Marcia Siegel could write of a performance of Drumming by Laura Dean's dancers: "With my western eyes and my lingering Romantic need to comprehend everything, I often wished there were less going on in Drumming.

But there came one moment of transcendence, when, during the second - marimba - section of the music, Dean abandoned rhythmic compliance altogether. Listening, perhaps, to a sustained ringing created by overtones in the percussive sound, the dancers spun in different tempos, in two concentric orbits around Dean. As they whirled and lifted their faces and palms to the resonating space above them, I thought of some great celestial orchestra made up of vibrations, energies, a universal pulse, not any single artist's tune at all".[147] But, as Eliade would have it, the rule is other, the community of modern man is doubly fallen: after the first fall religious sense remained with fragmented consciousness and secularization; in the second fall, within truncated consciousness and secularism, religious sense is forgotten, hidden, clamouring in the unconscious.[148] To recall a significant title, there is now <u>The Empty Space</u>.[149] We may have Happenings, in art or in liturgy, but they cannot systematically get beyond a primal scream. "A holy theatre not only presents the invisible but also offers conditions that make its perception possible. The Happening could be related to all of this, but the present inadequacy of the Happening is that it refuses to examine deeply the problem of perception. Naively it believes that the cry 'Wake up!' is enough, that the call 'Live!' brings life. Of course more is needed, but what?".[150] Elsewhere Brooke notes, " ... if we pretend there is such a source readily at hand we will go on cheating ourselves with rotten imitations. If we recognize how desperately far we have drifted from anything to do with a holy theatre we can begin to discard once and for all the dream that a fine theatre could return in a thrice if only a few nice people tried harder".[151]

Brooke notes some eccentric moderns with a sacred aim: Merce Cunningham, Samual Beckett, Jerzy Grotowsky; "the invisible made visible is of sacred nature, and as he dances Merce Cunningham strives for a holy art".[152] Certainly it is true that since the 1890's in St. Petersburg and the innovations of Duncan, Fuller and St. Denis in America at the same time, modern dance has moved towards non-representation, towards subjectivity, even towards the symbolization of the shift from Control to microautonomy. <u>The Rise and Fall and Rise of Modern Dance</u>[153] are only oscillations above the deeper issue of the crippled infrastructure of modernity. "By the social infrastructure is meant simple prolongations of prehuman achievement ... What once I described as intersubjective community, may be identified, I believe, with the infrastructure of some sociologists. It is any set of social arrangements that goes beyond prehuman attainment but does so with a maximum of obviousness, directness, simplicity".[154] So we are led, like Twyla Tharp,[155] out of the prescribed space of the dance into everyday space, from aesthetic tension to everyman's madness.

So: Here Comes Everybody![156] There is the daily tension-in-existence of each Penelope and Ulysses in the modern grotesque chapter of the Illiad of history, Bloomsdames and Finnegans Knights, plastic-cased seeds of speaking, touching, embracing, cast with hourly news that chokes aspiring lungs. Subway walls in the Jungle of Cities clutch the train, so that business eyes narrow beyond recognizing the woman opposite or the man within: "Theodora heard the difference between doing and being. The corn could not help itself. It was. But the man scrabbled on the surface of life, working himself into a lather of perspiration under his laundered shirt ... The man said that the population of Chicago had risen from 2,701,705 in 1920 to 3,376,438 in 1930. The population was being raised all the time. But in Chicago also, Theodora had seen the nun who danced along the sidewalk, unconsciously, for joy, and the unnatural natural face of the dancing nun had sung some song she had just remembered. The nun's feet touched grass. So that Theodora smiled now. And the man in the perfect shirt was encouraged. He leaned forward to tell the population of Kansas City, St. Louis, Buffalo, and Detroit".[157]

Marinetti, multinationals, military academies and MBA's move to "convert everything private and fugitive and driven in Nietzscheanism into the hearty noonday bustle of optimistic Milanese enterprize",[158] so that Dinosaurs with small truncated heads crib the core private fugitive drive of Everybody in the hearty biophobic bustle of university, hospital, government, business, war: all the structures of laws and profits. Each Hua or Bloom, Leopold or Molly, an ocean of survival, can stay seed-strangled, and still be thin-Tao-tunneled to Eternity. But the seed may take the white apocalyptic name as a beckoning: Bloom, A Hundred Flowers Bloom! Then refining splits

- ego, shadow, persona, anima - or more delicate multiplicities, are admitted as rites of passage.[159] The tension is admitted into total consciousness, so that anima may breath shadowed bedwords leading to Yes-saying,[160] the daybreak of ego and persona may close in the strategic solitude of a bath,[161] and doubly-fallen Finnegan may be waked, regressed,[162] redressed, to rise to larger living.

How large? The question of course is yours and mine. The beckoning may well lead to view with larger heart "distress of nations and perplexity whether on the shores of Asia, or in the Edgeware Road".[163] The largeness may be that of Mother Theresa. But if the largeness aspires to being academic in a contemporarily normative sense then - and this is the central issue of the paper - the four tensions-in-existence to be named shortly must be faced in personal discomfort. The issue is that of "the use of the general categories" as normative in functional specialization. How else is one to view adequately the present 600,000,000 stephens and stephanies under thirty, and the many more to come, in The Central Flower People's Republic, lacking a hundred foundation Blooms? How else can one tear that Chung-hua, that Central Flower, from the penhold of power and nominalism, if not by placing that flower in heuristic heart pocket, to hear the hidden language of those blooms?

I have been trying to give some impression of three human tensions that are both transcultural and available to common sense.[164] The four tensions-in-existence to be considered immediately, however, are all beyond the horizon of common sense: indeed they are tensions that I would relate[165] to the pursuit of generalized empirical method.

There is the tension-in-existence mediated by the epiphany, through theoretic answers, of the what-question: mediated to Plato by geometry, mediated to the contemporary thinker, if he seriously reverences history as revelation, by the centuries of science since Galileo. It grounds with present adequacy the second tension.

The second tension-in-existence is that mediated by the epiphany of the is-question in the appropriation of the meaning of its answers; mediated to Aquinas by the incomplete position of Aristotle and the facticity of the Incarnation; mediated to Lonergan by Aquinas and the first tension. It is a prerequisite for the third tension. The focal expression of that tension occurs in <u>Insight</u>, 388, but it has enlargements in the tension of mere facticity,[166] in the tension of the mystery of Is,[167] in the tension of the mystery of evil.[168]

The third tension-in-existence is mediated by the intussusception of other tensions into total consciousness, into nerves and bones and molecules. It is a third-stage-meaning tension that has preoccupied Robert Doran during the past decade.[169]

The fourth tension-in-existence is that of <u>Praxisweltanschauung</u> in the fivefold differentiated consciousness of the Sargawit. Clearly, its genesis and mediation are our present concern. It is a liberation of the Question that Voegelin discusses in his final chapter, and it escapes his criticism of doctrinal positions in being metadoctrinal. Central to its reality in the subject are the precised darknesses of nescience and mystery. HCE needs a story, an Odyssey within an Illiad, but the Foundations person's story normatively stretches flesh round a noetic possession of the heuristics of Total Process. The adequacy of future stories for everyman, bushman, chinaman, depends on the fidelity of a theological community to the intussusception of that <u>Weltanschauung</u> in their contribution to the emergence of an adequate genetico-dialectic systematics, a mark of the latter's adequacy being its incommunicability to common sense. From that systematic transposition of history, telling in remote vision stories of stories "better than it was", communications specialists would labour to select elements, symbols, stories, that would mesh, in dynamic gentleness, with cultures, communities, media.

Just as Voegelin's treatment of tension-in-existence calls for more adequate differentiations so does his identification of pathologies require enlargement through the heuristic specifications made possible by generalized empirical method. The topic is enormous, but some suggestions may enlarge perspective on both pathology and therapy.

A full heuristic consideration of tension and pathology would require the understanding of man, mediated by modern science, sublated by procedural analysis, as a six-levelled hierarchy[170] symbolically named

$$f(p_i, c_j, b_k, z_l, u_m, r_n),$$

where each of the variables denotes a level of conjugate forms, and the coincidental acts of one level (e.g., the level of physics, p_i: i ranges over the properties of fundamental particles and multiparticles) are aggreformically[171] related to the level above (e.g., chemical, c_j: j ranges over the periodic table relations, inclusive of the compound molecules that occur in chromosome, muscle and brain structures). Substructures (organs of digestion, of seeing etc.) can be similarly specified.[172] The level of wonder, u_m, has the familiar complexity of levels of consciousness as well as the openness to the supernaturality of r_n. Such a heuristic structure is a necessity for serious interdisciplinary efforts to adequately specify, for example, claustrophobia, chemotherapies, biorhythms, thirst,[173] psychoneuroses, insight, serenity, mysticism.[174] This interdisciplinary collaboration belongs to the future, but some suggestive comments on the three main pathologies that Voegelin touches on may throw further light on the enterprize.

Voegelin's main concern is with the withdrawal from the reality of the Vertical Metaxy, but two related pathologies emerge: the scared non-knower can cloak that state in nominalist rationalism or in mere power.[175] So, the noetic tension is expressed by Plato or Aristotle, the challenge is dodged, but the names become a Greek tradition. Again, "the principle of force, represented by Kuo swallows up the ecumene and its order. The foundation of the empire can be defined, therefore, in Chinese terms, as the victory of the Kuo over the t'ien-hsia: the empire was an inflated Kuo without spiritual legitimacy".[176] And in the West, long before Machiavelli, the terms Praxis and pragmatic history, received their technical meaning from Polybius:[177] "the attempts at ordering society by the truth of existence, be it the revealed love of God or the philosopher's love of wisdom, appeared to have come to their end".[178]

Voegelin's suggestions admit sublation into the heuristics of the transcendental dynamisms of the human spirit in their privations by atheism, common sense eclecticism and power seeking.

Heuristically, atheism is a complex pathology involving

unstable or closed[179] integrations of the various
levels of human intentionality. Clues to its transcendendal varieties can be found in Lonergan's reflections on the tones of aesthetic consciousness,[180] on the
genesis of scotosis,[181] on the manners in which the
question of God arises,[182] manners, then, in which
the question can be locked. Atheism can be as elemental as the spontaneous adulthood rejection of
early guilt. It can be as precise as a philosophic
failure to come to grips with the experience of
is-saying. It can be as subtle as the elder Jung's
move past the anagogic in a dream that called for a
different <u>Answer to Job</u>.[183] It can be as evil as the
emphatic moral and religious normality of a righteous
persona cloaking an egophanic core. It can be as
pathetic as the response of human ordinariness to such
righteousness. Many of its varieties are taken as
sanity in the Horizontal Metaxy, and so I would note
in conclusion that the issue here is not the relative
authenticity or the cultural viability of atheists:
there are many relatively authentic people, some locked
up, some at large, who are lunatic. The issue is the
specification of a predominant lunacy of the Horizontal Metaxy.[184]

Like atheism, common-sense eclecticism is a complex
pneumopathology, but its central sickness is the
avoidance and obscuring of the conversion to serious
understanding. Socrates' discomforting challenge
is echoed by the remark of Samuel Beckett, "I think
anyone nowadays who pays the slightest attention to
his own experience finds it the experience of a
non-knower".[185] Common-sense eclecticism is a
disease both of theology and of Marxism. In response
to the threat of larger horizons, such as are required
by a contemporary elitist Foundations or Systematics,[186]
it can be belittingly hostile,[187] or passionate, or
ice-cold.[188] It breeds most comfortably in a scholarship of post-systematic meaning where it criticizes,
corrects, or "lauds the great men of the past":[189]
Lenin or Leo I. Through the gap "between an understanding of verbal usage and an understanding of
what names denote"[190] it can march "with an air of
profundity".[191] It stands for "sound judgment",[192]
regularly with emphatic normality. It is too busy
with the flow of current opinion "to erect syntheses,
to embrace the universe in a single view".[193] And,
while common sense would wish to do the world's work,
common-sense eclecticism would guarantee that the work

be done badly.

It is perhaps necessary to note that the previous paragraph has only the appearance of common sense. It points, in fact, to a heuristic sublation of common-sense eclecticism continuous with Lonergan's discussion of common sense: "while common sense relates things to us, our account of common sense relates it to its neural basis and related aggregates and successions of instances of common sense to one another".[194]

Finally, there is need for an explanatory and therapeutic heuristics of the lunacy of mere power. It is a predominant lunacy of the Horizontal Metaxy, with its focus in a sickness of the dynamic of responsibility. It can have religious and theoretic trappings, but in its more vigorous forms - as in Mao Tse-tung's politics - it is supported "from above" by the lunacy of atheism and "from below" by common-sense eclecticism. And, as Karen Horney's book, The Neurotic Personality of Our Time, would suggest, it can have further dynamic components from below due to early disorientation of feeling. From a therapeutic heuristics, meshed into formal and informal education, one would hope for a discontinuous shift in its statistical disorientations in the third stage of meaning, so that what the eccentric Mo Ti marvelled at in Plato's day might become a marvel of common meaning: that a man who steals a pig is universally condemned and generally punished, while a man who invades and appropriates a kingdom is a hero to his people and a model to posterity.[195] That shift in common meaning would be a shift in power, for "the carrier of power is the community",[196] and in so far as the shift springs from the transcendental dynamisms, the shift is authentic, and there is progress. "Authenticity makes power legitimate. It confers on power the aura and prestige of authority. Unauthenticity leaves power naked. It reveals power as mere power".[197] The adequate therapeutic heuristics of power and authority lie in the future: Lonergan's short article, in the context of his foundational efforts, invites that future work.

We have been placing Voegelin's work in the larger context of Lonergan's Foundations, and perhaps some light has been thrown on aspects of those Foundations. So, for example, "the longer cycle of decline"[198] may

take on larger meaning when it is associated with
the fragmentations of compact consciousness and the
dynamics of the Horizontal Metaxy. One final enlargement remains which the reader may usefully relate
to the problem of specifying Cosmopolis.[199] The
specification carries us beyond the general categories
to the special categories of Christian Theology. My
present interest is in the systematics mediated by
Lonergan's general and special categories. The
collaborative functional specialist effort required
to generate the genetico-dialectic systematics that
would include, as one recent stage in man's noetic
reach for the Mystery of God, Lonergan's 1957-64
writings on the subject, is in the future. I turn
then to the systematics of the ongoing discovery of
mind and Mind, not in the genetic fullness that transposes the historic search,[200] but in the richness of
the operative component that has emerged in our time.
I began part two by noting the two apparently unconnected challenges of 1964, Lonergan's and Chinese
Communism's, and I will link them shortly. Lonergan's
challenge, it seems to me, has scarcely been noticed.
The issue is the subjectivity of God, and the reality of
history as absolutely[201] participative in that
conscious fellowship. Or, as Lonergan notes "the
issue may be put differently. One can ask whether
God revealed his love for us by having a man die the
death of scourging and crucifixion? Or was it his
own Son, a divine person, who became flesh to suffer
and die and thereby touch our hard hearts and lead
us to eternal life?".[202] Or one may bring the issue
into the present context by asking what this oriental[203]
Person of the Horizontal Metaxy, who so died at the
hour of the monkey, means in the fullness of elite
meaning[204] - for the orientals, and us?

The issue, then, is our Eternal Relations' design
and achievement of personal presence in history, and
I can be brief here only by writing in the rhythms
of an invitation to elements of a larger view.[205]

Earlier, two metaxies in history were identified. Is
it plausible that the metaxies are related intimately
to the subjectivity of God? Certainly the Second
Person is Middle Person in God: is the Second Person
not also Middle Man in history, whose secondary
existential act wraps[206] history in essential sacredness,[207] the sacredness of a real participation in
the Divine Paternity.[208] Is this not the axis of

the Vertical Metaxy? But is not the sacredness of history a reality of all human time through the related[209] gift to men of a soulfilling[210] participation in the originating energy of Speaker and Son with a concomitant gift of participative Alertness to the togetherness of Speaker and Son?[211] The fullness[212] of the Sacredness of Christ is the mediating actuality in history of the promise of adoption: the blighted spring of history is meshed in hope into the Second Person's bright spring from "Light and Love".[213] His reality of participation in all four Divine Relations contrasts[214] with our dark participation in the originating fellowship of Speaker and Word and the listening openness to them that is the Spirit. In the Is-answer of Faith, our What-question is an openness for eternal participation in Him as Word, for an adoption by Hidden Call. By His presence the ongoing discovery of mind and Mind is radically changed. His coming seeds truth, never essentially enlightening, but genetic of most fruitful understanding and larger kindness. Through His talk and His dangling we have a peg of hope on which to hand our metaxic hats. A Care absolutely beyond nature surrounds with mysterious personality the suprazoological. The fundamental tension-in-existence is the Trinitarian tension of Abundant Care, lifting the darkness out of history. And 600,000,000 young Chinese become 600,000,003 persons living in darkness and a great light.

"In accordance with the above views, I would like to make the following proposals:

1. We should place before the whole Party the task of making a systematic and thorough study of the situation around us ...

2. As for China's history in the last hundred years, we should assemble qualified persons to study it, in co-operation and with a proper division of labour, and so overcome the present disorganized state of affairs. First it is necessary to make analytic studies in the several fields of economic history, political history, military history and cultural history, and only then will it be possible to make synthetic studies.

3. As for education ... a policy should be

established of focussing such education on the study of the practical problems of the Chinese Revolution and using the basic principles of Marxist-Leninism as the guide, and the method of studying Marxism-Leninism statically and in isolation should be discarded".[215]

This quotation from Mao's essay brings us to our final topic: China and The Man.[216] I am evidently making my own Mao's proposals, where for "Party" one may real "Christian Theologians". The situation around us is history, its systematic study being a reach for adequate categories. Their adequacy will concern us shortly.

Mao's second proposal may be put in the context of Lonergan's dialectic, in particular, the task of Method in Theology, 250. The history that is revelation is not just the history of religious debate. "What is good, always is concrete",[217] and the "assembly"[218] of dialectic has reference to events and movements that are candidates for progress.

The third proposal can be considered in relation to the last four functional specialties, and I wish to dwell on it in these concluding pages, with China as focal problem.

It seems to me that the problem of these four specialties is intimately related to grasping adequately the intention of the general categories. That intention is a reach towards the future in the full vigour of the personal perspective of the generalized emergent probability of meaning and Faith. It envisages world history in its concrete emergence in terms of possibilities and probabilities. Whether its use is in Foundations or in Communications it is never abstract; on the other hand, neither is it ever obvious. So, for example, Communications is not popular theology: it requires sophisticated selections from a genetico-dialectic elitist systematics that would mediate larger life to diverse communities. Some particular instances of the relevant attitude would perhaps be useful.

Within the perspective of the general categories, the probability schedules of schemes of transcendental aliveness or alienation in China certainly include Voegelin's sober perspective: "Periods of

great establishment, such as a Communist government
in China or a Communist government in Russia, have
a habit of running for two hundred and fifty years".[219]
However, the inclusion involves the sublations that
have been indicated throughout this paper, and would
lead to a more optimistic statistic, pivoting however
on a creativity in the West that also is being envisaged here.   There is Chinese theatre, opera, dance.
There is an even longer stable tradition of poetry
and painting.   There is the more recent pressure
towards a new mandarinism of science.   All these,
within a creative global context, mediate the problematic of a third stage of meaning.   But the emergence of the creative context is delayed by the
necrophilia of the Western academy, so that instead
of the Trojan horse of transcendental method being
available to Chinese universities there is just
another version of truncated subjectivity.   Yet
history has habits grounding hope.   Of a Chinese,
as of an American, it can be said that "within the
walls of his individuality, there is more than a
Trojan horse.   He has no choice about wanting to
understand; he is committed not by any decision of
his own but by nature to intelligent behaviour; and
as these determinants are responsible for the emergence of social orders in the past, so they account
for their development, their maintenance, their
reformation".[220]   Moreover, history pushes towards
an epiphany of understanding as data through the
problem of emergent science.   One may well speak
of <u>The Coming Convergence of World Religions</u>, but one
should also reverence the nöosphere of what-answers,
including foundational economics, that are invariant
over nations.[221]

Mao Tse-tung wrote extensively on varieties of
contradiction among the people[222] and moved away from
Marxist-Leninism in asserting the continued presence
of non-antagonistic contradictions that can be
resolved within socialism through the formula unity-
criticism-unity.[223]   He discussed, at length, the
need to identify, at each stage of revolution, the
principal contradiction.[224]   But his truncated
subjectivity excluded him from envisaging the principal contradiction noted above, the tension between
truncation and transcendental dynamics in the people.
In this, of course, he differs little from Western
government, economics, education.   But he adds to
it the blunt strength of a "totalitarian integration
of common-sense practicality"[225] which guards, with

emphatic normality,[226] Party thinking from discovering the major principles of decline in general bias, and the minor principle of decline in group bias. So, the truncated analysis protects itself from discovering that the "confusing error of Marx was to lump together both progress and the two principles of decline under the impressive name of dialectical materialism, to grasp that the minor principle would correct itself more rapidly through class war, and then to leap gaily to the sweeping conclusion that class war would accelerate progress".[227]

But in the break with Russia in theory and practice, during the Great Leap Forward, lies a hope of a different statistics for Chinese Communism. However party-lined the slogans, ("Carrying out the policy of letting a hundred flowers blossom and a hundred schools of thought contend will not weaken but strengthen the leading position of Marxism in the ideological field"[228]), Mao opened the way to levels of democracy and dialogue.[229] Instead of declaring "that all new ideas are taboo",[230] he quotes Mencius, "The office of the mind is to think",[231] and speaks, without knowing it, the fundamental law of history: "much thinking yields wisdom";[232] the second stage of meaning mediates the third: the dialectic of the three plateaus of minding, and dialogue, reveal the transcendental reality of poet and peasant: "While the dialectic of history coldly relates our conflicts, dialogue adds the principle that prompts us to cure them, the natural right that is the inmost core of our being".[233]

The adequate heuristic envisagement of poet, peasant and dialogue is a requirement of the use of the general categories in the functional specialties of the second phase. What is needed are a hundred foundation Blooms, twentieth-century Leopolds who would envisage China as William Cobbett envisaged England in the nineteenth century on his Rural Rides,[234] and as many Mollys who would see the cities like Jane Jacobs[235] with a larger perspective. Moreover, the envisagement entails, in Communications, strategies of mediating transcendental expansiveness in cottage and commerce. So, for instance, criticism in the Yangi Commune of the use of canteens in Ten Mile Inn generated a consensus regarding six advantages of canteens " ... (2) They take a great load off the minds of those people who don't know how to plan and budget properly and so are always finding themselves in a fix ...".[236] This advantage, of course, echoes the orientation of centralization and planning in the West: one unburdens the mind and cultivates the pneumopathologies. Indeed, the Chinese Commune lunacy seems somewhat saner than much Western government and planning. History must educate, or reeducate, the globe to acknowledge that "the principle of progress is liberty, for the ideas occur to the man on the spot, their only satisfactory expression is their implementation, their only adequate correction is the emergence of further insights".[237]

But, again, I must insist on the concreteness, and the theoretical adequacy,[238] of the envisagement of possible and probable schemes of recurrence. So, I recall schemes of recurrence involving pigs. William Cobbett once remarked that what he most liked to see was "a pig in almost every cottage sty; that is the infallible mark of a happy people".[239] Emergent Chinese writing indicates parallel insights: "In the olden days the Chinese thought a pig under a roof was home ... A 'roof' with two 'pigs' under it means 'contentment'".[239a] The Communists missed the point and its related schemes of recurrence, but through the correction of oversights the family pig reappeared.[240] "During the Great Leap Forward certain industrial crops, like cotton, had done spectacularly well, but not everywhere, mainly because of the lack of fertilizer. The small communal industries did not produce enough fertilizer and there was less natural manure because there were fewer privately owned pigs. Certain orders did not take into account what the peasants knew from first-hand experience: for example, birds were exterminated on a large scale in 1959 because they devoured seeds, and this left the land defenseless against insects".[241]

Both East and West in these late modern times are massively and madly committed against the transcendental structure of man's dreams, feelings, insights. The madness can extend to discussion of that transcendental structure. There is a call at present for Theology to be empirical: if the call is not to be yet another ideology, it must become a boned-up[242] inner opening to people as they actually are and as they could probably or possibly be in the next year, in the next million years. It would perhaps be significant here to sum up the task in the words of the neglected Mo Ti:

These are what I call the Three Laws of Reasoning:

1. Where to find the foundation. Find it in the study of the experiences of the wisest men of the past.
2. How to take a general survey of it? Examine the facts of the actual experience of the people.
3. How to apply it? Put it into law and governmental policy, and see whether or not it is conducive to the welfare of the state and the people.[243]

To take that task seriously is to question present theology and present theological education. No doubt some will echo the complaint of a man in the Yangi Commune: "All this leaping forward takes it out of you".[244] But perhaps some will share the slogan on the Commune mudbrick walls "Three years of bitter struggle, ten thousand years of joy".[245]

I have commented on the orientation of general categories in relation to Voegelin's sober perspective. That sober perspective is sublated by the special categories, factualized through Doctrines[246] and fleshed out by a Christian Systematics. I conclude by drawing on Lonergan's systematics to ask of the Trinity's relation to the future of China. Before doing so an aside is necessary on the issue of "drawing on systematics", indeed in a foundational manner.

By "drawing on systematics" I mean, not doing the functional specialty Systematics, but profiting from its achievements. The functional specialties are tasks, and to continually enlarge Systematics is, indeed, a lifelong task. To profit from the enlargement is the privilege, obligation, and need of every theologian. One may be helped by a simple parallel. Anyone in the creative entertainment business knows the effort and the luck of discovering a new joke; but we can all enjoy the joke. I spoke of privilege, obligation, and need. The theologian is privileged and obliged by profession; if he or she has no need to understand God then he or she is pneumopathological. In the present context it is not irrelevant to recall Marx: "Take the case of Marx. He says he is fully aware that the question

of the Divine Ground of all things must be asked.
But were he to ask it, he couldn't insist that
material conditions are the base of that question
and of everything else he thinks. Therefore socialist man must not ask it. Now what goes on in
the mind of a man who makes such statements? Is
it a case of schizophrenia or of something entirely
different?".[247] A theologian may say that biblical
conditions or historical research or dialectic
issues are the preoccupying base. But can you
sanely be in love with a Divine Ground without the
itch to ask Who?[248]

Frederick Crowe's insights within Trinitarian Systematics provide a suitable starting point. In discussing the stages of the Trinity's entry into history
which were mentioned above, he remarks: "This seems
relevant to our missionary activity. The Risen
Jesus told his disciples, 'As the Father sent me,
so I send you' (John 20:21), so surely we can learn
from the Father's procedure. If, then, our apostolate
is analogous to his, it will be accomplished in word
and love, the love will always be total, while word
will be according to the condition of the time and
place. If in primitive times the Spirit came
<u>incognito</u> and did his work in secret while he awaited
the time when the fullness of the Word could be mani-
fested, the idea occurs that our own missionary
activity may consist for a long time in bringing our
charity to the missionary country while we help with
agriculture, housing, education, hospitals, etc.,
and bring conditions to the point where they can
receive the relevation we would transmit".[249]

Let us, briefly, relate the point to some further
elements of Lonergan's Latin Works.

The Word proceeds from an understanding of history.[250]
Eternally[251] and solely[252] spoken is the understanding
of all the "concrete patterns of diverging series of
scattering conditions",[253] that leave us groping for
light through emergent probability. History slowly
reveals to us the schedules of God's patience but we
are slower still to learn.[254] In 781 A.D. the
Nestorians raised a monument to Chinese tolerance,
and a short time later Rome raised a hullaballoo to
Ricci's tolerance; should we not try again?

As Fr. Crowe reminds us "the Son and Spirit were not

sent until 748 and 781 A.U.C.".[255] Further, the Son is graced as head of all men [256](t'ien hsia: i jen), history is eternally spoken as absolutely supernatural,[257] laced with an invitation to a friendship without a Name: the Hidden Perfection of Order invites a finite order to the limits of intimacy.[258] The invitation constitutes a state of Eternal and historical being:[259] the Globe, and China, are in that state of grace. In that state there is the image of the Divine Lovers that is private but also public,[260] and may even be identified as reality, yet not as image.[261] But that state is changed by the walk and the talk of the Man from the Middle East, among his own. "doing his own thing":[262] the Lowers are darkly[263] revealed to a group in simile, stride and suffering, and the group are invited to a new justice.[264]

Here we pass over the group's history of impatience, law, power, empire: there is the large task of future dialectic to reveal the goodness of the goings-on of the Christian West.[265] It is the focal normative element that is of immediate interest.

The Word in conscious hypostatic union,[266] cherishes us, known and loved, both in the Divine Nature and in the human nature,[267] in the complexity of Eternal Order and of his human graces.[268] The Word is with us, as a Person who shared global air, sensibly drawing us to inaccessible light.[269] In explicit Christian faith, we are drawn to speak interiorly our word of the Word, for the Word came in processional reality to be with us in graceful processional image.[270] And the graceful processional image for the theologian includes the present reach of Christian systematics.[271]

What of the non-Christian Chinese? I recall the quotation from Fr. Crowe regarding missiology, and I add to it the context of Lonergan's discussion of the two times of the temporal subject.

First, there is the Western challenge, and ours, of fostering the transition to generalized empirical method and the third stage of meaning in all fields and in our concrete living. It is a challenge to go beyond the madnesses of Western capitalism, of University life, of conventional Theology. Only thus can we adequately invite the Chinese into the third stage of meaning, into a larger presence of the Unnamed

Trinity. To Christ's admonition "tell no man that I am the One",[272] we might oddly add "Tell no one that We love them". Fr. Crowe has written of help in charity: I am complexifying the issue of help to require a help towards self-help grounded in Chinese insights. Further, the help is authoritative only through the collaborative achievement of the goal of help in the helpers.[273] Finally, there are three basic ways of bringing a subject to that second time which opens the road to integrality and hope: through understanding, through belief, through love.[274] The last leads to belief and to understanding.[275] It would seem to be God's way. It is not the way of an arrogant Christianity, pathologically intent on the 11th Commandment: "make sure that the others keep the first ten" (even perhaps adding "according to our culture and creed"). Help is genuinely given in the shedding of pseudo-theism, power and eclecticism. It is given in the Mystery of God, with limited authority and reverence for liberty, withdrawn from the sinful backwardness of common-sense eclecticism. Perhaps, after all, Christianity has not been tried. The Middle Man said: "if I be lifted up I will draw all things to myself".[276] "The cock crows today".[277] Might we not weep, repent,[278] reflect, leap forward?

> "The night was long and the
>   crimson dawn cracked slowly;
> For hundreds of years demons and
>   monsters danced frantically;
> Our five hundred million people
>   were disunited.
>
> Once the cock has crowed and all
>   beneath the sky is bright,
> Music rises from Khotan and a
>   thousand places
> To fill the poet with unparagoned
>   inspiration".[279]
>
>   (Mao Tse tung, 1950)

CHAPTER TWO

Report on a Work in Progress

Robert Doran

I. Introduction

After nearly a year of wrestling with the question of how to integrate a process of psychic self-appropriation, involving a good deal of dream analysis, with the dimensions of interiorly differentiated consciousness promoted by the work of Bernard Lonergan, in February of 1973 a basic insight occurred to me that I have been laboring to articulate, develop, test and amplify ever since. The insight was to the effect that there is a fourth aspect of foundational subjectivity, and so of conversion, beyond the three instances - intellectual, moral, and religious - whose objectification constitutes in Lonergan's work the theological functional specialty, Foundations.[1] I have called this fourth aspect of conversion, psychic conversion. Quite recently I have been moved to clarify for myself where my work is going from here, and so to locate the work of the past nine years within a new and more inclusive context. In the present paper I will describe this newly explicit context and will then offer an interpretation of the two stages through which my work of the preceding nine years has passed.

This new context is one neither of method nor of psychology, as the previous two phases, respectively, have been, but explicitly one of theology, and, more precisely, of Systematics. I am beginning work on a Systematics that I will entitle <u>A Theology for a World-Cultural Humanity</u>. The first volume of this work will be devoted to two themes: the cultural matrix of a contemporary systematics and the meaning of integrity or authenticity within that matrix. It will present a vision of a religiously and theologically transformed cosmopolis. The section dealing with integral interiority will include a statement, more thorough and refined than any that appears in my previous work, regarding the structure of a psychology of orientations. But - and this is the most important point - the context even of this psychological theory is explicitly theological.

The cultural matrix with which a contemporary Christian Systematics must mediate the significance and role of the Christian religion is global. I understand the global cultural matrix of our age as constituted by several competing and escalating sets of totalitarian ambitions, which for purposes of hypothetical generalization, or at least of "idealtype" articulation, can be reduced to variations on one or the other of the two major myths of post-Machiavellian modernity: the progressionist myth of automatic expansion, unlimited progress, and exponential growth, whose paradigmatic resultant in our day is found in transnational corporational capitalism, and the myth of class conflict as the indispensable and infallible means to social harmony and justice that finds similar paradigmatic expression in the Marxist states. A common structural error regarding the order of values infects both of these sets of ideological assumptions and their corresponding and competing social-systemic objectifications: namely, a subordination of the cultural values in terms of which groups live in a world mediated and constituted by meaning to the social values that constitute a particular social order. I understand the significance and role of Christianity, then, within such a global cultural matrix to consist in the promotion of a mentality that would become incarnate in alternative communities and that would proceed in the order of _Praxis_ on the grounds of a rectified conception and articulation of the genuine order of values. In such a conception religious values condition the possibility of personal integrity, personal integrity conditions the possibility of genuine cultural values, such cultural values condition the possibility of a just social order, and a just social order conditions the possibility of an equitable distribution of particular goods. The network of alternative communities arising from the _Praxis_ of such a mentality must extend across both cultural and religious boundaries. I adopt Lewis Mumford's expression, world-cultural humanity, as an appropriate denomination.[2]

The ground of the values that motivate a world-cultural humanity I locate in the four aspects or modalities of conversion - religious, moral, intellectual and psychic - whose objectification constitutes "theological foundations". The conversions will ground the _Praxis_ of world-cultural humanity. This _Praxis_ will be both superstructural and infrastructural. The superstructural Praxis will consist in the interdisciplinary collaboration required to reorient the human sciences. My work up to this point indicates what the reorientation of one of these sciences, depth psychology, entails, and argues that this particular reorientation is itself a dimension of theological Foundations. The infrastructural Praxis of world-cultural subjects is intent on the transformation of the myriad varieties of common sense by integrating the cosmological, anthropological, and soteriological modes of spontaneous self-understanding that constitute the authentic heritage of the various cultural traditions, and by reversing the mechanomorphic self-understanding that informs the common-sense of totalitarian societies.[3] The bulk, if not the totality, of my intellectual energies will be devoted, for the foreseeable future, to working out a theology that can mediate Christian faith with the global cultural matrix in such a way as to promote the emergence of a world-cultural community.

My work of the previous nine years I now understand as a methodological, and consequent psychological, preface to a theology for a world-cultural humanity. Methodologically, this work complements Lonergan's objectification of the interiority of the integral human subject, and so further specifies what constitutes authenticity. Thus, it is heading toward a specification of the grounds of orthopraxis. Psychologically, this work articulates the aesthetic sensitivity of the converted subject. I have moved to this articulation by way of a dialectical confrontation with Jungian depth psychology. Thus both of the aspects or phases of my work are a fitting preparation for my present concerns: the methodological aspect because of the transcultural structure of consciousness disengaged in Lonergan's writings, and the psychological because of the potential of Jung's insights for promoting cross-cultural understanding. The scope of my attempt to reorient Jung's work is limited to articulating the nature of converted psychic sensitivity. This articulation is obviously dependent upon Lonergan's understanding of self-transcendence. Thus, the methodological phase of my work precedes the psychological, and grounds the latter in an extension of Lonergan's notion of generalized empirical method. Let me add that I believe that a reorientation of much of 20th-century depth psychology could follow from my attempt to outline the structure of a psychology of orientations. But I have decided to turn my own energies to the theological task consequent upon the first two phases of my work.

I have not yet proceeded very far in pursuing this goal. My book, Psychic Conversion and Theological Foundations,[4] specifies the superstructural dimensions of the endeavor to form a global alternative to the totalitarianisms. It speaks of the reorientation of the human sciences on the foundation of the objectification of authenticity. But I have yet to relate my understanding of the global cultural matrix to various prevalent interpretations of culture and politics, or to begin constructing a systematic theology to mediate Christian faith with this matrix. I have written very little about the infrastructural transformations that would be promoted by a world-cultural humanity, though I have received much encouragement concerning my ideas in this regard from my students in a course on "Religion and Culture" at Regis College in Toronto.[5] I was fortunate enough to have a class in which twelve distinct cultural backgrounds were represented, so I consider the encouragement something of a confirmation that I should continue along the path of my explorations.

II. Background

Prior to the completion of any of my work to date, my concerns went through two stages, which are reflected in the two phases of the written work itself. The first concern emerged between May of 1972 and October of 1973, when, with the assistance of Dr. Charles Goldsmith in Milwaukee, I began a process of dream analysis that promoted a process that I call psychic self-appropriation. During these months I resolved to begin in my doctoral dissertation the work of complementing Lonergan's intentionality analysis with the psychic self-appropriation that I was about. This stage of concern is reflected in the first, or methodological, phase of my written work to date, which includes the book, Subject and Psyche,[6] and the articles, "Psychic Conversion"[7] and "Subject, Psyche, and Theology's Foundations".[8] The principal function of this phase is to generate categories for expressing an understanding of the psyche that would be continuous with Lonergan's articulation of intentionality. I also argue in these works that these new categories are foundational. They are expressive of a dimension of converted subjectivity, and so they articulate an aspect of foundational reality. I became convinced at this time that these categories afford a necessary complement to Lonergan's account of this reality, and so that his notion of foundational reality was to this extent incomplete. This claim, which I still maintain, has proved to be the most controversial aspect of my work among Lonergan's students. Put briefly, my conviction is that the self-knowledge that is gained through psychic analysis is methodologically just as important and personally just as transformative as is that acquired through intentionality analysis, and that <u>the latter can neither supply nor substitute for the former</u>. Four new foundational categories are generated during this phase of my work: second immediacy, the imaginal, psychic conversion, and the anagogic.

My second conviction, which is as controversial among Jungians as the first is among students of Lonergan, is that Lonergan's intentionality analysis is needed if one is critically to ground a psychic analysis that avoids the perils of self-deception concerning our authentic possibilities. This conviction reached articulate form while I was in Zürich from October to December of 1974. There I came to see that, while psychic analysis is a necessary <u>complement</u> to Lonergan's intentionality analysis, the latter stood in a relationship of <u>dialectic</u> with Jung's science of the psyche. Jungian depth psychology, as it stands, is not complementary with Lonergan's intentionality analysis, and the problem lies in mistaken assumptions on Jung's part concerning the three aspects of foundational reality that Lonergan had articulated: knowledge, morality, and religion. Jungian psychology needed to be reoriented on the basis of Lonergan's intentionality analysis. While this conviction is clearly present even in the writings of the first phase of my work, the actual task of attempting the reorientation could not be undertaken until I had arrived at the notion of the anagogic, and had distinguished the anagogic from the archetypal. These developments emerge in the last work of the first phase, the paper, "Subject, Psyche, and Theology's Foundations". The

second phase begins to display positively what a
reoriented depth psychology would be, and thus I
refer to this phase as psychological. The concerns
of the third phase, which I described in the introductory section above, begin to become apparent in
some of the later works of this period.

III. The Methodological Phase

The generation of additional foundational categories
is the preoccupation of Subject and Psyche. These
categories would serve to integrate psychic self-
appropriation with Lonergan's account of method,
and so would fill a need that was left unaddressed
by Lonergan and that had to be met before the
structure of foundations was complete. Since my
first thorough absorption in Lonergan's work in
1967, I had been engaged in the slow and laborious
process of explanatory self-knowledge. In May of
1972 I began with Dr. Goldsmith a similarly intense
journey through another dimension of inner life.
It did not take long before I realized that the
process of recovering, telling, and making the
story of my life in which I was engaged bore striking resemblances to some of the work that I had
been engaged in under Lonergan's tutelage for some
five years, and was definitely aided by what I had
learned about myself from Lonergan, but also that
the dimension of interiority that I was now coming
to understand and take responsibility for was different from the one to which Lonergan had introduced
me. Thus I began to formulate the question of how
I could integrate these two processes of self-explor-
ation, not simply in the unthematic manner of living
from the basis of both, but in the thematic manner
of articulating their integration in a theoretic
or explanatory fashion. Subject and Psyche,
completed in 1975, was the first articulation of
my convictions that Lonergan's account of foundational subjectivity had to be complemented by a depth
psychology, and that psychic interiority was indeed
important and significant enough to deserve to be
considered a dimension of "foundational reality".
The opening of my own intentional consciousness to
a willingness to negotiate psychic sensitivity in
an intelligent, reasonable, and responsible fashion
was such a change in myself, and instituted such a
new horizon, that I felt justified in referring to

it as a fourth mode of conversion, which I called psychic conversion.

I have already referred to a second concern that appeared but was left undeveloped in Subject and Psyche. In Zürich I became quickly disillusioned with Jungian psychology, which previously I had thought could be integrated in a fairly straightforward way with Lonergan's thought. I had supposed that the integration would require little more than a purging from Jungian thought of its at least implicit Kantianism in the realm of epistemology and metaphysics. But in Zürich I saw that much more was demanded, that the existential problems in Jungianism were far more profound than the cognitional difficulties, and that in fact a quite radical religious and moral crisis lies behind the epistemological and metaphysical counterpositions in Jungian literature. In effect, a new psychology had to be proposed, if Lonergan was to be appropriately complemented by psychological self-knowledge. My own readiness to carry out this task was quite incomplete at the time of writing Subject and Psyche, and so I deliberately contented myself with indicating the scope of the problem, and then devoted my attention to the first concern of suggesting the manner in which Lonergan's thought left itself open to, and demanded, a psychological complement which it had already begun to anticipate.

The anticipation to which I refer is found in Method in Theology, where Lonergan speaks of the relations, first, between feelings and values,[9] and then, in a distinct context, between feelings and symbols.[10] I concluded to a relation between values and symbols, because of their common relatedness to feelings, and I claimed that the spontaneous symbols that emerge from the psychic depths of the subject, particularly in dreams, but also in such deliberately undertaken exercises as those proposed by Ira Progoff,[11] provide significant help in the appropriation of that level of intentional consciousness whose distinctness from the cognitional emerges in Lonergan's later work: the fourth or existential level. The relationship between intentionality analysis and psychic analysis consists in the fact that psychic analysis is one necessary key to the appropriation of the fourth

level of intentional consciousness. Psychic
analysis helps one to know what one actually wants,
what one truly values, the real state and orientation of one's desires. The spontaneous symbols
of the sensitive psyche constitute the principal
data for the differentiation of one's existential
orientation to the objectives that constitute the
human good, objectives whose pursuit or neglect
constitutes world-constitutive and concomitant
self-constitutive praxis.

This insight serves to integrate psychic conversion
with the other dimensions of foundational reality.
When Lonergan speaks of intellectual, moral, and
religious conversion, of their order of emergence,
and of their reverse order of sublation,[12] he creates
a problem that he leaves unanswered, in my view.
For intellectual conversion, at least as this
expression is usually used in his work, is in fact
intellectual self-appropriation.[13] It is a precise,
theoretic, explanatory self-understanding that guides
a responsible self-determination in matters cognitional. But religious and moral conversion precede
intellectual conversion thus conceived, and so they
are not a matter of explanatory - or, for that matter,
even descriptive - self-thematization. But if they
are to sublate intellectual conversion, they must be
raised out of their compactness and be subjected to
the process of self-appropriation, the process that
leads to interiorly differentiated consciousness.
Only then will cognitional theory find that higher
integration in existential world-constitutive agency
that is implied when one speaks of sublating intellectual by moral conversion. Now, it is psychic
analysis that makes moral self-appropriation possible,
and so that enables the sublation of intellectual by
moral conversion. The dominant theme of <u>Subject and
Psyche</u> is the following: by exploiting the clue
mentioned earlier - the relation of feelings both to
values and to symbols - one can develop a depth
psychology, integrate this psychology with Lonergan's
intentionality analysis, and raise moral and religious conversion into the stage of meaning governed
by interiorly differentiated consciousness.

The integration of psychic analysis with intentionality analysis, as I have stated, gave rise to three
new foundational categories in <u>Subject and Psyche</u> -
second immediacy, the imaginal, and psychic conversion - and to a fourth that emerged a bit later, the

anagogic.

Second immediacy can be explained by contrasting it with the spontaneously operative infrastructure of the subject-as-subject that I call primordial immediacy. Primordial immediacy is the immediacy of the operating and feeling consciousness to the symbols, concepts, and judgments through which the world is mediated and constituted by meaning, and to the evaluations through which the world is motivated by values. The operational aspect of primordial immediacy is mediated in Lonergan's work. My proposals speak of a complementary mediation of the affective dimensions of immediacy. Both mediations result in objective self-knowledge, the subject-as-object. But the subject-as-object is not yet what is meant by second immediacy. The latter emerges as objectivity in one's own regard changes one's spontaneity as a subject as a result of one's decisions to operate in a manner consistent with what one has come to affirm regarding one's most authentic possibilities. New habits of perception, insight, judgment, feeling, and deliberation begin to be formed, the habits that constitute interiorly differentiated consciousness. When this most subtle of all differentiations becomes habitual, it establishes one in a condition that I call second immediacy and that I describe as "the probably always asymptotic recovery of primordial immediacy through method".14 Lest such a claim appear either outlandish or Gnostic, let me emphasize that what one becomes asymptotic to is wrapped in the non-luminosity that is the very reason that primordial immediacy is, as I put it in my later writings, a search for direction in the movement of life. We are not speaking here of anything continuous with the lumen gloriae, the luminosity in which we shall know even as we are known, but of a differentiated appropriation of our own nescience and so of the process of inquiry through which, step by step, we discover the direction that is to be found in the movement of life. In the humility that reflectively owns its own nescience in a differentiated fashion is to be found the integral foundation of theology, of human science, and of world-cultural humanity.

A discussion of Paul Ricoeur's understanding of the symbol precedes my treatment of the imaginal. I find Ricoeur's efforts to mediate the conflict between

restorative and reductive hermeneutics essential for
my own insistence on psychic analysis as an intrinsic
ingredient of existential self-appropriaton. I also
find his discussion of the structure of the symbol
quite illuminating. But I take issue with him on
three counts. First, I do not accept his insistence that self-appropriation is to be mediated
radically by an encounter with the externalized
objectifications of religious and cultural history;
I propose rather that, however contributory such an
encounter is to our self-understanding, our very
interpretation of these expressions is grounded in
our understanding of ourselves, and so, that the
grounds of the hermeneutic of symbolic <u>expressions</u>
lie in our understanding of our own spontaneous
symbolic <u>experience</u>. Second, I find that Riceour
mistakenly undervalues the symbolic power and worth
of dreams. Finally, I propose that the teleological counterpole to the Freudian archeology of the
subject must be found in the same dimensions of the
subject as were studied by Freud, in the sensitive
psyche itself, and not in the fictive Hegelian <u>Geist</u>
to which Ricoeur appeals, nor even in the very real
dimensions of intentionality, however much the
teleology of the psyche may be explained in terms
of its orientation to a participation in the objectives of our intentional operations. Jung has
correctly insisted on a teleological orientation
within the psyche itself and so on the inclusion
of teleological considerations in any science of the
psyche, even if he misplaces and in fact dislocates
the direction of psychic intending. The dialectic
of archeology and teleology is experienced in sensitivity itself. This is due to the psyche's inter-
mediate status or position between and participation
in the schemes of recurrence of the bodily organism,
on the one hand, and the unrestricted reach of
intentionality, on the other hand. The symbols
released in our dreams are exploratory of the
dialectic of the subject within the dialectic of
history. But they can be produced as they are
only because of the dialectic within the psyche
itself. That dialectic, I later came to see, can
be understood in Lonergan's terms of limitation and
transcendence.15

<u>The imaginal</u> is that sphere of being that is known
in true interpretations of elemental symbolic prod-
uctions. I extend the processes of sublation to

the imaginal, in an effort to account for how such interpretations are possible. Thus the dream is sublated into waking experience by memory, into intelligent consciousness by interpretation, into rational consciousness by reflection, and into existential consciousness by decision. The decision has to do with how I am to deal with the self-knowledge gained in the interpretation of the dream. In this way, and through the negotiation of the interpreted materials, the sensitive psyche is gradually conscripted into the self-transcendent dynamism of intentionality. The teleology of the psyche is to be understood in terms of its potential orientation to and participation in the objectives of intentional consciousness. This potential is actualized only as the detachment and disinterestedness of ordered intentionality permeates one's affectivity.

This specification of psychic teleology differs from the Jungian position. The elemental symbols of our dispositionally conscious energies reflect the emergence or non-emergence of the subject as an originating value. Their ground theme consists in the conflict between the intention of the transcendentals and the flight from genuine humanity. This drama is <u>a priori</u>, in Lonergan's operative-heuristic sense of "notions", rather than in the content-objective sense of Kant's categories. In the first volume of <u>A Theology for a World-Cultural Humanity</u>, I will elaborate its theological, and so most radical, meaning.

Psychic conversion, the third foundational category generated in <u>Subject and Psyche</u>, is the process that enables a person consciously to sublate imaginal data by intentional process. The psychically converted subject has learned to sublate the elemental symbols that reflect his or her affective orientations in a world mediated and constituted by meaning and motivated by value. In the article, "Psychic Conversion", I spoke of this process as one in which the undertow of sensitive consciousness is subjected to the same kind of self-appropriation as was brought to bear on cognitional activity in Lonergan's work. This means that psychic self-appropriation as I am conceiving it is a matter of <u>interiorly differentiated consciousness</u>. It corresponds to the philosophic variety of intellectual conversion that results from answering correctly the three questions: What am I doing when I am knowing? Why is doing that knowing? What do I know when I do that? It would be artificial and arbitrary to try to elaborate parallel questions to promote the process of psychic conversion. It is more accurate to say instead that the detachment and disinterestedness of the notions of being and value which the process of philosophic conversion reveals as constitutive of authenticity move one to the further question of how one can negotiate one's affective spontaneities so that they further the emergence of genuineness in one's own conscious behaviour rather than obstructing that emergence. Where self-knowledge becomes explanatory, as it does in philosophic conversion, one wants the same rigor of interiorly differentiated consciousness to extend to one's familiarity with one's psychic spontaneities. "Psychic conversion", then, as I am using this term, refers to more than the spontaneous affective self-transcendence of the well-ordered psyche, or even the spontaneous sublation and correction of affective energies by the morally good person, just as "intellectual conversion" in Lonergan's work usually refers to more than the cognitive genuineness of a person who happens to be using his or her mind intelligently and rationally as it is meant to be used. "Psychic conversion" means rigorous, explanatory appropriation of one's sensitive psychic experience and of its existential meaning just as "intellectual conversion" means rigorous, explanatory appropriation of one's intellectual and rational activity.

The fourth foundational category generated in my early work is that of the anagogic. It is introduced, not in Subject and Psyche, but in the article, "Subject, Psyche, and Theology's Foundations". It is further elaborated in many of the articles of the second or psychological phase of my work, where my concern shifts from that of complementing Lonergan to that of reorienting Jung. Jung spoke of two kinds of elemental symbolism: the personal symbols of the personal unconscious, and the archetypal symbols of the collective unconscious. I want to speak of a third variety, which Jung includes under the rubric of archetypal symbols, but which I consider quite distinct. Archetypal symbols are taken from nature and imitate nature in a generic and highly associative way. They correspond to the symbolization that Eric Voegelin calls cosmological. Anagogic symbols, on the other hand, while they may be borrowed from nature or from history, express the relation of the person, the world, or history to the reality disclosed by the anthropological and/or soteriological "leaps in being" by which consciousness is explicitly related, through philosophy or faith, to a world-transcendent measure of integrity. This distinction enabled me to address myself to the reorientation of Jungian psychology, and more specifically to come to grips with the moral and religious crises that lie behind the epistemological and metaphysical counterpositions in Jung's thought. The crucial issue in Jung's work is the problem of evil. The symbolism of the negotiation of evil is anagogic, not archetypal, and the resolution of the problem of evil calls, not for an integration of evil with good in such a way that both good and evil can be cultivated, as would be the case if they were archetypal contraries, but for the decision between contradictories, a decision made in the freedom that we are given by our relation with the world-transcendent and redeeming measure of our integrity.

With the emergence of this fourth category, the first phase of my work, that of complementing Lonergan's intentionality analysis with an account of the structure of psychic analysis, comes to a close, and the second phase, that of suggesting a reorientation of Jungian psychology, begins.

IV. The Psychological Man

My efforts at reorienting Jungian psychology began in an article that I wrote for a Festschrift honoring Frederick E. Crowe on the occasion of his sixtieth birthday.[16] Jung had written a number of works in which he treated the symbolic significance of the person of Christ. His late work, Aion,[17] is perhaps the most thorough presentation of his thought in this regard. Here he tries to understand Christ's psychological importance and meaning by considering Christ as an archetype of the self. Now, for Jung, wholeness, conceived as the integration of opposites, is the paradigm for understanding the self. Good and evil are among the opposites that must be integrated. Christ functions as a symbol of the self-as-good, and Satan as a symbol of the self-as-evil.

Wholeness demands that Christ's psychic significance be complemented by and integrated with Satan's, through the cultivation of dimensions of the self that Christianity had rejected as evil during the astrological Age of Pisces, in which the warring fish symbolized the conflict of opposites. The emerging Age of Aquarius will witness the cessation of the conflicts, the reconciliation of the warring elements, the rapprochement of Christ and Satan. I contend that Jung limited himself to archetypal or cosmological symbolizations as expressions of the reality of God. God is to be understood as emergent within the world, in a manner not unlike Hegel's Absolute Spirit; in fact God is to be redeemed from his own unconsciousness by individuating persons. God's unconsciousness is to be attributed to the exclusion from his conscious being of the fourth personal element of divinity, of God' shadow, i.e., Satan. As human subjects integrate good and evil in themselves, Satan will be reintegrated into the conscious being of God, and God will be at rest with himself.

The leap in being to a world-transcendent God who redeems human subjects and communities from evil seems never to have been taken by Jung. There is for him no further dimension of symbolism beyond the archetypal, for there is nothing beyond the cosmological to be symbolized. His autobiographical Memories, Dreams, Reflections, records a dream in which Jung is invited to acknowledge the transcendent God into whose mystery we are introduced by the experience of innocent suffering.[18] But in the dream Jung refused the invitation. The dream itself is anagogic in its symbolism; but, paradoxically, it reflects the choice in which Jung ruled out an acknowledgement of the relations to which anagogic symbols refer. The irony is that Jung has provided a superb avenue to an appropriation of the dimensions of our inner being that stand in need of God's redemptive love, and yet he missed or rejected the connection between his own discoveries and the Christian life of grace. The problem of evil is resolved, not by an apocatastatic reconciliation of evil with good, but only by the transformation of evil into a greater good by participation in the "just and mysterious Law of the Cross".[19] Jung has penetrated so deeply into the recesses of the psyche that he has uncovered the need for a theological grounding of depth psychology. But he did not acknowledge the necessary grounding, and so he ends up offering a system of thought that must, in the last analysis, be regarded not as a complement but as an alternative to Christian theology and to Christian religious praxis.[20]

Another article written at the same time, "The Theologian's Psyche: Notes toward a Reconstruction of Depth Psychology",[21] pursues the question of the transformation that Jungian psychology will undergo when it is encountered dialectically by an analysis of intentional self-transcendence. In this article the Jungian notion of the self is examined. This notion, as we saw, was central to Jung's critique of the Christian ethos in Aion. I redefine the self as the subject, and I understand the subject as inextricably involved in the dialectic of authenticity and inauthenticity. I speak of good and evil, respectively, as the intelligent, reasonable and responsible negotiation of the tension of limitation and transcendence, matter and spirit, on the one hand, and the failure or refusal so to negotiate this tension, and thus its displacement to one or other pole, on the other hand. Thus I argue that good and evil cannot be listed among the contrary opposites to be negotiated by a process that establishes their complementarity, i.e., the opposites that can be discussed under the general rubric of limitation and transcendence. Rather, good and evil are qualifications of that very process of negotiation itself, depending on whether it has or has not been characterized by the genuineness that is constituted by the taut balance of limitation and transcendence. There is no "both/and" here, but only an "either/or".

Further nuances are introduced in the two papers, "Aesthetics and the Opposites"[22] and "Aesthetic Subjectivity and Generalized Empirical Method".[23] The first of these papers speaks of the context of psychic self-appropriation as being quite beyond the narrow psychotherapeutic framework that my earlier works are still presupposing. Furthermore, it correlates the psychic or aesthetic dimension of subjectivity with the dramatic character of world - and self-constitution. The appropriation of this dimension will thus take the form of a narrative which may or may not require a psychotherapeutic setting to get one started, but whose purpose is "beyond therapy". The second paper proposes that the differentiation of the psyche is more accurately

conceived as a process of developing one's aesthetic
sensitivities than as a matter of psychotherapy as
we usually think of the latter, and of developing
these sensitivities primarily in the area of artistry
in which all of us are inevitably involved, the
dramatic artistry of making a work of art out of our
own lives.

This theme is resumed in "Dramatic Artistry in the
Third Stage of Meaning",[24] where psychic conversion
is argued to be the key to a self-appropriating
genuineness, i.e., to a genuineness that reflectively
mediates the duality of limitation and transcendence.
Sensitive participation in both the organism's
schemes of recurrence and the spirit's intention of
objectives that are not restricted by space and time
makes of the psyche the locus in which the tension
of limitation and transcendence is experienced. This
paper also proposes that in psychic conversion the
healing and creative vectors of conscious development
are conjoined. The retrieved genuineness that results
from the mediation, through interiorly differentiated
consciousness, of limitation and transcendence involves
sensitivity itself in the divinely originated solution
to the problem of evil. This sensitive participation
is manifest especially in the spontaneous release of
the anagogic symbols that reflect the penetration of
gratia sanans to the physiological level of the person.

The world-constitutive praxis of the converted subject
has been emerging as a more central theme in these
last few papers. In "Metaphysics, Psychology, and
Praxis",[25] it comes to center-stage. The debate
with Jung continues in this paper as well, for the
question with which the paper deals has to do with
the contribution of a transcultural psychology of
orientations to the emergence of a world-cultural
humanity. In my response to this question I insist
on the penetration of sensitive consciousness by the
detachment that makes one able to think and choose on
the level of history. Such detachment is quite other
than what develops if one submits to Jung's prospect-
ive swallowing up of intentionality and its objectives within the horizons of a merely archetypally
symbolizing psyche. Jung's discovery of archetypal
symbols is an important contribution to cross-cultural
communication. But equally important is the insight
that in all cultures authenticity consists in the
participation of the sensitive psyche in the pursuit
of the transcendental objectives of intentionality.

Most of the remaining articles in the second phase resume the central task of reorienting Jungian psychology. "Primary Process and the 'Spiritual Unconscious'"[26] recasts the Freudian notion of primary process so that it includes the operations of intentional consciousness as well as all of the motivations and orientations of the sensitive psyche. Thus it becomes, not libido, but the search for direction in the movement of life. It is constituted by the tension of limitation and transcendence. Secondary process, then, becomes a term referring to all attempts to objectify primary process. Among these attempts are those which issue from philosophic and psychic conversion, and so which admit into consciousness in an explanatory fashion the ineluctable tension, felt in the sensitive psyche, between the schemes of recurrence of a body-bound sensitivity whose imaginal horizons are constituted by time and space, on the one hand, and the intention of the true and the good, the notions of being and value, on the other hand, which are unrestricted by time and space. The philosophies that we adopt in secondary process have a constitutive influence on the psyche and its symbolic deliverances. This explains why persons undergoing different kinds of psychotherapy will experience different kinds of dreams - "Freudian", "Jungian", etc. And this means that a therapy of pneumopathology[27] is more radical than a therapy of psychopathology, and that an accurate science of the psyche is dependent on a critical retrieval of spiritual intentionality. One's imaginal experience depends on one's fidelity or infidelity to the transcendencal precepts, which, along with grace, are the ultimate operators of one's psychic development. One implication of this is that the Jungian symbols of wholeness, such as the mandala, symbolize only temporary plateaus of integration. They will be continually and relentlessly dissolved by the self as operator, in favor of more comprehensive integrations that are reached only through the difficult process of advancing differentiation. Jung's compacting of all transpersonal symbolism into the archetypal images of wholeness reflects too one-sided an emphasis on the self-as-integrator and a relative neglect of the unceasing process of differentiation as this process moves to ever more comprehensive synthesis of the tripartite self-bodily organism, sensitive psyche, and spiritual intentionality. When wholeness is over-emphasized, the danger is incurred that the person will be derailed from the search for direction in the movement of life. What should be regarded as the goal of psychic development is, not wholeness, but the affective self-transcendence which enables the psyche to participate ever more spontaneously in the person's fidelity to the transcendental precepts, to the normative order of inquiry through which direction is found. Wholeness is a relative and temporary integration of various stages of development along the way.

"Jungian Psychology and Lonergan's Foundations: A Methodological Proposal",[28] lists the changes that would take place in Jungian psychology if it were to be reoriented on the basis which I am suggesting. The operative heuristic notion guiding the process of individuation would become, not wholeness, but self-transcendence. Jung's romantic mysticism, where affectivity bogs down in intracosmic archetypal symbolization, would be replaced by an intentionality mysticism that would be reflected in the anagogic images released by a psyche that participates in the spirit's openness to a world-transcendent and redeeming God. These images would themselves be negotiated "anagogically". They would not be clung to, but would lead one beyond themselves to participation in the very life of God. Moreover the symbols of our dreams, whether personal, archetypal, or anagogic, would be regarded as a narrative whose theme is the emergence of the authentic world-constitutive agent. In the theoretic real, the psyche would be more sharply differentiated from the spirit. The spirit is not an unknowable <u>Ding au sich</u>, but is rather what one knows when one affirms oneself as the subject of intelligent, rational, and responsible operations. The issue of good and evil would be understood in terms of one's emergence as a self-transcendent agent. The integration proposed by Jung would become patently absurd, for one cannot be simultaneously and willingly both an intelligent, rational, and responsible person and a stupid, silly, sociopathic drifter. The symbolic significance of Christ and Satan reflects the ultimate context of grace and sin, where the problem of evil is decided, not by the cultivation of darkness in the illusory hope of integrating it with the light, but by the even further transformation of the realm of our darkness by the therapeutic vector of redemptive love.

I published in Review for Religious three less technical articles on Jungian psychology and Christian spirituality.[29] They conclude with the affirmation that the divinely originated solution to the problem of evil invites us to the existential decision to "let ourselves fall into the incomprehensibility of God as into our own true fulfillment and happiness" (Karl Rahner).[30] This is precisely what Jung's dream, referred to above, shows that he would not let himself do. This existential refusal is the root of the most serious intellectual problems in his psychology. No clearer instance can be provided of the spiritual causation of the psyche's symbolic manifestations. By the time of the article, "Psyche, Evil, and Grace",[31] then, I am calling for the construction of a new psychology that would articulate the psychic dimension that permeates all intentional orientation. I have been presenting the outline of this psychology in my course at Regis College on "Psychic Conversion and Contemporary Spirituality", and I will include it in the book that I am now writing, in the context of a discussion of authenticity within the global cultural matrix that invites the formation of a world-cultural, communitarian alternative to the competing and escalating totalitarian systems.

V. Psychic Conversion and Theological Foundations

The anticipation of a world-cultural community begins to take more definitive shape in my second book, Psychic Conversion and Theological Foundations. The book is essentially a sustained argument to the effect that the processes of intellectual, psychic, moral, and religious self-appropriation must ground not only a contemporary doctrinal, systematic, and practical theology, but also an interdisciplinary collaboration geared to the reorientation of the human sciences on the basis of the positions in which authentic subjectivity is objectified. This collaboration will constitute the superstructural dimension of the cosmopolitan alternative to totalitarianism. The first of the human sciences to be reoriented is depth psychology, because its data are among the data of interiority whose explanatory objectification constitutes the foundations of further endeavor in the human sciences. In this sense the book returns to the concerns of the first phase of my work, that of complementing Lonergan's methodological positions. I begin to draw out the implications of Lonergan's suggestions regarding a hierarchy of values, and I root totalitarianism in the instrumentalization of rationality and the concomitant neglect of psychic sensitivity that coincide with the collapse of the scale of values into the two levels of the good of order and the acquisition and distribution of particular goods. As I argued in the first section of this paper, this collapse is predicated on a neglect of the manner in which religious values condition personal integrity, personal integrity conditions cultural values, and cultural values condition a just social order. A global alternative to competing totalitarianism will take its stand on the integrity of the full scale of values. It is in terms of this full scale of values that I wish in the near future to discuss as well the infrastructural dynamics of a world-cultural community. But I intend as well to ground this dynamics in an advancing position on interiority in which there would occur an integration of the truth of the cosmological, anthropological, and soteriological symbolizations through which various cultures have expressed their experience of the search for direction in the movement of life. This integration depends above all on a reversal of the mechanomorphic symbolization of the totalitarian systems, that is, of symbolization that results from the utilitarian collapse of the scale of values and that threatens a deaxialization of history, a regression to a compactness that would forget even the limited but essential ecological truth of the cosmological or archetypal symbolizations.

Two further attempts to complement Lonergan's work appear in Psychic Conversion and Theological Foundations. The first draws out the implications of the distinction drawn in Method in Theology between the notion of being and the notion of value. This distinction is not as clear in Insight, for Lonergan had not yet arrived at the differentiation of the fourth level of consciousness, the intention of value, from the three levels that constitute the cognitive intention of truth. When existential consciousness emerges as a distinct level that is both the ground and the objective of cognitional praxis, the notion of value is no longer interchangeable with the notion of being. The real human world as it is and the good human world as it ought to be are not coincident. With this distinction, and perhaps only with it, transcendental method moves definitively beyond a classicist orientation, and so beyond the danger of its becoming an agent, however unwilling, of right-wing ideologies. Moreover, with this distinction, psychic self-appropriation, as the key to the objectification of the fourth level, becomes the narrative through which we express what we do when we strive to transform the human world as it is into the human world as we judge it ought to be. With this qualification, psychological self-knowledge transcends the narcissistic concerns that, as Peter Homans has shown, undermine the Jungian enterprise from beginning to end.[32]

Secondly, I attempted to draw an explicit link between the sensitive psyche and the transcendental notion of the beautiful. The beautiful is the objective of affective intentionality. In beauty there is articulated in sensible form the splendor of truth and goodness. Thus one more argument is forged for the assertion that the sensitive psyche cannot be brought to the realization of its own proper objective except to the extent that the person remains faithful to the spiritual exigencies that prompt us to be intelligent, rational, responsible, and in love. The paradigmatic enjoyment of and creative participation in beauty lies in the affective integrity of the subject who has been healed by redemptive love and thus freed to implement the creative vector of consciousness through whose operations one's constitution of the world and of oneself becomes a work of art.

CHAPTER THREE

Dialectically-Opposed Phenomenologies of Knowing: A Pedagogical Elaboration of Basic Ideal-Types

Michael Vertin

I. Introduction

I should like to introduce this paper by first recounting briefly something of my own history as a student of human cognition and then specifying exactly, against that background, the enterprise to which the body of the paper is devoted.

A. The Background of this Paper

In the summer of 1973 I completed work on a doctoral dissertation entitled, The Transcendental Vindication of the First Step in Realist Metaphysics, according to Joseph Marechal.[1] The project had grown out of my longstanding interest in what has come to be called the "critical" problem, that of establishing the real objectivity of human knowledge. How, if at all, can one ever be certain that what one concludes to be so is really so? How, if at all, can one escape the possibility that even one's most fully substantiated and seemingly incontrovertible judgments of real existence are finally not necessarily more than just subjective? I had been disturbed by this most basic of epistemological problems first during undergraduate work in physics and then, from a markedly different angle, during graduate work in theology. Subsequently, through a modest investigation carried out near the beginning of my graduate studies in philosophy and focussed on the writings of Bernard Lonergan up to that time, especially Insight: A Study of Human Understanding,[2] I had gained a more exact appreciation of the problem and learned of the "critical realist" proposal for solving (or, more accurately, dissolving) it. A certain personal uneasiness with that proposed solution had remained, however. Consequently, in an effort to lay to rest that residual uneasiness through a more extensive historical and philosophical investigation of critical realism as such, and encouraged by Father

Lonergan's assurance to me that the work of Marechal was very much to the point in this regard, I had undertaken the study of the Belgian Jesuit.

Marechal's fundamental philosophical theme, already present in his early studies of the psychology of the mystics[3] and developed at great length in the five-volume work for which he is best known, Le Point de depart de la metaphysique,[4] is the natural finality of the human intellect. Speaking now in metaphysical terms and now in phenomenological ones, Marechal argues that human intellectual cognition is essentially a matter of identity and perfection, active, dynamic, and constructive, rather than a matter of duality and confrontation, passive, static, and receptive. And, most importantly, the judgment of real existence, the culminating moment of the cognitional process, is discursive or affirmational and not intuitive or perceptual. To judge is not intellectually to intuit, perceive, see, real existence in some concrete intelligible. On the contrary, to judge is to affirm of, assert of, attribute to, that concrete intelligible a relation to the ultimate objective term of intellectual finality, the ultimate cognitional goal which one anticipates a priori and which is the plenitude of what in fact one means, at least implicitly, by "real existence". For humans, to know a concrete intelligible as really existing is nothing other than to affirm that concrete intelligible as related to the ultimate objective term of intellectual dynamism. The critical problem, Marechal claims, arises precisely insofar as one overlooks the discursive character of actual judgments, mistakenly asserts that an intuitive grasp of real existence is requisite for objective knowing, and then notes - correctly - that concretely the requisite intuition does not occur.

Marechal's approach to the question of the real objectivity of human knowledge, then, is simply to argue that even at a very primitive level of awareness the human subject makes judgments that are indeed discursive or affirmational. On the basis of what purportedly is a transcendental analysis, Marechal avers that a transcendental condition of one's _having_ some concrete intelligible as _phenomenally_ objective is that one _affirm_, at least implicitly, that concrete intelligible as fundamentally _really_ objective, really existing, related to the ultimate objective term of intellectual finality. But it is undeniable that one frequently has concrete intelligibles as phenomenally objective. Consequently, says Marechal, the real objectivity of human knowledge stands essentially vindicated, and the critical problem is dissolved.

After many months of studying the long and detailed historical and systematic argumentation by which Marechal builds his case,[5] I concluded that his chief contentions, notwithstanding certain misleading expressions and dubious metaphysical conceptions that encumber them, are substantially correct. The basic (if seldom explicit) meaning of "real existence" is indeed "goal of intellectual finality"; one actually does know real existence via judgments that are discursive or affirmational in character; and the critical problem really is a false problem, one which arises because of the human propensity ot suppose, in the absence of adequate concrete self-knowledge, that cognitional operations can achieve real objectivity only if they are intuitive, perceptual, at least analogous to ocular vision. I felt content with critical realism at last.

Nonetheless, a difficulty with Marechal's account continued to nettle me, a difficulty that was highlighted when I compared his account with that of Lonergan. Marechal, in his analysis of judgment, clearly rejects the "cognitional myth" that holds "that knowing is like looking, that objectivity is seeing what is there to be seen and not seeing what is not there, and that the real is what is out there now to be looked at".[6] Thus he has achieved what Lonergan by now is labelling "intellectual conversion".[7] On the other hand, the two thinkers differ significantly in their respective accounts of the primitive self-awareness of the subject in general and of the judging subject in particular. For Lonergan, the subject's primitive self-awareness is intrinsically non-reflexive; and the judging subject's primitive self-awareness is at best not just self-manifestive but rationally self-constitutive as well. Consequently, by discussing variations in the judging subject's commitment to, and skill at, rational self-constitution, Lonergan is able to provide a highly nuanced phenomenology of cognitional error.[8] For Marechal, by contrast, the subject's primitive self-awareness is intrinsically reflexive, albeit only "partially" or "incompletely" so; and the judging subject's primitive self-awareness does not constitute the self-as-judging but merely manifests it, reflectively, as already pre-reflectively or "naturally" constituted. Thus Marechal cannot avoid maintaining that in their originating moments judgments, like other activities of the subject, proceed "sourdement et necessairement",[9] a position that leads to what surely is one of the most striking deficiencies of PD, namely, the absence of any account of cognitional error.

"Given that Marechal is intellectually converted, why does he still retain the 'ocularist' position that primitive self-awareness is a kind of 'looking at self'?". "Does Marechal's notion of primitive self-awareness, and his resultant inability to account for cognitional error, ultimately jeopardize his rejection of the 'ocularist' notion of knowing?". Bothered by questions such as these, but tentatively answering the latter in the negative, I consigned my discussion of the matter to the second of two appendices in my dissertation.

In the years since completing my doctoral dissertation I have continued to pursue my philosophical study of human cognition, proceeding mainly in two complementary ways.

First, in meeting my assigned responsibility to design and conduct a number of year-long advanced undergraduate courses under the titles, "Epistemology" and - later - "Metaphysics",[10] I have had a splendid opportunity to increase both the depth and the breadth of my acquaintance with basic philosophical issues as arising in the work of others, both past and present. After initially structuring these courses simply as interpretive thematizations of the history of philosophy, thematizations (with a distinctly Marechalian flavor!) designed to illustrate the relatively small number of possible positions on basic philosophical issues, I soon began also to consider the relations between those basic position-sets and the current disputes over method in selected "trans-philosophical" disciplinary areas. I was greatly influenced throughout this enterprise by my continued reading and re-reading of both Marechal and Lonergan; and the general pattern upon which I finally settled is exemplified by my description of a recent course entitled, "Metaphysics":

"This course investigated two basic theses: (1) that any solution of the metaphysical problem of the one and the many presupposes at least implicitly solutions of the phenomenological problems of the one and the many and the epistemological problem of objectivity and subjectivity; and (2) that differences over the solutions of these philosophical problems constitute a fundamental, though often unnoticed, part of disputes over method within the various empirical disciplines. These theses are explored dialectically through reference to selected systematic controversies from the history of philosophy and selected methodological debates in current physics, historiography, literary criticism, and theology. A general orientation is provided by selections from the philosophical writings of Bernard Lonergan".[11]

Those familiar with the work of Lonergan will recognize, in the first part of this program, my attention to what he labels the basic issues of "knowing, objectivity, and reality".[12] The major figures whose works I have usually employed to raise these issues dialectically are Plato, Aristotle, Epicurus, Aquinas, Hume, Kant, Hegel, and Lonergan. The disciplinary areas and figures upon which I have concentrated in the second part of this program have varied somewhat from year to year, in function of my own immediate interests. (Besides the areas noted above, I have also made forays with the students into psychology, sociology, and ethics). In the most recent course, the persons whose works I used for dialectically illustrating the methodological issues were these: in physics, Israel Scheffler, Wilfrid Sellars, and Patrick Heelan; in historiography, Carl Hempel, R. G. Collingwood, and W. H. Walsh; in literary criticism, I. A. Richards, Northrop Frye, and H.-G. Gadamer; and in theology, Peter Berger, Paul Ricoeur, and Lonergan.[13]

The second way in which I have been able to extent my philosophical study of human cognition is through preparing a sequence of scholarly papers. Though having the usual variety of particular aims, collectively the papers have allowed me to articulate, consolidate, and implement certain advances that I have made in thinking about basic cognitional issues since completing my doctoral work.[14]

B. The Aim of this Paper

It will scarcely surprise the reader to learn that the effort to which the body of this paper is devoted flows from the prior work of my own that I have just discussed, work that in its theoretical aspect I now explicitly locate mainly in the functional specialties of Dialectic and Foundations and, more precisely, in the cognition-regarding (by contrast with the further, decision-regarding) parts of those two functional specialties.[15]

Specifically, then, the body of this paper is a pedagogical effort in the functional specialty of Dialectic and, more exactly, in that part of Dialectic concerned with the phenomenology of knowing. Let me expand this characterization, in six steps.

First, as located in, rather than beyond, the order of functional specialties, my effort here is concerned immediately with theory (including theory about praxis) and not immediately with praxis itself.[16]

Secondly, as in a fourth-level rather than a lower-level functional specialty, my effort is concerned with **theory in** its merely structural, simply heuristic, purely transcultural, strictly philosophical[17] aspect, by contrast with theory insofar as in addition it is content-inclusive, heuristically complemented, culturally conditioned, empirical.[18]

Thirdly, as in Dialectic rather than Foundations, my effort is simply to articulate something of the comprehensive set of those basic dialectically-differing integral supposition-sets (ultimately reflecting dialectical differences among theorists in their fundamental, if not always explicit, intellectual, moral, and religious outlooks) by virtue of which individual theories in any given area of inquiry may be opposed in their strictly philosophical aspects, without yet proclaiming which one of those supposition-sets I take to be correct.[19]

Fourthly, as in that part of Dialectic concerned with knowing rather than deciding, my effort is oriented, more narrowly, toward the supposition-sets from the aforementioned comprehensive set that regard cognitional acts (and, by inclusion, their contents) by contrast with decisional ones.[20]

Fifthly, as in that part of Dialectic concerned with the phenomenology rather than the epistemology or metaphysics of knowing, my effort is oriented, still more narrowly, toward the supposition-sets from the aforementioned comprehensive set that regard cognitional acts (and their contents) from the standpoint of <u>description</u> as distinct from both <u>vindication</u> and <u>explanation</u>.[21]

Sixthly, as pedagogical rather than originating, my present effort is to articulate something of the comprehensive set of dialectically-differing integral sets of basic phenomenological suppositions about cognition in such a way as to help <u>the reader</u> make progress toward adopting, as his[22] own, the supposition-set that I take to be correct. The contrast is with my earlier work of spelling out dialectical alternatives for <u>myself</u> and deciding among them.[23]

As a supplementary characterization, I should say that my aim in the body of this paper is to display, in a comprehensive schema, the basic theoretical correlatives of both the concrete (and concretely implemented) self-knowledge that is the fundamental component of what Lonergan labels "intellectual conversion", and the varieties of that component's absence.[24]

II. Elaboration

A. <u>The Phenomenology of Knowing: The Ten Basic Questions</u>

Consider the collectivity of basic descriptive philosophical - or basic phenomenological - suppositions regarding human knowing that either have been made explicitly by individual philosophers or are implicit in the work of individual philosophers and empirical theorists.[25] So far as I can determine, this collectivity suggests that human cognitional acts may occur on any of as many as five distinct levels and may have as many as two distinct dimensions. While not yet assessing the accuracy of any supposition in that collectivity, I would claim that the collectivity itself can usefully be envisioned as a group of diverse responses to ten basic phenomenological questions about the occurrence, distinction, and characteristic structure of those five levels and two dimensions and, moreover, that no phenomenology of human knowing can be complete without addressing each of those ten basic questions.26

The five supposed levels of cognitional acts are the sensory, the ideational, the judicative, the evaluative, and the fiducial levels.27 The supposed first, <u>sensory</u>, level is that whose characteristic contents include colors, sounds, odors, tastes, etc.28 The supposed second, <u>ideational</u>, level is that whose characteristic contents include intelligibility, i.e., the intelligible unities that constitute things and the intelligible similarities that constitute properties.29 The supposed third, <u>judicative</u>, level is that whose characteristic contents include factuality, i.e., the existence and occurrence, beyond the mere intelligibility, of things and of properties.30 The supposed fourth, <u>evaluative</u>, level is that whose characteristic contents include value, i.e., the genuine goodness, beyond the mere factuality of things and of properties.31 And the supposed fifth, <u>fiducial</u>, level is that whose characteristic contents include holiness, i.e., the redolence of unrestricted lovability, beyond the mere value, of things and of properties.32

The two supposed dimensions of cognitional acts are in the <u>intentional</u> dimension, the dimension in which sensible contents, intelligibility, factuality, value, and holiness become cognitionally present to the knowing subject, and the <u>conscious</u> dimension, the dimension in which, in utterly primitive fashion, the cognitional acts themselves - and, underlying them, the cognitional actor, the knowing subject - are cognitionally self-present.33

The ten basic phenomenological questions, then, fall into two groups, five regarding cognitional intentionality, and five regarding cognitional consciousness: In fact, do cognitional acts possess an intentional dimension on a sensory level, and, if so, precisely what is their structure in this regard? on an ideational level? on a judicative level? on an evaluative level? on a fiducial level? And, in fact, do cognitional acts possess a conscious dimension on a sensory level, and, if so, precisely what is their structure in this regard? on an ideational level? on a judicative level? on an evaluative level? on a fiducial level?

B. The Phenomenology of Knowing: Dialectically-Opposed Answers to the Five Basic Questions regarding Cognitional Intentionality

The collectivity of basic phenomenological suppositions regarding cognitional intentionality may be organized in terms of the five basic questions to which those suppositions constitute responses; and thus one has suppositions about sensory, ideational, judicative, evaluative, and fiducial intentionality, respectively. The collectivity may also be organized in terms of the dialectically-opposed kinds of responses that those suppositions constitute; and in that case one has absentialist, reductionist, immediate-receptionist, pure-productionist, and mediate-receptionist suppositions about cognitional intentionality.[34] I shall give priority to the latter organizing principle in the present section of this paper.

<u>Absentialist</u> suppositions about cognitional intentionality postulate in common that alleged cognitional acts in whose intentional dimension the contents in question become cognitionally present to the knowing subject do not occur at all, on any level. Thus, the absentialist supposition about sensory intentionality is that colors, sounds, odors, tastes, etc., are not to be found at all among the contents of human knowing. The absentialist supposition among ideational intentionality proposes the total cognitional absence of intelligibility. The absentialist supposition about judicative intentionality is that there is no cognitional achievement of factuality; about evaluative intentionality, of value; and about fiducial intentionality, of holiness.[35]

<u>Reductionist</u> suppositions about cognitional intentionality agree in hypothesizing that alleged cognitional acts in whose intentional dimension the contents in question become cognitionally present to the knowing subject do indeed occur, but that they occur not on the level in question but rather on a different level - higher or lower, as the case may be - such that the contents in question are not these levels' <u>characteristic</u> intentional-dimension contents. Thus, for example, reductionist suppositions about sensory intentionality are that colors, sounds, odors, tastes, etc., are indeed among the contents of human knowing, but not as characteristic

contents of a first, sensory, level. Instead they are to be found on the second level, as aspects of intelligibility, or on the third level, as aspects of factuality, or on the fourth level, as aspects of value, or on the fifth level, as aspects of holiness. Or, again, reductionist suppositions about fiducial intentionality are that there is indeed a cognitional achievement of holiness - not, however, as the characteristic content of a fifth, fiducial, level of human knowing but only on the fourth level, as an aspect of value, or on the third level, as an aspect of factuality, or on the second level, as an aspect of intelligibility, or on the first level, as an aspect of sensible contents.[36]

Suppositions in the three remaining groups agree in theorizing that alleged cognitional acts in whose intentional dimension the contents in question (i.e., sensible contents, or intelligibility, or factuality, or value, or holiness) become cognitionally present to the knowing subject both do occur, and occur precisely on the level in question (i.e., the sensory, or ideational, or judicative, or evaluative, or fiducial, respectively), with the contents in question as these levels' <u>characteristic</u> intentional-dimension contents. They differ in how they portray the intentional structure of those cognitional acts.

<u>Immediate-receptionist</u> suppositions about cognitional intentionality all propound that the intentional structure of the cognitional acts that they regard is immediately receptive. That is to say, the knowing subject - precisely as such - makes contents cognitionally present to itself by acts which in their intentional dimension are acts of accepting contents as given to the subject-as-knower from beyond the subject-as-knower and, moreover, accepting them directly rather than through any intermediary contents.[37] Accordingly, the immediate-receptionist suppositions about sensory, ideational, judicative, evaluative, and fiducial intentionality are that sensible contents, intelligibility, factuality, value, and holiness, respectively, become cognitionally present through sensory, ideational, judicative, evaluative, and fiducial acts that in their intentional dimension are acts of direct, unmediated acceptance.[38]

Pure-productionist suppositions about cognitional intentionality all suggest that the intentional structure of the cognitional acts that they regard is simply productive. That is to say, the knowing subject - again, precisely as such - makes contents cognitionally present to itself by acts which in their intentional dimension are acts of creating, fashioning, fabricating contents entirely out of the subject's own resources. Hence, the pure-productionist suppositions about sensory, ideational, judicative, evaluative, and fiducial intentionality are that sensible contents, intelligibility, factuality, value, and holiness, respectively become cognitionally present through sensory, ideational, judicative, evaluative, and fiducial acts that in their intentional dimension are acts of simple fabrication.[39]

Finally, mediate-receptionist suppositions about cognitional intentionality all speculate that the intentional structure of the cognitional acts that they regard is mediately receptive. That is to say, the knowing subject - once again, precisely as such - makes contents cognitionally present to itself by acts which in their intentional dimension are acts of accepting contents as given to the subject-as-knower from beyond the subject-as-knower, but accepting them indirectly, through intermediary contents. There is a distinction, therefore, between the contents that are received and the contents in which they are received.[40] The former, the known contents, are fundamentally beyond the subject-as-knower.[41] The latter, the intermediary contents, are simply within the subject-as-knower; and they arise from the productive action of the subject upon contents received on the prior level(s) of knowing.[42] Thus, the mediate-receptionist suppositions about ideational, judicative, evaluative, and fiducial intentionality are that intelligibility, factuality, value, and holiness, respectively become cognitionally present through ideational, judicative, evaluative, and fiducial acts that in their intentional dimension are acts of indirect, mediated acceptance, where the respective media are subject-produced concepts, judgments-of-factuality, judgments-of-value, and judgments-of-holiness.[43]

C. The Phenomenology of Knowing: Dialectically-
   Opposed Answers to the Five Basic Questions
   regarding Cognitional Consciousness

The collectivity of basic phenomenological suppositions regarding cognitional consciousness may be organized in terms of the five basic questions to which those suppositions constitute responses;[44] and thus one has suppositions about sensory, ideational, judicative, evaluative, and fiducial consciousness, respectively. The collectivity may also be organized in terms of the dialectically-opposed kinds of responses that those suppositions constitute; and in that case one has absentialist, reductionist, immediate-receptionist, and internal-presentialist suppositions.[45] I shall give priority to the latter organizing principle in the present section of this paper.

Absentialist suppositions about cognitional consciousness postulate in common that alleged cognitional acts possessing the conscious dimension - the utterly primitive cognitional self-presence - in question do not occur at all, on any level.[46] The premises of such suppositions can be that cognitional acts with the corresponding intentional dimension do not occur at all,[47] and that cognitional acts cannot occur with a conscious dimension unless they also occur with the corresponding intentional dimension.[48] Alternatively, the premises can be that cognitional self-presence is correlative with reflection: it occurs only insofar as the subject's acts, initially oriented toward contents distinct from themselves, return upon themselves, receiving themselves as their own contents.[49] But in any given instance such reflection either does not take place at all (in which case the acts are not cognitionally self-present at all), or else it takes place more or less completely (in which case the acts are cognitionally self-present more or less fully and not just in a primitive way).[50] On one of these two sets of premises or the other, accordingly, the absentialist suppositions about sensory, ideational, judicative, evaluative, and fiducial consciousness are that there are no sensory, ideational, judicative, evaluative, or fiducial acts, respectively, that are cognitionally self-present simply in primitive fashion.[51]

Reductionist suppositions about cognitional consciousness all suggest that alleged cognitional acts

possessing the consciousness in question do indeed
occur, but that they occur not on the level in question but rather on a different level - higher or
lower, as the case may be - such that the consciousness in question is not these levels' <u>characteristic</u>
consciousness. Thus, for example, reductionist
suppositions about sensory consciousness propose that
there are indeed conscious acts in whose intentional
dimension colors, sounds, odors, tastes, etc., become
cognitively present to the knowing subject; but
that just as these acts' intentionality is not the
characteristic intentionality of a first, sensory,
level of knowing, so their consciousness is not the
characteristic consciousness of a first, sensory,
level. Rather, it is to be found on the second
level, as but an aspect of ideational consciousness,
or on the third level, as but an aspect of judicative consciousness, or on the fourth level, as but
an aspect of evaluative consciousness, or on the
fifth level, as but an aspect of fiducial consciousness.[52] Or, again, reductionist suppositions about
fiducial consciousness propose that there are indeed
conscious acts in whose intentional dimension there
is a cognitive achievement of holiness; but that
just as these acts' intentionality is not the characteristic intentionality of a fifth, fiducial level
of knowing, so their consciousness is not the characteristic consciousness of a fifth, fiducial, level.
Instead, that consciousness is on the fourth level,
as but an aspect of evaluative consciousness, or on
the third level, as but an aspect of judicative
consciousness, or on the second level, as but an
aspect of ideational consciousness, or on the fifth
level, as but an aspect of sensory consciousness.[53]

Suppositions in the two remaining groups agree in
hypothesizing that alleged cognitive acts possessing the consciousness in question (i.e., the conscious
dimension of acts whereby colors, sounds, odors,
tastes, etc., or intelligibility, or factuality, or
value, or holiness become cognitively present)
both do occur, and occur precisely on the level in
question (i.e., the sensory, or ideational, or
judicative, or evaluative, or fiducial, respectively),
with the consciousness in question as these levels'
<u>characteristic</u> consciousness. They differ in how
they conceive the conscious structure of those acts.

<u>Immediate-receptionist</u> suppositions about cognitive

consciousness all propound that the conscious structure of the cognitional acts that they regard is one of immediate receptivity. That is to say, cognitional self-presence is indeed correlative with reflection - the subject's acts returning upon themselves, receiving themselves as their own contents. But although a complete self-return, and thus full cognitional self-presence, either may or may not take place in any given instance, at least a partial and unmediated self-return, and thus primitive cognitional self-presence - consciousness - takes place in every instance. Hence, immediate-receptionist suppositions about sensory, ideational, judicative, evaluative, and fiducial consciousness are that sensory, ideational, judicative, evaluative, and fiducial acts, respectively, are cognitionally self-present in utterly primitive fashion precisely because they are at least partially and immediately reflective.[54]

Internal-presentialist suppositions about cognitional consciousness all propose that the conscious structure of the cognitional acts that they regard is one of internal presence. That is to say, there are two distinct kinds of cognitional self-presence. There is the advanced cognitional self-presence that arises by virtue of the subject's reflective self-reception.[55] But there is also a prior, utterly primitive cognitional self-presence that is not reflective in any way. The former arises insofar as the subject's acts take themselves as their own external terms. The latter, by contrast, is originally and immediately given. It is the internal presence of the acts (and, underlying them, the actor), the presence to which all external terms - whether of non-reflective acts or of reflective acts - become cognitionally present. Accordingly, the internal-presentialist suppositions about sensory, ideational, judicative, evaluative, and fiducial consciousness are that the utterly primitive cognitional self-presence of sensory, ideational, judicative, evaluative, and fiducial acts, respectively, is original, immediate, and non-reflective.[56]

D. The Phenomenology of Knowing: Dialectically-Opposed Integral Sets of Answers to the Ten Basic Questions

My central claim thus far in the body of this paper has had two main parts.

First, I have argued that the collectivity of basic

descriptive philosophical - or basic phenomenological - suppositions about human knowing that either have been made explicitly by individual philosophers or are implicit in the work of individual philosophers and empirical theorists may be construed as a group of diverse responses to ten basic phenomenological questions. These questions regard the occurrence, distinction, and characteristic structure of alleged cognitional acts that, taken collectively, go forward on five distinct levels (i.e., sensory, ideational, judicative, evaluative, and fiducial) and, taken distributively, possess two distinct dimensions (i.e., intentional and conscious). A complete phenomenology of human knowing must address each of these ten basic questions; consequently, the number of basic phenomenological suppositions in an integral set is ten.

Secondly, I have sketched what I take to be the fundamental dialectically-opposed kinds of basic phenomenological suppositions that are suggested by the aforementioned collectivity.[57] I have argued that any given theorist's suppositions about sensory, ideational, judicative, evaluative, and fiducial intentionality inevitably are either absentialist, or reductionist, or immediate-receptionist, or pure-productionist, or mediate-receptionist[58] in character, though not necessarily the same about each; and, moreover, that any given theorist's suppositions about sensory, ideational, judicative, evaluative, and fiducial consciousness inevitably are either absentialist, or reductionist, or immediate-receptionist, or internal-presentialist in character, though - once again - not necessarily the same about each.

Let me now define dialectically-opposed integral sets of basic phenomenological suppositions as those integral sets possessing suppositions that address at least one of the ten basic phenomenological questions in dialectically-opposed ways.[59] The comprehensive set of such dialectically-opposed integral sets may be made explicit by first articulating one integral set, then replacing one of its suppositions by that supposition's series of dialectical opposites to give a series of further integral sets, then replacing a second of its suppositions by that suppositions series of dialectical opposites to give a second series of integral sets, etc., until all of the possible internally-consistent[60] integral sets have been spelled out.[61]

I shall not speculate on how many of these possible dialectically-opposed integral sets of basic phenomenological suppositions about human knowing have actually been maintained in the history of thought to date, except to say that the number of theorists who have explicitly and consistently addressed all ten issues would seem to be rather small.[62] However, insofar as the patterned set of dialectically-opposed integral sets that may be made explicit by the procedure that I have just outlined is in fact both correct and comprehensive, it constitutes a heuristic framework within which can be located any basic phenomenology of knowing (or, indeed, any element thereof) that any theorist ever has maintained or ever could maintain.[63]

III. Conclusion

A. The Personal Assessment

My effort in the body of this paper has been simply to articulate something of the comprehensive set of basic dialectically-opposed integral phenomenological theories about human knowing. Even if the success of that effort were wholly unchallengeable, however, the reader would still be left with nothing more than a very large number of mere theories; and he might fairly be expected to ask, "Which of those theories is the correct one?".

Should that question be asked, the appropriate initial response to it would be, of course, not substantive but procedural: "You must determine that for yourself!". For to verify one phenomenological theory of knowing and falsify the others is ultimately nothing other than to grasp the former as the uniquely adequate theoretical account of the only concrete knowing of which one is directly aware, namely, one's own.[64]

Assuming that the reader recognizes the ultimately personal character of phenomenological verification, however, I should like to offer - in three main points - my own substantive response to the foregoing question, in the hope of facilitating the reader's performance of his personal verificational task. This response is ultimately based, of course, upon my own concrete knowledge of myself as a knower; and my articulation of that concrete self-knowledge carries me beyond the functional specialty of Dialectic and into that of Foundations.[65]

First, then, the ten suppositions that constitute the correct basic integral phenomenology of knowing are the following: regarding sensory intentionality, the appropriate <u>immediate-receptionist</u> supposition; regarding ideational, judicative, evaluative, and fiducial intentionality, the respective <u>mediate-receptionist</u> suppositions; and regarding sensory, ideational, judicative, evaluative, and fiducial consciousness, the respective <u>internal-presentialist</u> suppositions. That is to say, there are indeed cognitional acts that, taken collectively, go forward on sensory, ideational, judicative, evaluative, and fiducial levels and, taken distributively, have intentional and conscious dimensions. The knowing subject makes colors, sounds, odors, tastes, etc., cognitionally present to himself by sensory-level acts that in their intentional dimension are acts of direct, unmediated acceptance. He makes intelligibility, factuality, value, and holiness cognitionally present to himself by ideational-level, judicative-level, evaluative-level, and fiducial-level acts, respectively, that in their intentional dimension are acts of indirect, mediated acceptance, where the respective <u>media</u> are subject-produced concepts, judgments-of-factuality, judgments-of-value, and judgments-of-holiness. And the utterly primitive cognitional self-presence of all of these acts is original, immediate, and non-reflective.[66]

Secondly, in one's concrete cognitional performance the activities terminating in the concepts, judgments-of-factuality, judgments-of-value, and judgments-of-holiness whereby one knows intelligibility, factuality, value, and holiness respectively are not activities that are mechanical, unwitting, purely other-determined, simply other-constituted. Quite to the contrary, they are activities that pre-eminently are self-determining, self-constituting. That is to say, there is the (at best) <u>intelligent</u> self-constituting that characterizes one's acts of inquiring, having direct insights, and formulating concepts; there is the (at best) <u>rational</u> self-constituting that distinguishes one's acts of reflecting, achieving reflective insights, and making judgments-of-factuality; there is the (at best) <u>responsible</u> self-constituting that marks one's acts of ethical deliberating, having apprehensions-of-value, and making judgments-of-value; and there is the (at best) <u>unrestrictedly loving</u> self-constituting that typifies one's acts of agapic deliberating, having apprehensions-of-holiness, and making judgments-of-holiness.[67] But cognitional self-constituting presupposes non-reflective cognitional self-presence; for there could be no cognitional self-constituting where there was not even cognitional self-presence, and acts that became self-present only through reflection would lack self-presence in the moment of their original, pre-reflective, constitution.[68] Thus, in one's actual knowing of intelligibility, factuality, value, and holiness the non-reflective conscious dimension of one's cognitional activities has a certain methodical priority over the intentional dimension; and, correlatively, within the correct integral supposition-set the internal-presentialist suppositions regarding consciousness are methodologically more basic than the mediate-receptionist suppositions regarding intentionality.[69]

Thirdly, the inadequacies which can arise in one's phenomenology of knowing (and thence negatively influence one's epistemology and metaphysics) are of two main types: mere deficiencies and outright errors. The deficiencies arise from insufficient (or insufficiencly implemented) concrete knowledge of one's own cognitional acts (and their contents). The errors (other than mere inconsistencies) arise from insufficient (or insufficiently implemented) concrete knowledge of one's own cognitional acts (and their contents), together with the application - permitted by the absence of such self-knowledge - of some mistaken cognitional principle that itself is finally nothing else than an unwarranted generalization of some cognitional feature that concretely one <u>does</u> know. Thus, absentialist suppositions of all kinds are utterly deficient, reflecting the theorist's failure to grasp concretely even the occurrence of those of his cognitional acts (and contents) that the suppositions regard. Reductionist suppositions of all kinds represent some advance but are still greatly deficient. They manifest that the theorist has grasped concretely the occurrence of those of his cognitional acts (and contents) that the suppositions regard, but not yet their distinction from other acts (and contents). Immediate-receptionist and pure-productionist suppositions are even less deficient, but, on the other hand, they are positively erroneous. They reveal that the theorist has grasped concretely both the occurrence of those of his cognitional acts (and contents) in question and their distinction from other acts (and contents) but that he has misunderstood their structure in some way. Immediate-receptionist suppositions regarding the upper four levels of cognitional intentionality and/or any of the five levels of cognitional consciousness show that the theorist, influenced by the mistaken principle that all human knowing is fundamentally like the intentional dimension of sensory knowing, has concretely attributed an immediacy to the intentional dimension that those dimensions on the levels in question simply do not possess.[70] And pure-productionist suppositions regarding any of the five levels of cognitional intentionality indicate that the theorist, influenced by the mistaken principle that the intentionality of human knowing is purely constructive, has concretely attributed a self-sufficiency to the intentional dimension of his knowing that it just does not have.[71]

B. This Paper and the Work of Lonergan

In working, during the past several years, toward the conclusions that I have set forth in this paper, I did not bind myself in advance to making my results harmonize with the work of Bernard Lonergan.[72] Nonetheless, I would contend that as a matter of fact my conclusions here not only harmonize with Lonergan's work but finally do little more than differentiate and bring together certain fundamental elements that are already present, though as compact or unintegrated, within that work itself. While not attempting to document this contention here,[73] I should like at least to amplify it slightly by suggesting that my schema adds both generality and detail to what Lonergan has said about the radical personal advance that he calls "intellectual conversion" and about its absence.

For Lonergan, the fundamental component of "intellectual conversion" is an adequate (and effectively implemented) concrete knowledge of oneself as a knower; and the theoretical expression of that component is the basic cognitional phenomenology that itself is adequate or "positional". Again, the absence of the fundamental component of "intellectual conversion" is nothing other than an inadequate (or ineffectively implemented) concrete knowledge of oneself as a knower; and the theoretical expression of that absence is a basic cognitional phenomenology that itself is inadequate or "counter-positional".[74]

Now, I am claiming that my schema makes explicit that the "positional" phenomenology (1) regards no less than two dimensions of cognitional acts on no less than five levels; (2) reflects the theorist's concrete grasp of the occurrence, distinction, and characteristic structure of each of those dimensions on each of those levels; and, more fully, (3) manifests the theorist's concrete recognition that (i) in their intentional dimension cognitional acts (a) on the first level are immediately receptive and (b) on the second, third, fourth, and fifth levels are mediately receptive, and (ii) in their conscious dimension cognitional acts on all five levels are internally self-present.[75] Again, I am claiming that my schema makes explicit that (1) phenomenologies can be "counter-positional" either through mere deficiency or through outright error; (2) the deficiencies mirror the theorist's failure concretely either to grasp even the occurrence of both dimensions of cognitional acts on all five levels or to grasp at least their mutual distinction; and (3) the errors arise because concretely the theorist mistakenly takes the cognitional acts (i) in their intentional dimension (a) on the second, third, fourth, and/or fifth levels to be immediately receptive and/or (b) on any of the five levels to be simply productive, and/or (ii) in their conscious dimension on any of the five levels to be immediately receptive.[76]

More simply, I am claiming that my schema makes explicit that in its fundamental moment the radical personal advance lebelled "intellectual conversion" (1) must, if it is to be complete, regard not just three but rather five levels; (2) consists not just in eliminating one's incorrect concrete understanding of oneself as a knower but also, and initially, in overcoming one's inadequate concrete attention to oneself as a knower; and (3) eliminates not just the error that "all knowing is looking" but also the error that "all (intentional-dimension) knowing is making".[77]

I conclude with a terminological suggestion. Since what we have been discussing is a radical advance in one's concrete grasp not simply of one's "intellectual" knowing, the knowing that culminates on the third level of conscious intentionality, but also of one's "moral" and "religious" knowing within the total sequences of operations on the fourth and fifth levels respectively, I propose that in the interests of clarity this radical advance be called not "intellectual" conversion but, more broadly, "cognitional" conversion.[78]

CHAPTER FOUR

The Human Good and Christian Conversation

Frederick Lawrence

I. Introduction

For the past six or seven years I have been tantalized by a passage from Lonergan's economics manuscript; and I have been trying to come to grips with it directly and indirectly in my work as a teacher and theologian for the same period of time. I have had an overwhelming sense that it points to the transformation in society and culture at stake in contemporary political theology and locates the arena in which the most basic questions for political theology lie. The passage goes as follows: "Now to change one's standard of living in any notable fashion is to live in a different fashion. It presupposes a grasp of new ideas. If the ideas are to be above the level of currently successful advertizing, serious education must be undertaken. Finally, coming to grasp what serious education realizes, and, nonetheless, coming to accept that challenge constitute the greatest challenge to the modern economy".[1]

The change in living, in ideas, in education indicated here has to do with the issues of revolution and conversion associated with the achievement of a new identity. In this paper, I want to discuss issues connected with meeting the challenge and understanding what Lonergan is talking about in terms of the metaphor of learning a new language.

A. Learning a New Language

This metaphor, of course, is not just a metaphor, because language as I am using the term here is a component integral to the processes of communal and personal self-constitution. If human self-becoming is chiefly a matter of asking and answering questions for understanding, reflection, and deliberation and then living by the answers, it is clear just how important language is to us. Besides the verifiable correlation between aphasia and apraxia, we need language to pose questions to the situations we encounter in life. Language leads us along both preconceptually and imaginally as well as within the spontaneously ordered operations of intelligent, reasonable, and responsible consciousness. With Rosemary Haughton and Stephen Crites, indeed, we could articulate the meaning and value of the major transformations in our lives by studying the changes in language usages that are correlative with the different conversions.

But aside from its intrinsically methodical appropriateness, the metaphor of learning a language presents itself to us with a more special urgency at the present time. In a time that is felt to be a period of almost unprecedented crisis we Christians speak languages stemming from traditions, the meanings and values of which are at odds both with Christian faith and with Lonergan's foundational language. Thus, the problem of the watering down or distortion of one's tradition about which Lonergan has written so eloquently enters our lives with a vengeance. These alien and alienating languages may be generating not merely lives of inauthentic authenticity, but lives of unconverted inauthenticity almost as a rule within the Christian traditions. And when Christianity gets co-opted into supplying a legitimating veneer for meanings and values that are unchristian, then probabilities mount that even well-intentioned speakers and doers of what they think is the Word will not only not be doing so, but they will be unaware of the existential contradictions in which they are involved. The urgency becomes all the more pressing when we realize that "they" are we ourselves.

I have found that expressing in word and deed the horizon to which one has been moved by Christian conversion is almost as much a matter of unlearning the languages that have possessed us hitherto as of learning to speak a new language. But this general problem of learning and unlearning is particularly delicate when one tries to operate in the specialty of foundations; especially if one tries to speak with Lonergan's general and special categories. To show more exactly what I mean, I have decided to use Lonergan's structure of the human good to convey a notion of the hindrances to speaking authentically his language, especially as they arise from other competing languages by which we are already liable to be dominated.

B. The Structure of the Human Good as Language

Let us recall first of all the structure of the human good developed by Lonergan in the second chapter of Method in Theology:[2]

Individual		Social	Ends
Potentiality	Actuation		
capacity, need	operation	cooperation	particular good
plasticity, perfectibility	development, skill	institution, role, task	good of order
liberty	orientation, conversion	personal relations	terminal value

This structure is a component in a technical language - what I shall be calling Lonergan's foundational language. As a language in the most serious sense, it is heuristic, and so it will be learned or mastered according as we are able to use it in asking our own real questions about the human situation. Its overwhelming suitableness for political theology becomes obvious, for instance, as soon as we grasp that it names at the outset what it is we are looking for when we ask the very questions from which philosophy as practical and political first originated: "What's the right way to live?". "What's the best, the most choiceworthy, way of life"?. I want to illustrate what I mean by learning a new language and unlearning old languages by setting the structure of the human good in the contexts of ancient and modern political philosophies and comparing the range of meaning intended by their languages with that intended by Lonergan.

II. The Human Good and the Alternative Answers of Antiquity and Modernity

A. The Context of Ancient Political Philosophy

The premodern breakthrough in posing the practical-political question was crystallized in the Greek and Christian apprehension of it as a question about the good of order. Plato's Republic and Aristotle's Politics ask, "What's the best regime?". The key to the question is the clear and consistent discrimination between mere life as physical, vital, and sensitive spontaneity and the good life.[3] The latter is coordinate with "rational appetite, (and) with the specialized object of the reasonable good".[4] The following rather lengthy quotation from a 1943 article by Lonergan may provide a summary of the salients uncovered by the classical response to the question about the best regime.

> Throughout, nature is characterized by repetitiveness: over and over again it achieves mere reproductions of what has been achieved already; and any escape from such cyclic recurrence is per accidens and in minore parte or, in modern language, due to chance variation. But in contrast with this repetitiveness of nature is the progressiveness of reason. For if it is characteristic of all intellect to grasp immutable truth, it is the special property of the potential intellect of man to advance in the knowledge of the truth. Nor is it merely the individual that advances, as though knowledge were classically static, a fund whence schoolboys receive a dole. On the contrary, to the historian of science or philosophy and still more to the anthropologist, the individual of genius appears no more than the instrument of human solidarity; through such individuals humanity advances, and the function of tradition and education is to maintain the continuity of a development that runs from the days of primitive fruit-gatherers through our own of mechanical power on into an unknown future. But not only are nature and reason contrasted as repetitive and progressive. There is a contrast between the organistic spontaneity of nature and the deliberate friendships of reason. By 'organistic' spontaneity I would denote the mutual adaptation and automatic correlation of the activities of many individuals as though they were parts of a larger organic unit: This phenomenon may be illustrated by the antheap or beehive; but its more general appearance

lies in the unity of the family, a unity which nature as spontaneously and imperiously attains in the accidental order as in the substantial it effects the unity of the organism. Now it is not by organistic spontaneity but by mutual esteem and good will that reason sets up its comparable union of friendship: and in accordance with our eternal viewpoint we may note that human friendship is to be found not only in the urbanity and collaboration of contemporaries' esteem for the great men of the past on whose shoulders they stand, and in their devotion for the men of the future for whom they set the stage of history for better or worse. A third contrast between nature and history is in point of efficiency. While nature with the ease of a super-automaton pursues with statistical infallibility and regularly attains through organistic harmonies its repetitive ends, the reason and rational appetite of fallen man limp in the disequilibrium of high aspiration and poor performance to make progress of reason a dialectic of decline as well as of advance, and the rational community of men a divided unity of hatred and war as well as the indivisible unity of fraternity and peace".5

From this summary we need to notice a number of points. First, then, treating the question about the right way to live in terms of the second level of the structure, that of the good of order, brings with it a tendency to subordinate elements located on the third level of that structure to the second level. In Thomas Aquinas' Of Princely Government, for example, needs on the level of particular goods motivate and call for a civil or political society (Bk.I, Ch.1), and friendships (personal relations) are acknowledged to be the aim or goal of political rule (Bk.I, Ch.10); but the intelligible content of civil society is handled most profusely in terms of virtues and types of regime, etc.). Although almost all third level components are present and treated in the ancient accounts, they do tend to get subordinated to the second level.

Secondly, the ancients conceive the practical and

political question about the right way to live not merely empirically (i.e., as an account of possible ways of life as verified), but ethically or morally. Thus, Aristotle's <u>Nicomachean Ethics</u> is integral to his <u>Politics</u>, with the former being devoted to habits and skills (the moral and dianoetic virtues) and the latter to the institutional set-up with its appropriate roles and tasks. This same unity of the political and moral is also evident in Plato's famous parallel between the order of the polis and the order of the soul, with its tripartite division into desire (for sensible or material pleasure), spiritedness (anger, the root of the war-like virtues), and reason (the faculty for seeking the true, the good, the beautiful). As Gadamer, Arendt, and a host of others in our day have discovered, by treating the question of the good of order as a question of morality and ethics, the ancients kept questions for practical intelligence distinct from questions for technical expertise; by never reducing the former to the latter, they did not make sheer feasibility in a technical sense into a criterion for practical judgment, but normally judged against advances in technology when it was thought to jeopardize the common good.

However, this approach to practical issues also went hand-in-hand with what Lonergan calls a normative notion of culture, or what he spoke of as "the great republic of culture" in the passage cited above. This was an ambiguous achievement. To begin with, there is the normative function of culture delineated by Lonergan in the following fashion: "Corresponding to judgments of value, there is cultural community. It transcends the frontiers of states and epochs of history. It is Cosmopolis, not as an unrealized political ideal, but as a long-standing, nonpolitical, cultural fact. It is the field of communication and influence of artists, scientists, and philosophers. It is the bar of enlightened public opinion to which naked power can be driven to submit. It is the tribunal of history that may expose successful charlatans and may restore to honor the prophets stoned by their contemporaries".[6] Within the structure of the human good, Lonergan has brought out the differentiation of culture as the domain in which society reflects upon and appraises its way of life in distinguishing between the second and third levels. The second level regards the <u>social</u> dimension of the human good, the concretely verifiable way of life as embodied in laws, technology, economy, polity, family life; the third level comprises the <u>cultural</u> domain in the light of which the social is (to be) judged and evaluated. By this distinction, both the "social" and the "cultural" have an utterly empirical meaning, but "culture" retains the connotation of a normative function without being classicist in Lonergan's pejorative sense.

In the best of the ancients, culture and the poltical order are identical only in the ideal and highly improbable case where the philosopher becomes the ruler; otherwise and (we can almost always suppose) in fact, culture is only the forum before which the political order is judged, and within which justice is realized not in deed but in speech alone. This sense of balance got lost as the "Greek mediation of meaning" was transformed into classical culture with its science of man. As Lonergan came to discover, classical culture performed the above-mentioned normative function of culture by means of "a somewhat arbitrary standardization of man".[7] Classical or classicist culture transformed the Greek breakthrough - "a necessary step in the development of the human mind"[8] - into a timeless criterion in which the content of the classically oriented science of man "easily obscures man's nature, constricts his spontaneity, saps his vitality, limits his freedom",[9] because it "concentrated on the essential to ignore the accidental, on the universal to ignore the particular, on the necessary to ignore the contingent".[10] Since it omitted so much of the data on human being, its explanations could not help but be provisional in some respects, which is understandable. The overwhelming problem with classicist culture is its inability to acknowledge these limits and its apparent unwillingness to keep learning.

B. <u>The Context of Modern Political Philosophy</u>

1. <u>The First Wave of Modernity</u>[11]

The ancient answers to the question about the right way to live focused on the common good understood as a complex good of order; and they were preoccupied with virtue. What happened in the first phase of the shift to modernity has been suggestively encapsulated in the following passage by Allan Bloom: "The Ancients talked only about virtue and not about well-being. That in itself is perhaps harmless, but the moderns contended that the concentration on virtue contradicts the concern for well-being. Aristotle admitted that 'equipment' as well as virtue is needed for happiness, but said nothing about how that equipment is acquired. A careful examination of the acquisition of equipment reveals that virtue impedes that acquisition. Equipment is surely necessary, so why not experiment with doing without virtue?".[12] In other words, thinkers like Bacon, Hobbes, Descartes, Spinoza and Locke judged that in the light of humanity's "disequilibrium of high aspiration and poor performance",[13] taking care of equipment not only means doing without virtue if need be, but displacing the desire to know elevated to normative status by the ancients with the desire for self-preservation.

When the summum bonum gets replaced in modernity by the fear of death as summum malum, the psychology of orientation gets replaced by a psychology of motivations. Motivated by the anxiety about death, only the accumulation of power and property seems a choiceworthy good; and so comfortable self-preservation becomes the primary end of human beings.

In tandem with modern science's myth of productivity, modern political philosophy undertook the vast "humanitarian" project of taking care of equipment by parleying private vices into public welfare. But this was to subordinate the second and third levels of the structure of the human good to that of needs, desires, and particular goods. It follows that the common good no longer refers to the good of order as normative, but to particular goods as satisfying needs and desires as correlative with life in contradistinction to the good life. As a mere collectivity of private goods, the common good is "common" only in the sense of an accidental genus or species instead of as the objective of rational choice correlative with the human capacity for intellectual development. Furthermore, in relation to the normative order of vital, social, cultural, personal and religious values, the preference for mere life over the good life means the supremacy of vital values. The dominant practical question becomes not merely, "What's in it for me or my group?", but "What's the value of being good if you're not well off?".

The purpose of civil society and government on the early modern account is to protect pre-existent rights to life and the pursuit of property. Its key means will not be morality or religion, but the spirit of acquisitiveness at the root of property. Hence, governments are legitimate to the extent that they, as <u>The Federalist</u> put it, protect different and unequal faculties of acquiring wealth. This implies that the motive for political society according to the ancients becomes transformed into its criterion; even as action for the private good (conceived of as enlightened self-interest) is elevated into the standard for assessing rightness or wrongness overall.

Concerns for the third level are acknowledged by the early moderns under the rubric of natural right. Friendships are relevant as long as they are based on utility or pleasure. Liberty means either the freedom to design institutions that will provide mutual security and rules that guarantee the public good by enabling each individual to pursue private goods without obstruction from others, or at least the freedom to consent to such a design. It is clear, then, that the notion of natural right, inalienable, underivable from any authority, is an eminently selfish idea. As the product of an attempt to define human equality independently of any religion or metaphysics, it also meant to leave open the answer to the question of the right way to live, at least in principle; but in fact, that openness was a void the early moderns were content to see filled by commerce. Taking care of equipment is realized as taking care of business.

2. The Second Wave of Modern Political Philosophy

In his <u>First and Second Discourses</u> Rousseau laid bare the opposition between nature (now identified with the satisfaction of needs on the level of organistic spontaneity) and culture or civilization. He thus set the stage for the modern use of the term culture. As Bloom has written, "(A)ccording to Kant, Rousseau in his later works, <u>Emile</u>, <u>Social Contract</u>, <u>Nouvelle Heloise</u>, proposed a possible unity that harmonized the low natural demands with the high responsibilities of morality and art. This unity Kant called 'culture'".[14] Rousseau, therefore, unleashed the first cultural critique of the mercenary morality of liberalism.

94

From the point of view of the structure of the human good we can say that Rousseau's scathing attack was actually an ambiguous breakthrough to the second (social) and third (cultural) levels in reaction to the early modern reduction of all elements to the first level. Both the breakthrough and its ambiguity are signaled by the notorious modern dichotomies between nature and freedom, nature and history, and nature and art, which were exploited till our own day by the movements of idealism, historicism and romanticism. No less than Hobbes and Locke, however, Rousseau conceived of liberty without any reference to divine transcendence. Though he did not confine freedom to the limits of scientific calculation and technical control and debunked early liberalism's utilitarianism and instrumentalism, freedom for him was coordinate with the perfectibility of the amiable but brutish human being he uncovered in the state of nature; and its matrix was that animal's "simple feeling of existence", its "conscience" as "the science of simple souls".

Out of the framework built with these ideas Rousseau eventually developed the idea of the "general will". On the one hand, the general will was to be understood in terms of national custom, national "philosophy", or the "mystique of the nation". We have become familiar with these ideas under the guise of such terms as Hegel's *Zeitgeist* or Whitehead's "climate of opinion". On the other hand, Kant drew out the more idealist implications of the general will, for example, in his moralistic grounding of human rights. Earlier liberalism's "natural" rights to life, liberty, and the pursuit of happiness were founded not so much in the state of nature theory as on factual evidence on the dominance within human beings of the natural inclinations toward security and comfort. But Kant uses the ability (shown by Rousseau to be human and rational, but not natural) humans possess of universalizing their desire in order to subordinate the older liberalism's self-interest in safety and prosperity to rights conceived of as universal principles that serve to define human beings as free and independent.

One can appreciate the high moral tone of this transformation of so-called natural rights into human rights. It does seem to give primacy to the moral demands proper to the second and third levels. However, the apriorism, abstractness, and formalism of Kant's thought not only divorce his grounding from any concrete practical relevance; but his intelligible ego with its good will is so isolated from the empirically verifiable process of communication within which subjects grow to maturity that we are forced to concede that it is quite utopian (not to say unreal) as well. Kant had no way of tethering his "normative" realm of freedom to empirically verifiable fact; and so he buttressed it with postulates about God, freedom, and immortality on the one hand; and with a speculative philosophy of history on the other. Even on Kantian grounds the former threesome may be argued not to exist; and Kant's philosophy of history finally settles for a distinction between morality and mere legality which represents a compromise of rational faith with <u>Realpolitik</u>.

As a result of the two waves of modernity, there are two chief forms or languages of Western liberalism. They both depart from the modern assumption that the chief concern or issue of modern politics is power. First, <u>commercial democracy</u> is based on consent to governmental power as guarantor of public safety and comfort and on the doctrine of classical political economy that if there are no restrictions to free economic activity other than enlightened self-interest, social harmony and well-being will necessarily prevail. Second, <u>socialist politics of compassion</u> grounds the legitimacy of governmental power upon the extent to which it bolsters equality not merely of opportunity (i.e., the political right to endeavour to acquire and dispose of one's property within the limits of the law and the civil right to freedom of expression and to self-government), but of the satisfaction of aggregate societal needs (under the heading of economic, social, and cultural rights to such things as health, housing, education, employment, sanitation, etc.) by attempting to reconcile older liberalism's means with socialist or collectivist ends in what has been since called welfare economics. Both versions of liberalism are staunchly convinced of the efficacy of scientific prediction and control and of institutionally contrived solutions to political problems. In general, and by way of oversimplification, advocates of commercial democracy believe that enlightened self-interest in private good is the operator of <u>common weal</u>, and they preach the ideal of as much freedom as possible for the individual and the equality of opportunity. In the

United States we tend to label this stance conservative. Secularist proponents of the socialist politics of compassion depend upon "culture" to supply the link between the self-regarding individual and disinterested respect of the law or the rights of others by generating a secular kind of compassion which educes gentle and beneficient concern for others from natural selfishness. They advocate a greater equality of conditions or results in life and preach equality of influence and power for all. In the United States we tend to reserve the name liberal for people who are considered politically progressive in this sense.

The most noteworthy proponent of the socialist politics of compassion is Karl Marx. The industrial revolution, especially after its "take-off", made plain to him that the liberal capitalist belief in a pre-established harmony between private interest and public welfare was an idealogy. As he argued in The Jewish Question, the natural rights enshrined in such revolutionary documents as the Declaration of Independence (1776) and the Declaration of the Rights of Man and Citizen (1789) are really only bourgeois rights; they hold good for the capitalist class, but not for the proletariat. Commercial democracy in its intention to supply the equipment for freedom turns out in the final analysis to be a struggle between capitalists and workers. Marx tried to analyze that struggle by re-introducing social (second level) and, at least in his youthful writings, ethical (third level) concerns into political economy in opposition to the "possessive individualism" of liberal capitalism. However, this important attempt to redress the biases of liberal democratic political economy unfortunately got derailed by Marx's uneasy blend of idealism and materialism. That idealism trivialized the underlying problem of evil just as Rousseau and Kant had done. The materialism kept him from breaking cleanly from the utilitarianism and instrumentalism of his early liberal predecessors. He failed altogether to appreciate Rousseau's insight that to achieve freedom in equality requires small communities with religious foundations. And however much the romantic model of artistic creation was his privileged model for the making of history by human subjects, his revolutionary idea was ultimately just a project of technical mastery, which not even a classless and stateless society would be capable of redeeming.

3. The Third Wave of Modern Political Philosophy

a. Nietzsche

As the inaugurator of the third wave of modernity, Nietzsche realized that the outcome of both liberal democracy's dedication to preservation and comfort and social democracy's well-fed, well-clothed, well-sheltered human beings with their up-to-date educations, entertainment, and psychiatry would be the abolition of all ideals and aspirations. To the degree that liberalisms of both left and right choose mere life over the good life, they produce the "last man" - healthy, but without heart or convictions.

Nietzsche, therefore, has the overwhelming importance of trying to re-establish the importance of the level of liberty and terminal values. He stands just at the threshold of the religiously mediated insight so nearly formulated in the title of the book by Dorothee Sölle: *Death by Bread Alone*. He sets the stage for the rescuing consciousness of the unorthodox Jew, Walter Benjamin, and for the Christian theologian, Johann Baptist Metz. The latter's short definition for religion is interruption - interruption of the modern project of subjugating human and subhuman nature. But for Nietzsche Christianity is just Platonism for the masses; and all the supports for ultimate values in nature, God, or reason are gone. The only option left open in the face of the abyss is a creative transvaluation of all previous values on the part of solitary individuals creative enough to respond to the implications of the will-to-power, especially, that human beings are originating values in the absolute sense of being able to posit values arbitrarily. In Nietzsche, the most radical breakthrough to the third level of terminal values also presents us with the epitome of human disorientation, rebellion, and disorder.

b. Weber: Between Kant and Nietzsche

Nietzsche's perhaps most influential disciple, Max Weber, domesticated his master's concept of value for the academy by marrying it to Kant's synthesis of culture performed in his three *Critiques*. Weber thus spawned the fact/value distinction as it is commonly and erroneously understood. The realm of nature investigated by science and exploited by technology becomes the value-free domain of fact; whereas both the realm of freedom and responsibility and that of art and religion become the domain of value. As a result of this fateful distinction, the normative moment of culture intended by Lonergan's notion of terminal value gets sunk into the quagmire of the arbitrariness and caprice of values as the creation of the Nietzschean will-to-power.

The devastation wrought thereby for apprehending the third level is exacerbated by the common understanding on the part of the contemporary social sciences of the way the Weberian distinction between facts and values is to govern the relationship between social science and social policy. Social science is confined to facts: it describes, and its descriptions are expected to yield information on the basis of which social policy can predict and control. Any normative judgment - either as classical intelligibility or as true judgements of fact and value - gets systematically excluded. The individual, group, or general bias of those in power leads them to repudiate true terminal values (beyond the desires and needs of organistic spontaneity) and to reject any intelligibility yielded by science that does not afford means of prediction and control. The point is to increase managerial efficiency even at the cost of human liberty or social, cultural, personal, or religious values.

Again, within the perspective of Weber's fact/value distinction, a Nietzschean slant can hold sway in personal and communal thinking and action. For it is difficult to avoid the, either benevolently or malevolently, nihilist conclusion that all standards of meaning and substantive order are relative in the last analysis. Nihilism simply eliminates the insight that "though the things seen are at different times in their internal temporal relationships, still it is possible and proper for the human intellect to imitate the divine and by abstraction stand outside the temporal flow in which really, though not of necessity intentionally, it is involved".[15] The nihilist operates instead on the assumption that judgments of fact or value are no more than the historically conditioned illusions - the humanly posited horizons - without which the human animal can not live. For the benevolent nihilist, this becomes the premise for a "soft tyranny" of cultural manipulation of the many by the few - for profit. For the malevolent nihilist, this becomes the premise for the "big lie" enforced by terror.

Fortunately, however, the response to Nietzsche's call to the best of a generation to become true selves and form a new aristocracy has often been based less on nihilism than on the Kantian rational belief (so congenial to secularized Protestantism) that in principle if not in fact a human person ought never to be used as a means to any aim or purpose not freely chosen by himself or herself; no one can ever be an object of manipulative control by another. For Kantians, of course, this conviction has the cognitive status not of objective truth, but of a postulate, so that the value of the person may never be affirmed as ontic, as it is in Christian faith or in a critically realist philosophy such as Lonergan's. It follows that the inchoate acknowledgement of the human person as an originating imperative rather than in the concrete goodness meant by terminal values, goods of order, and particular goods in Lonergan's sense.

Unfortunately, the salutary Kantian doctrine of the unconditionality of the human person gets relegated to pragmatic irrelevance by Weber's separation of "the ethics of conviction" from the "ethics of responsibility". The ethics of conviction regards ultimate ends, while the ethics of responsibility regards only the pragmatic consequences of means in relation to ends established irrationally and arbitrarily. Doesn't this make Kant's idealistic faith just a matter of conviction? Moreover, this separation would have the effect of sealing off the third level of the human good from the second level.

The ongoing mutual impenetrability of second and third levels becomes all the more disastrous when it comes to Weber's reconstruction of the reasons why people historically have obeyed authority. On the one hand his construct of the charismatic form of legitimation is one of the only 19th century instances of evaluating religiously based existence positively, since for Weber charismatic authority is the privileged force or agency for social change. On the other hand, his hypothesis about modernity as a process of rationalization, combined with his analysis of bureaucratic control, spells out in a way that is verifiable the meaning of Nietzsche's critique of liberal democracy and socialism on the level of the good of order. Because, for all the preoccupation of liberal and socialist democracy with being emancipated from religious, feudal, monarchical, or aristocratic control; for all their preoccupation with the use of scientific prediction and manipulation "for the relief of man's estate", and of either consent and bargaining (liberal reformism) or violence (socialist revolution) to bring about an order of freedom in equality - it all seems only to have paved the way for bureaucracy and centralization: Weber's "iron cage".

III. Learning Foundational Language

A. Conflicts of Meanings and Values

The different political philosophies of antiquity and modernity have all shaped implicit or explicit answers to the question about the right way to live; and the latter have engendered languages that pervade our schools, homes, media, and cultural channels today. These languages often contain verbal equivalents to the language used by Lonergan to define implicitly the structure of the human good. As a result, when we speak about the human good, we are liable either to be intending meanings proper to these languages rather than Lonergan's, or at least to be mistaken by others in this way.

Take, for example, the word, liberty, in the structure of the human good. Liberty was acknowledged by the Greeks, but it was not a theme for them. They had a commonsense apprehension of the difference between slave or free. Theoretically, Aristotle was explicitly clear about the contingency of terrestrial events, which implies the contingency of all human agency. But he did not distinguish clearly between the specification and exercise of free will. And in spite of having a theory of habit, a notion that intellectual virtues liberate human beings more than even the moral virtues do, a recognition that most men know what is good yet choose what is to their own advantage, he had no theory of moral impotence. In short, we have no reason to suppose that the ancient Greek meaning of liberty coincides with Lonergan's in a more than partial way.

On the other hand, liberty has been a theme for the moderns. Indeed, some modern thinkers might agree with Lonergan that liberty is not just indeterminacy but self-determination and even perhaps that "we experience our liberty as the active thrust of the subject terminating the process of deliberation".[16] But none of the modern thinkers I have mentioned would agree with him either that "implicit in human choice of values is the absolute good that is God";[17] or, correlatively, that freedom of choice is grounded in our ability to criticize any finite course of group or individual action.[18] And similarly, despite their realization that _the_ god must be a being beyond the intracosmic gods, the Greeks did not affirm an explanatory notion of divine transcendence, any more than the moderns do.

In the course of my whirlwind survey of ancient and modern philosophical approaches to issues cognate with Lonergan's structure of the human good, I adverted repeatedly to ways the range of meaning made available in Lonergan's structure suffer major reductions when shifted into the perspective of any of the various languages discussed. From my brief critical comments, it may be plain how the many different interpretations of elements and levels within the structure have the effect of reducing one's ability to ask significant questions about our concrete situation. These contrasting languages express a reduction of Lonergan's horizon of meaning and value. Since the horizons of our speech and living have been constituted by _those_ languages, we must ask ourselves how we can learn the foundational language Lonergan uses so that we can mean what he meant.

When we take seriously language as operative within the matrix of conscious intentionality and as a component in human self-constitution, the issue that comes to the surface when appropriating Lonergan's foundational language is the fourth aspect of understanding any text listed by Lonergan in Method in Theology's chapter on Interpretation: "One arrives at such understanding through a process of learning and even at times as a result of conversion".[19] It is the issue Lonergan put so starkly in the chapter on History and Historians: "For any notable change of horizon is done, not on the basis of that horizon, but by envisaging a quite different and, at first sight, incomprehensible alternative and then undergoing a conversion".[20] Although I could multiply citations at some length, this issue even gripped Lonergan in 1926, when, at age 22 he had to preach to 250 students in the Heythrop College dining room and selected for his text: "You may hear and hear but you will never understand. You may look and look but you will never see".[21] The issue Lonergan had to face is one we may have to face, too. It is the issue of conversion and repentance.

My own sense is that conversion and repentance are crucial to the process of learning Lonergan's foundational language precisely because the languages of liberalism or nihilism are so dominant in our culture. They do not just exist "out there" or "in *them*". If my own experience is not unique, these languages have invaded us. They affect our day-to-day life-choices and our overall way of life both in the manner in which we individually and collectively interpret our desires and needs and in the ordering of the values incorporated in the already understood and agreed upon-solutions to the problem of living together that make up our institutions. These languages are *the* symptom of our implicatedness in what today is commonly called "structural sin". And so the heart of relinguishing the languages and the start of the process of learning a new foundational language - which, as I have tried to show, does not necessarily mean using different words or inventing neologisms - is metanoia, conversion and repentance.

B. Christian Conversion as Conversational

1. The Christian Situation of Conversion

Frederick Crowe has written with theological intelligence about the situation in which one appropriates Christian conversion:

> "At one end of the spectrum, we have ourselves ... with our religious interiority to be pondered and understood. At the other end we have Jesus with his human consciousness and the religious interiority of God's Son in human form. In between we have the apostles, prophets, evangelists, etc.; as well as the mystics of all ages, but especially from those

times when they began to describe more helpfully their experience ... (T)here would be the inner word of Jesus finding expression in his spoken words and deeds, in his silence and his suffering. This expression, an outer word in the broad sense, is received, assimilated interiorly, and re-expressed by the ... intermediaries between Jesus and the people of God. It becomes then an outer word for us, to be received in faith but given new expression in virtue of our own inner word, the gift of the Spirit, on the foundations, that is, of our interiority".[22]

In being converted, in repentance, we enter a conversation within what might be called a redemptive tension as we experience the interplay between inner word (gift of the Spirit) and outer word (Jesus, who lived, suffered, died, and rose again) in the process of ongoing conversion, since conversion as Christian involves a two-sided response to God's outgoing love: a response to the operative grace of conversion which bestows a universal antecedent willingness through the gift of the Spirit; and a (not necessarily separate) response to the outer word of the Risen Lord.

2. Conversation with the Outer Word: Its Redemptive Function[23]

I want to underline Lonergan's statement: "Without the visible mission of the Word, the gift of the Spirit is a being-in-love without a proper object; it remains simply an orientation to mystery that awaits its interpretation".[24] Perhaps for most of us, Christian conversion involves encountering "the Christ, the Son of God, whose story is to be read in the Gospels and the significance of that story in the Old Testament and the New Testament"[25] in the light of God's gift of his love. As with the original disciples, it is the Risen Lord who first reveals to us our own very real implicatedness in personal and structural sin; who reveals us to be the co-causes of his suffering; he who shows us the extent of suffering our sin cost him, and who communicates to us the judgment of his Father on the sheer horribility of that personal and structural sin. Confronted by our responsibility for our part in sin, we want to repent,

to change; but we cannot change ourselves. And so the
Risen Lord forgives us for our involvement in personal
and structural sin; he thereby gives us the strength
at once to take responsibility for our sin and to claim
a new identity by uniting us with his redemptive suffering. He enables us to accept consciously, knowingly,
responsibly the de facto intelligibility of this concrete
universe: the law of the cross as the movement through
death to life eternal.

3. Conversation with the Outer Word: Its Constitutive Function

When we put in terms of language the issue of conversion
as a radical change in our horizon or orientation, then
we need to speak of story in the sense intended by Lonergan when he wrote that "we have hunches we cannot formulate so we tell a story".[26] Let me cite at greater
length his way of handling the category of story:

> (B)eing human is being-in-the-world (in der
> Welt sein), ... one can rise to full stature
> only through full knowledge of the world, ...
> one does not possess that full knowledge and
> thus makes use of the elan vital that, as it
> guides biological growth and evolution, so
> too it takes the lead in human development
> and expresses its intimations through the
> stories it inspires. Symbols, finally, are
> a more elementary type of story: they are
> inner or outer events, or a combination of
> both, that intimate to us at once the kind
> of being that we are to be and the kind of
> world in which we become our true selves.[27]

In terms of language, then, being converted means radically changing the story by which one lives. Thus, J.
B. Metz has identified the emancipatory stories implicit
in the liberal languages in which we have been educated,
socialized, acculturated. As success stories they
cover over the lives human beings really lead by making
us oblivious to the full scope of human suffering
throughout history. Metz has contrasted these success
stories with the redemptive story of Jesus who suffered,
died, and rose again.

Response to the linguistic and incarnate meaning of the

outer word of the Risen One meets head on our need to be conversationally opened up and made sensitive to the depth of our involvement in the sinfulness of the situation brought about by the stories that have grown out of the waves of modernity in our culture; our need to absorb in detail how much we have constituted ourselves individually and collectively in these stories to the detriment of others, even Jesus. Contact - however mediated it may be - with the Risen Judge who has been victimized by our sin can open up this conversation for us. But, on the other hand we also need to be forgiven and empowered by his spirit in order to gradually displace the "hunches" about our future cultivated in us by the dominant liberal languages in favor of the story of the one who suffers and dies for us, the one who rises and forgives us in befriending us. Thus, we need both his Spirit and meditative exegesis of his story in order to make his orientation toward the suffering and loss in the world our own. When we have been forgiven, loved, and illumined in faith by his story, a shift in probabilities takes place, and we have much more of a chance to become like the man Jesus whose overall approach to the world is portrayed by Mark's transfiguration story where Jesus moves from being utterly absorbed in conversational immediacy with the Father, Elijah, and Moses, to inquire with simple, direct, and genuine concern about the epileptic child: "How long has he been like this?".

And so, the question has been urging itself upon me with increasing force whether a concrete entry into the conversation with the outer word may not be a prerequisite as a matter of fact for speaking Lonergan's foundational language, somewhat in the way he affirms that religious conversion is required not de jure but de facto for a correct conception and affirmation of the existence of God.

4. Conversation and Community

I have been speaking of the communication of Spirit and Word in terms of its redemptive and constitutive functions. Let us return to the two sides of Crowe's spectrum to recall the conversational situation of Christian conversion. On the one side there is the outer word originally generated by the consciously elicited acts of meaning and value of the mind and heart of Jesus as

he sought to discover how to share with us the meaning
and value of being in love with his very dear Father.
On the other side there are our Spirit-enlightened
questions for intelligence, reflection, and deliberation, as we enter into communication with the outer
word. In either case, Jesus's and ours, we are con-
stituting ourselves humanly by acts of meaning and value
that are conversational. The conversation begins, as
Lonergan once put in, in "the experience of a transformation one did not bring about but rather underwent, as
divine providence let evil take its course and vertical
finality be heightened, as it let one's circumstances
shift, one's dispositions change, new encounters occur,
and - so gently and quietly - one's heart be touched.
It is the experience of a new community ...".[28]

We find in our experience that one's gift of the Spirit
surges or rises up gradually to the forefront of consciousness as one falls in love with someone who lives
a life of self-transcendence. One feels oneself invited
or challenged to live up to a new standard, because the
one or ones with whom one has fallen in love speak a
language with their lives that embodies a different
orientation and different judgments of value than one
was used to. The eyes of being in love bring one to
appreciate the implicit or explicit meanings and values
that make the beloved "tick". If it is explicitly
Christian, the life of the new community will have the
shape, as Richard Holloway has so beautifully expressed
it, of being taken, blessed, broken, and given away;
if it is not explicitly Christian, similar life-patterns
will be in evidence together with the vital sense of
living out of a gratuity to which one cannot simply
lay claim. At any rate, when one is drawn by love
into such a relationship, one wants to become identified with the new community, and one begins to accept
the pattern or shape of its life and its story, not
as theories or explanations but as a framework of
beliefs. As time passes, one finds oneself assenting
not only notionally but really to the meanings, facts,
and values that are constitutive of the group's identity,
not because one has grasped their underlying intelligibility or the sufficiency of the evidence, but because
of what can only be described as the beauty of the
lives inspired by them. "In thy light we see light".
As believed and lived, such meanings and values become
constitutive of oneself, "for they crystallize the inner

gift of the love of God into overt Christian fellowship".[29]

5. Christian Identity and Its Cognitive Function

Besides being redemptive and constitutive, the communication of the Son and Spirit is also cognitive. The constitutive Christian story gives an existential answer to the question about the right way to live; but this answer gives rise to questions for intelligence, reasonableness, and responsibility as the Christian community tries to live out the answer it believes in the different circumstances, stages of meaning, and cultural milieux in which it exists. Hence, to keep its identity clear and to mediate its redemptive and constitutive power to every culture and every domain of human life, the Christian community focuses on its meaning and value as cognitive within the diverse stages of meaning.

Because, as Augustine made so clear in The City of God, there is a strict correspondence between what we individually and communally love and the identity of the selves and communities we are becoming, the cognitive function of meaning which clarifies the objective of our faith and love has a great practical importance. This practical and existential correlation between the identity of self and community on the one hand and the identity of the God of the self and the community on the other was in the forefront of the Christian community's concern "on the way to Nicea" and in the course of the patristic and conciliar debates of the first seven or eight Christian centuries, when it made the transition from a commonsense control of its basic meanings to second-order theoretical control. If the Arian question whether Jesus was the highest creature or God's son in the strictest sense reached its cognitive resolution on the explanatory level of logical operations on predicative statements, the need for such a resolution was practical, constitutive, soteriological: if Jesus was not God, are we really saved? Moreover, Erik Petersen, Matthew Lamb, and others have stressed the demolition of Eusebian civil theology consequent upon the Athanasian orthodoxy. These are examples of the way the cognitive function of meaning contributes to the foundational purification of the stories by which the Christian community expresses its terminal values and constitutes its identity.

An even more telling example of the foundational significance of Christianity's cognitive function in the second stage of meaning regards the speculative theology of the Trinity based on the Church doctrines worked out in those early ecumenical councils. I am referring, of course, to Augustine's breakthrough to the first non-material analogy for the immanent processions of the Son and the Spirit. His discovery of the most adequate created _imago Dei_ in the human mind and heart was a great watershed of Christian and human speculation on the divine nature. It came into its own only in the mature trinitarian theology of Thomas Aquinas; yet this hypothesis of the _emanatio intelligibilis_ was buried by Scotist, Ockhamist, and even Thomistic conceptualism promptly after his death. His explanation of the intrinsically conversational nature of the godhead, of its immanent processions, of its economic missions, however, is not something that could have been demonstrated outside the ambit of the stream of tradition generated by the outer Word, Jesus Christ. But its virtualities both for the self-understanding of the Christian community and for the focusing of its God-given orientation to the suffering world have, I am sorry to have to say, lain almost dormant, as far as Christian theology has been concerned.

At the present time, the Christian community in its cognitive function is making the tortuous passage from the second into the third stage of meaning. Perhaps the most unsettling manifestations of the breakdown of the theoretical, logically oriented, classical control of meaning have been connected with the widespread, wholesale jettisoning of specifically Christian meanings and values in favor of one or another "progressive" product of modernity. In its preaching and its liturgies, in its counselling and its conduct, in its theology and its catechesis, Western Christianity has been in the process, as one of my colleagues at Boston College has well put it, of diluting the Good News into "nice" news. Or in another suggestion articulated by Joann Wolski Conn and Walter Conn, the oscillations in Christian self-understanding between the attitudes of self-sacrifice and self-realization have tended to cover over the attitude of genuine self-transcendence demanded by the Christian gospel.

What is at stake in the Christian community's changeover

from second to third stage control of meaning is evident in Karl Rahner's foundational concentration in the thirties (in Geist im Welt) on the seventh article of Question 84 of the first part of the Summa theologiae, which used phenomenological means to comment on Thomas Aquinas' cognitional metaphysics. It is even more apparent in Lonergan's Verbum articles of the early forties and signaled again by the epigraph to Insight (1957) taken from Artistotle's de Anima. The pivotal issue in all these works was the prepredicative, prepropositional, phenomenologically ostensible act of direct insight into imaginatively elaborated symbolisms which grounds intelligent articulation in either other symbols or concepts, and of reflective insight into the sufficiency or insufficiency of evidence to ground true judgments. Lonergan, indeed, explicated the genuinely conversational basis of Thomas' trinitarian hypothesis within the realm of human interiority to uncover the most full-bodied and differentiated expression to date of the foundations of Christian theology in the third stage of meaning. By explicitly appropriating the way the authentic asking and answering of the eminently conversational questions[30] - "What are we doing whenever we really understand? What are we doing whenever we are really speaking? What are we doing whenever we are really listening to or really dedicating ourselves to someone or something?" - Lonergan discovered the concrete basis for theology as an integrally conversational discipline which mediates between past and future by passing from indirect discourse (research, interpretation, history, dialectic) to direct discourse (foundations, doctrines, systematics, communications). When Lonergan got clear about the last of the conversational questions, "What are we doing when we are loving?", his findings meshed with his own remarkable retrieval of Aquinas' intricate and second-stage theories on grace and freedom. That is to say, the clear differentiation of the further levels of consciousness engaged in deliberating and loving coalesced with the transposition into a third-stage framework of Thomas' doctrine on operative grace and, consequently, he was able to thematize the foundational reality for theology within the converted subject-in-love-with-God. This astounding transposition by Lonergan of Aquinas' fidelity both to Church doctrines and to the systematic exigence of meaning lays the groundwork for general and special categories and a renewal of theology in a new key with implications that are immediately practical and political.

The third-stage-of-meaning systematics already inaugurated by Lonergan allows us to put the theology of God, Trinity, Christology, Pneumatology, and Eschatology into explicitly conversational terms. In this framework, the interplay between the conversational self-meaning essential to God and the conversational self-meaning by which we are personally and communally constituted can be integrated into a complete revision of foundational theology. Here I would like to give an example of what I mean by sketching out how the structure of the human good can be transposed into the context of the communication of the Son and the Spirit as redemptive and constitutive meaning.

IV. The Human Good and the Christian Conversation

God's self-communication in grace involves not merely an entry into a new entitative, supernatural order of being; but the catching up of our human being as conversationally stunted or deformed self-meaning into the self-meaning constitutive of the Trinity. The gift of God's love liberates human <u>liberty</u> when we fall in love with God. But the <u>conversion</u> by which we fall in love with God is also an <u>entry into</u> a new set of <u>interpersonal relations</u> with Father, Son, and Spirit.

As sharing in the relationship of the Spirit to the Word and the Father, we are

- oriented (with the Son) toward the Father in the beatific vision in the afterlife, and in the present life, given the faith, hope, and love by which our conscious intentionalities can respond here on earth to God's outgoing love in a life of self-transcendent listening, devotion, and self-dedication;

- made ever more receptive to the goodness, truth, and intelligibility of the linguistic and incarnate meaning of the Word;

- introduced into a dynamism of discernment by which we gradually become more pure and disinterested toward the expression of God's will in the concrete world order comprised of ranges of <u>goods of order</u>, <u>particular goods</u>, and natural schemes of recurrence.

As sharing in the Son's relationship to the Father (filiation), we actively desire the strictly supernatural fulfillment of the beatific vision as a <u>particular good</u> that relativizes all other <u>needs</u> and <u>desires</u>.

As sharers in the mission of the Word, listening to the Word expressed in history by Jesus under the Spirit's tutelage is just the beginning; we have also to

- use our <u>capacity for intellectual development</u> to enter into solidarity with the poor and the victims of injustice by envisaging and helping to bring about the concrete realization of God's rule on earth by understanding correctly and making wise judgments about the complex interlocking of familial, legal, technological, economic, and political <u>goods of order</u>; and by acquiring the needed <u>skills</u> and <u>habits</u> for playing the requisite <u>roles</u> and <u>tasks</u>;

- use our faith-enlightened intelligence, reasonableness, and responsibility to transform our conversation on earth, especially the meta-institution of language, and to transvalue all vital, social, cultural, personal, and religious <u>values</u>, about us, by moving toward <u>institutions</u> and <u>personal relations</u> in which people can be more intelligent, reasonable, responsible, free, and <u>friendly</u>.

These are no more than just hints and guesses - paltry intimations - of the way the Christian community can appropriate for its foundations the intrinsically conversational character of its God and itself in the third stage of meaning.

CHAPTER FIVE

Lonergan's Search for Foundations: The Early Years, 1940-1959

Frederick E. Crowe

The title of this volume suggests the aim of its chief contributors: the constructive work of laying foundations in specific areas of culture. It also obliges me to justify the contribution I am offering, for I have not attempted, and would not attempt, that kind of constructive work. Still, my justification need not be farfetched. The other studies are all inspired by, and would carry forward, the seminal ideas of Bernard Lonergan. Now I know that their authors share the conviction that a basic task, still far from finished, is that of understanding Lonergan himself, that a developmental work such as this volume would be, is an effort in a sense to go beyond a point we have not yet reached. That is not fatal to the enterprise. On the contrary. Genuine progress is often an oscillation, maybe a dialectic, between going beyond our sources and returning to them for new inspiration. Thus, as this project may serve to force us back to our origins, so that return may contribute in its own way to the total enterprise. That, anyway, is my hope as I begin this study of Lonergan's early years, during which he was searching, in a way that gradually became more explicit, for his own foundations.

The material limits of my study should be stated. It covers the period from 1940, the date of Lonergan's dissertation, to 1959, the year in which he gave a course at the Gregorian University under the title, De intellectu et methodo, and brought the question of foundations into sharp focus. There is good reason for regarding this year as marking a halfway point, and some reason (beyond the personal one of pressure of time) for stopping the present study there, for not only has Lonergan's thought reached a kind of plateau but the route he followed is relatively easy to trace, whereas documenting the next stage of the journey, especially through the crucial years from 1963 to 1965, is more difficult. We should be clear at any rate that the foundations of 1959 are not yet those of 1972, as set forth in his Method in Theology. The early years offer contrast, then, as well as positive input, and to some extent I will be showing the influences Lonergan had to overcome in order to make his own creative contribution. I would not exaggerate that aspect, but it is well to realize at the outset that we have here the problem, recurring in any thinker of stature, of keeping in perspective the elements of continuity and discontinuity in his development.

****

Lonergan completed his dissertation, a study of the development of operative grace in the thought of Aquinas, in the spring of 1940.[1] The results of his positive investigations, considerably rewritten, were published soon after in Theological Studies and re-edited a few years later in book form.[2] But the original Introduction, whose main part is called - significantly, as we shall see - "The Form of the Development", was never published. David Tracy provided a welcome summary and evaluation in The Achievement of Bernard Lonergan,[3] a photocopy of the Introduction is available in the Lonergan Centre of Research at various institutions,[4] and for several years, and with increasing interest, students of Lonergan have been making it the starting point of their investigations. Quite rightly, for it allows us a valuable glimpse of his early thinking on what theology is and how it should proceed.

For my own purpose it will be preface enough to say that this Introduction sets forth the aim of the dissertation, which is to be an historical study, and indeed an historical study of a speculative development, that it shows a concern for determining the objectives of such a study, especially those of an inductive method that is not positivist and of a scientific objectivity that rises above the hopeless disputes of the previous three centuries, and that the strategic device it proposes for achieving those objectives is a general theory of development which would function as an a priori, somewhat in the way mathematics does for the quantitative sciences. Readers will recognize here the beginning of a long wrestling with the notion of the a priori, in which the movement will be back from logical principles to heuristic structures and to the real principles found in the dynamism of human consciousness. Similarly, the notion of generalizing will have a history -

presently we will refer to the general form of inference, and one remembers the later role of generalized empirical method - though again there will be an important modification: the addition of attention to the particular (meaning and interpretation, plurality of cultures, etc.).

But now to the point. This developmental law of the greatest possible generality will be stable; there will be "a point of vantage outside the temporal dialectic, a matrix or system of thought that at once is as pertinent and as indifferent to historical events as is the science of mathematics to quantitative phenomena".[5] The stability has a basis: "the human mind is always the human mind".[6] Here, stated with utmost simplicity, we find an orientation that will guide Lonergan throughout his career. We will be disappointed, however, if we look for detailed anticipations of later thinking; Lonergan's a priori at this time is quite prosaic: "The general law is perfectly simple. The mind begins from the particular and works to what is most general; it then returns from the most general through the specific differences to the particular".[7] It is true, the general law is made somewhat more complex here to deal with the data on grace, but it would be a digression to go into that now.

What is relevant now and can be documented is that we are dealing already with an interest in foundations, and that the foundations are located where they will be thirty years later, that is, in the human subject, and rather more specifically at the moment, in the human subject's mind. But, when Lonergan has pursued foundations to that point, he is content and drops the search; he does not go on to an epistemology. An epistemology would, no doubt, result in an imbalance in a dissertation whose introduction was now long enough. In any case Lonergan's creative energies are not directed at this time to further exploration of that area, but rather to the complexification of his a priori and its application to the immense field of data on divine grace.

The next work to interest us is a short article on the nature and form of inference, published in 1943.[8] Its immediate aim: "an empirical investigation of the nature of inference";[9] but it is conceived also as "a first step in working out an empirical theory of human understanding and knowledge".[10]

That latter statement is bound to excite the historian of Lonergan's thought, but I draw attention to this essay for other reasons: it is another instance of a bent for generalized understanding, and it records an early concern for rigorous demonstration, the process "from implier through implication to implied".[11] This concern was later balanced by other factors but, as far as I know, never abandoned. Not in the polemic against conceptualism and its syllogisms, of which more presently. Not in Insight's study of the non-logical paths of discovery. Not even in Method in Theology, which seems to do an about-face with its claim that "objectivity is the fruit of authentic subjectivity";[12] for in that work the subject "still needs truth ... The truth he needs is still the truth attained in accord with the exigences of rational consciousness".[13] Nor does the primacy accorded conversion dispense with the role of proof; only now it is clear that "proof becomes rigorous only within a systematically formulated horizon", and that it is conversion that establishes the horizon.[14] These remarks, inserted out of context, may help us maintain a proper perspective on a difficult question. To be noted, finally, in the 1943 work: inference is not affirmation (Newman's influence here surely). That is implied in the last paragraph where both induction and deduction are distinguished from "the more ultimate process from sense through intellection to judgment",[15] and it is made explicit some years later.[16]

The search for foundations takes a distinct step forward, though almost entirely in the cognitional field, a few years later in the series of articles on the concept of verbum in St. Thomas Aquinas.[17] Like a great inland waterway, with branches and fingers reaching into remote areas, they penetrate the whole vast plain of cognitional theory. Omitting then the wrestling with the thought of St. Thomas, and merely noting that Lonergan's contemporary purpose was to get behind a conceptualism that deals with terms, judgments, and syllogisms, to an intellectualism that studies the source of all these, we may quote his stated historical purpose: "to understand what Aquinas meant by the intelligible procession of an inner word",[18] and record his sense of "intelligible procession", that "an inner word not merely has a sufficient ground in the act of understanding it expresses; it also has a knowing as sufficient ground, and that ground is operative precisely as a knowing, knowing itself to be sufficient".[19] Now the second article, appearing first in March, 1947, and then as the second chapter of the later book,[20] deals extensively with foundations under the heading of the critical problem. For we are talking about "the reflective act" of understanding, which "generates in judgment the expression of consciously possessed truth through which reality is both known and known to be known",[21] in which the issue is "not knowledge as true or false but knowledge as known to be true or false".[22]

Three headings are distinguished here: assent, criteriology, and epistemology, this latter not so named in the listing.[23] I delay on assent only to note that it is not just a synthesis of subject and predicate, but the positing of that synthesis as true[24] - assent therefore in Newman's sense, going beyond inference. Criteriology is the business of telling true judgments from false, "measuring by a standard",[25] which means a return from judgments to their sources. Those sources are found "in sense and in intellectual light";[26] or, again, "in sense and in naturally known principles".[27]

Now an infinite regress is repeatedly rejected,[28] but "naturally known principles" do raise the question of the "nature" by which they are known; and, if that nature be the "light" of intellect, then that light too must be studied. So we come to the section on wisdom[29] and to questions of epistemology. Wisdom is ultimate for Aquinas, for it "validates even first principles themselves".[30] The ontological explanation of this: we can make "true affirmations of existence ... in virtue of our intellectual light, which is the participation of eternal Light".[31] But epistemologically that is not enough, for the issue is not just knowing but knowing our knowing: "intellectual knowledge is not merely true but also aware of its own truth".[32] And here Lonergan finds a Thomist epistemology inchoate in the notion of intellect's reflecting on itself to know its own nature; "and if it knows its own nature, intellect also known its own proportion to knowledge of reality".[33]

The next section, "Self-knowledge of Soul",[34] is Lonergan's deepest penetration here of this question of grounding our knowledge in its ultimate cognitional basis. The key point: with certain restrictions "we may say that the light of agent intellect is known per se ipsum"[35] - not known as an object is known, but known in illuminating objects and making them known,[36] and so going beyond Aristotle's agent intellect[37] but also replacing the Augustinian "vision of eternal truth".[38] Thus far we have Aquinas as guide; but Lonergan feels we must carry Aquinas forward to an epistemological position based on "a development of understanding by which we come to grasp just how it is that our minds are proportionate to knowledge of reality", namely, through "a grasp of the native infinity of intellect".[39]

The verbum articles then, though their direct concern is the thought of St. Thomas, are a significant stage in Lonergan's own search for foundations. The phrase, ultimate ground, occurs and is used in an ontological sense, but with implicit extension to the epistemological.[40] And the concern is clearly Lonergan's own. After what may seem a pejorative reference in the first article to "the epistemological bog",[41] he makes a point of bringing out the inchoate Thomist epistemology, expressly tries to go beyond it, and would heighten the "echo in a modern mind".[42] Thus, he sees the modern critical problem as one not "of moving from within outwards" but "of moving from above downwards, of moving from an infinite potentiality commensurate with the universe towards a rational apprehension that seizes the difference of subject and object in essentially the same way that it seizes any other real distinction".[43] His own epistemology in simplest summary: "We know by what we are; we know we know by knowing what we are".[44]

But I would note that it is only a "stage" in his search; even in the search for cognitional foundations, it is only a stage. It will take time and effort to move out of the Thomist context, replace Thomist language, refine the Thomist solution, and move fully into the twentieth century. The metaphor of light, useful though it be, will give way in Insight to direct appropriation of interiority, of "the dynamic orientation of intelligent and rational consciousness", that is, the notion of being.[45] The knowledge of light per se ipsum will be replaced by a self-authenticating grasp of the virtually unconditioned. The native infinity of intellect will

likewise yield to the unrestricted objective of
intelligence, to the permanently self-transcending
nature of a consciousness that never ceases to ask
questions, that can be known empirically to be
oriented to the All, and to suppose by its very
activity the intelligibility of the All. But
intellect as a faculty, and wisdom as its highest
realization, make a slow exit; they emerge again
after Insight, to disappear almost completely only
in the post-1965 regrouping of forces for the writing
of Method.[46] There is work to be done also in the
subjective conditions of knowing. And maybe most
fundamental, though elusive and hard to document, is a
mentality that seems to change subtly at this time.
I mean that there is, in 1947, almost a hint of
proving antecedently that we can know; deduction
is expressly excluded, but there is "a sort of reasoning" which is "a development of understanding"[47]
in the way intellect knows its capacity to know.
Such language, I think, would be alien in Insight;
in fact, we may be surprised to learn, the critical
problem gets rather short shrift in that work.

I pause, on the way to Insight, to notice two relevant articles. The symposium paper, "The Assumption
and Theology",[48] dated 1948, is an instance of the
actual founding of a dogma in the sense which foundations would then have had for Lonergan, and it
shows the principles by which he would provide those
foundations. Unquestioned is the given starting
point: "a divine revelation which already is in
the order of truth".[49] But since the assumption
of Mary is not explicit in our sources of relevation,
we have to seek an additional principle. Lonergan
defines it as "a development of understanding, an
opening of the eyes of faith, upon what had been
long revealed but ... not ... apprehended".[50]
So he tries to do here with the data of the New
Testament what Jesus himself had done for the two
disciples on the way to Emmaus with the Old Testament
data.[51] It is a matter of the "implication" of
scripture,[52] "grasped as human understanding ...
penetrates the economy of man's fall and redemption
and settles our Lady's place in it".[53] On the
question of foundations, then, I would say that this
is the classical type of theology, but brought
forward by Newman's notion of development, and
further refined by Lonergan's view of the act of
understanding. I have no doubt that it is still

valid, but also by the standards of Method it is a long way from being complete.

The other article is "A Note on Geometrical Possibility",[54] dated 1950. We may note the rather extrinsic point that Lonergan refers to Forder's book on The Foundations of Euclidean Geometry,[55] and himself speaks of "the problem of consistency of foundation propositions"[56] - an indication of his familiarity then with foundational language. But what I find more interesting is the application of such language to possibility and intelligibility, for we think of it more commonly in the context of actuality and truth. Thus, "the ground of possibility is intelligibility",[57] and so likewise "knowledge of possibility rests on knowledge of intelligibility".[58] It is true that Lonergan is speaking of "true judgment of possibility", with the two groundings it may have, the consequent ground of known actuality and the antecedent ground of known intelligibility.[59] Still, grasp of intelligibility seems to have this peculiarity that no further positive input is required to know it. At any rate this article suggests to me the analogy of foundations. We know that Lonergan does not talk much of analogy as such, but does draw up, repeatedly, creative analogies: the analogy of being, of matter, of intelligence, of meaning, etc. So we might draw up an analogy of foundations: foundations of being and of knowing; in the former, of actuality and of possibility; in the latter, foundations of truth, of inference,[60] and also, presumably, of intelligibility.

So we come to Insight, dated more usefully in 1953 when, except for a few revisions, it was finished, than in 1957 when it was published.[61] We find that the focus has shifted now away from an earlier concern with epistemology to a concern with the nature and forms of knowing, and with its subjective conditions understood in a somewhat more existential sense. This I will explain in due course.

It is worth making the preliminary point that Insight as a work bears the general character of Lonergan's work: that is, it is itself an exercise in foundations, in the analogous senses just indicated. One can easily verify this in what we have seen him name criteriology. Three samples of his criteriology in action: the first is his writing style; one may

take a few test pages (try pp.ix-xv) and see how
often the phrase, it follows, occurs there. The
second might be a couple of his more famous formal
arguments, that from latent to explicit metaphysics,[62]
and that for the existence of God.[63] The third:
his frequent reference to the role of the a priori,
especially for the upper blade of heuristic method.
- A large question, all this, but my sketchy paragraph may help us maintain an ever difficult perspective.

To turn from practise to its thematizing, I would
say that a chief contribution of Insight to our
question is its displacement of the critical problem,
a displacement announced in the first paragraph of
the Introduction: "In the first place, the question
is not whether knowledge exists but what precisely is
its nature".[64] Rarely does an opening salvo find so
unerringly its target, for in Insight's analysis of
what knowing is we have not only the positive foundation for an expanding correct knowledge but also
the dialectical factor that can either lead to aberrations or, if recognized, enable us to account for and
reverse the aberrations. The point is: "in each of
us there exist two different kinds of knowledge ...
separated and alienated in ... rationalist and empiricist philosophies".[65] The resulting duality does
not mean we should reduce them to one in a kind of
self-mutilation. "The problem set by the two types
of knowing is, then, not a problem of elimination but
a problem of critical distinction. For the difficulty
lies, not in either type of knowing by itself, but in
the confusion that arises when one shifts unconsciously
from one type to the other. Animals have no epistemological problems".[66] Thus we have "two quite different realisms ... [one] incoherent ... half animal
and half human ... [the other] intelligent and reasonable".[67] The whole of Insight can be read, it seems
to me, as an extended effort to establish a coherent
realism based on a proper recognition of the duality
of our knowing. This lies behind the repeated statement that the real is being, that is, what can be
intelligently grasped and reasonably affirmed - not,
as might be thought by a naive realist, what can be
seen or touched. If I may venture an opinion after
years of mulling over these matters ("venture"- hoping
it will not be taken for a shibboleth), I would say that,
if one understands what Lonergan is after in proclaiming

the real to be identical with being, one possesses the master key to Insight.

I spoke above of criteriology in action. But it can be set forth as a position too, on the basis of chapters nine and ten. To be noted: we are still in the first part of the book, on insight as an activity and not as knowledge; hence, the critical problem can hardly be an issue yet. What is at issue is where to find the measure of our knowledge. Thus, chapter ten speaks of judgment as resulting from the marshalling and weighing of evidence, and asks: "But what are the scales on which evidence is weighed?". The answer takes us to "the grounding act of reflective understanding", illustrated "from the form of deductive inference"[68] as showing the meaning of the virtually unconditioned, but not to be identified with deduction at all: "deductive inference cannot be the basic case of judgment, for it presupposes other judgments to be true".[69] A further step takes us to the invulnerable insight that "there are no further, pertinent questions".[70] But to recognise that we have reached that stage we need a "happy balance between rashness and indecision".[71] So Lonergan concludes with what are essentially practical rules for judgment: give the questions a chance to arise; let the question we try to answer be in a familiar field; let the process of learning break the vicious circle in which judgment on any insight seems based on previous correct insights.[72] That is, the "self-correcting process tends to a limit ... reaches its limit in familiarity with the concrete situation and in easy mastery of it ... while the limit is not marked with a label, still its attainment is revealed by a habitual ability to know just what is up".[73]

This does not sound much like direct confrontation with the critical problem, and in fact it is not that. It is criteriological, in the sense of the verbum articles. It is strategic. It takes us behind "our conceptual distinction between correct and mistaken insights" to "an operational distinction between invulnerable and vulnerable insights".[74] But it does not and cannot, and neither can any criteriology or strategy, offer an ultimate rule, criterion, norm, standard, scales, for judging judgment simply and universally. "Were there some simple formula or recipe in answer to such questions, then men of good judgment could be produced at will and indefinitely".[75] What we can achieve is what Lonergan in chapter seventeen will call a "proximate criterion" of truth.[76]

The critical problem in the standard sense belongs, then, in Part Two of the book, which deals with insight as knowledge; and it does emerge in chapter eleven, to receive, I would say, rather quick riddance. The chapter has to do with what is called "Self-affirmation", but the point lies in the <u>kind</u> of self that is affirmed, namely, a self that <u>is</u> conscious empirically, intelligently, and rationally. Section six, "Self-affirmation as Immanent Law",[77] offers a negative and a positive solution to the critical problem. First, there is the contradiction of self-negation, seen in the traditional device of getting the skeptic to talk. In Lonergan's formulation: the skeptic is involved in contradiction because he has no choice but to be conscious empirically, intelligently, rationally, once he chooses to talk.[78] The negative statement, then: rational consciousness can criticize everything else, but "only on condition that it does not criticize itself".[79] The positive counterpart is an operating reality and our appropriation of it. The reality can be given many names: a dynamism, an eros, a spontaneity, an inevitability, a necessity, an immanent Anagke; it can be seen as operative in the whole process from experience through understanding to judgment, as giving us no rest till we arrive at the realm of fact to which the dynamism committed us from the beginning. To write such lines (based on this section six) is to try to give expression to an appropriation of the reality. Maybe it can be put more simply still:

> "Behind that contradiction [of self-negation] there have been discerned natural inevitabilities and spontaneities that constitute the possibility of knowing, not by demonstrating that one can know, but pragmatically by engaging one in the process. Nor in the last resort can one reach a deeper foundation than that pragmatic engagement. Even to seek it involves a vicious circle; for if one seeks such a foundation, one employs one's cognitional process; and the foundation to be reached will be no more secure or solid than the inquiry utilized to reach it".[80]

The preceding paragraph is a statement of Lonergan's epistemology, of his solution to the critical problem as that problem is commonly posed, of the foundations he assigns for knowledge. It is a brief statement, as was the original, the section studied being only four pages out of nearly eight hundred, and the epistemology occupying only one page of the four. Why say more? Negatively, the opposite claim is self-destructive; positively, Lonergan's position rests ultimately on fact, not on talking about the fact. The need of talking arises when there is confusion about the nature of knowing or about the subject himself or herself, when there are biases, when there is flight from understanding. We can still call this a discussion of foundations, if we will, but only in an analogous sense.

We come, then, to discussion of subjective factors in knowledge, a feature of _Insight_ that I did not attend to properly when I made the Index twenty-five years ago.[81] I bring it in now in reference to the remote criterion of truth, about which the reader may be wondering since my mention above of the proximate criterion. As defined it is simple enough. "The remote criterion is the proper unfolding of the detached and disinterested desire to know".[82] But far more complex is the actual unfolding: "The subject becomes more or less secure or anxious about the genuineness of his inquiry and reflection, and further inquiry and reflection will in their turn be open to similar questioning. What is in doubt is the subject himself, and all his efforts to remove the doubt will proceed from the same suspected source".[83]

It is worth the while to collect some of the data on this subjective side, for they anticipate _Method_ to a quite remarkable extent. Thus, we read in the Introduction to _Insight_: "Prior to all writing of history, prior to all interpretation of other minds, there is the self-scrutiny of the historian, the self-knowledge of the interpreter"[84] - surely a sentence that could be set without change in the Introduction to _Method_. Take another sounding in chapter six: "common sense relates things to us. [But] ... who are we? ... an account of common sense cannot be adequate without an investigation of its subjective field".[85] The chapter on judgment, too, can be reread with the same question to guide us: "It is only when I go to the root of the matter and become efficaciously critical of myself that I can begin to become a reliable judge".[86] To take but one more sounding, chapter fourteen on the method of metaphysics goes deeply into the question of the polymorphic human consciousness, and sees it as the source of diverse philosophies, of positions and counter-positions on knowing, objectivity and reality. A revealing pair of sentences: "Metaphysics ... is not something in a book but something in a mind",[87] and, "the starting-point of metaphysics is people as they are".[88]

A few notes now to relate Insight more accurately to Lonergan's other writings, and first its general relation to the verbum articles. Insight makes much of its focus on the nature of knowledge, but we saw something quite a bit like that in the articles. The differences, I would say, are these. The articles talk of the nature of intellectual light, but Insight of the nature of our knowing, and then with a view to distinguishing two types of knowing. More important: the articles almost make the "known" nature of light an antecedent ground for knowing that we can know, and this through a reasoning process, and that does not fit in Insight, which distinguishes more sharply, and abides by the distinction, between nature and existence of knowledge, and gives little time to either the existence or the possibility of knowing. Finally, both works appeal to what we are as a foundation, but the articles to what we are in virtue of a light proportionate to the universe, and Insight to what we are in virtue of a eros, an immanent Anagke, a commitment to the realm of fact.

A second note concerns Thomist wisdom. It appears in Insight but only in a historical overview of positions on being. Still, Lonergan is reluctant to abandon the term. To the two Thomist uses - the wisdom which is a gift of the Spirit, and the wisdom which is "first philosophy ... as the knowledge of all things in their ultimate causes"[89] - he would add a third which our times require and we can piece together in cognitional terms from the works of Aquinas, an obvious reference to the verbum articles. Thomist wisdom will continue to haunt Lonergan's work on foundations in his summer institute of 1957, and in his courses De intellectu et methodo in 1959 and De methodo theologiae in 1962, to disappear almost completely, at least as a category under this name, in the Method of 1972.[90]

My third note relates Insight to its own second
edition. I suppose that is the edition used by
most of my readers, and they may have wondered why I
did not mention the little section that appears under
the title "Foundations" on page 98; and, even more,
why I did not notice the references on pages 340-341
to the third constitutive level of knowing as "both
self-authenticating and decisive". The reason in
both cases is that those usages appear in the revised
edition of 1958 but not in the first edition, and
are almost certainly due to the Boston College lectures of 1957. For foundations is a theme in those
lectures, and "self-justifying horizons" almost is.
I do not think that is the case in Insight (one
learns to be cautious on those 300,000 words and
more), though "foundation" occurs in a passage quoted
already,[91] and we read of "limiting structures that
carry their own guarantee",[92] the equivalent of
self-authenticating grasp of the virtually unconditioned.[93]

We come then to 1957 when Fr. Frederick Adelmann, of the
Boston College Department of Philosophy, invited
Lonergan to give a summer institute there, with a week
of lectures on mathematical logic and a week on existentialism. Records of those lectures I find illuminating for the direction of his development at this
time.[94] The first week offered five lectures: the
general character of mathematical logic; the history of its development; the truth of its systems;
the foundations of logic; and the relation of mathematical logic to scholasticism. The third lecture
not only assigns to the systems of logic "the verbal
type of truth that pertains to the analytic proposition",[95] but would also grant them fragments of
a form of factual truth, that is, factual truth of
"the provisional type".[96] So lecture four, dealing with foundations, is dealing with the foundations
of truth, and they are clearly stated. "The subject in this self-knowledge [that is, that of
Insight] is the foundation of logic; it is a foundation in the reality of the subject himself, and in
every experiencing, intelligent, reasonable subject;
it is a foundation in a reality and so it is beyond
formulations ... of philosophic position".[97]
Lonergan goes on at once to extend the same foundations to other branches of philosophy. More
clearly still in the next lecture: "Hence, in the
fourth lecture, I sought the foundations of logic

in the subject's personal appropriation of his own empirical, intellectual, and rational consciousness; on this view the foundations of logic are by identity the solution of the epistemological problem, the foundations of metaphysics, the foundations of ethics, and the foundations of natural theology".[98] Succinct and clarifying statements, these, locating foundations in the reality of the subject, and extending its foundational role over the range of philosophic disciplines.

Two notes on this week of lectures. The first: the reader will have noticed the verbal usage in my last quotation, where we have "the foundations of metaphysics" but "the solution of the epistemological problem". This surely represents a deliberate and careful choice. Sciences that, methodically, are derivative have a foundation; but that from which they cognitionally derive cannot strictly have a cognitional foundation, and that is the field of epistemology; so we "solve" the critical problem by appropriation of our knowing, but basically the knowing is self-authenticating. Our second note: there is a clarification on Thomist wisdom. Still holding wisdom to be "ultimate and decisive" but still feeling the need to modify the Thomist account, Lonergan tells us that in Insight he tried to work out "a genetic account" of wisdom.[99] We shall see him in 1959 study the genesis in some detail.

The lectures of the second week, on existentialism, bring to focus many scattered elements in previous work and make thematic the existential subject that will figure so largely in Method.[100] Actual lecture divisions are not clear in the records we have, but topical headings are: for example, On Being Oneself; The Dilemma of the Subject; Subject and Horizon; Horizon and Dread; Horizon and History; Horizon as the Problem of Philosophy - all these topics following some historical lectures, mainly on Jaspers, Husserl, and Heidegger. Our locus of interest is the last heading of the lectures, "Horizon as the Problem of Philosophy" (I suspect we should read "the Problem"), where we find the following: "The multiplicity of horizons as philosophic issue arises when we ask: Is some horizon the field, or is there not field? If some horizon is the field, how can it be determined?".[101] The distinction had been made, "The field is the universe, buy my horizon defines my universe".[102] Lonergan, of course, opts for a field, so the problem does arise of determining this horizon-field and justifying it.

It is not a simple problem, for any answer "arises within a stream of consciousness and so arises within what already is constituted as a horizon". The horizon cannot then be justified by the realities which are known within that horizon and are regularly consonant with it; if it could, every horizon would "automatically be self-justifying". This applies not only to objects known but equally to the subject known as object, for it becomes then one of the realities known within the given horizon. If neither the object known as object, or the subject known as object, can provide justification, that is, "constitute a self-justifying horizon", where shall we look? Lonergan's answer is the subject as subject: "The prior reality that both grounds horizons and the critique of horizons and the determination of the field is the reality of the subject as subject".[103]

These ideas surely flow into the revisions of *Insight* that were drafted in the spring of 1958 for the second edition. They just as surely flow into the abstract of the talk never actually given on "Philosophic Differences and Personal Development".[104] In fact, some lines of the latter are taken almost verbatim from the lectures on existentialism:

> "A new higher viewpoint in the natural sciences ordinarily involves no revision of the subject's image and concept of himself, and so scientific advance easily wins universal and permanent acceptance. But a higher viewpoint in philosophy not only logically entails such a revision but also cannot be grasped with a 'real apprehension' unless the revision actually becomes effective in the subject's mental attitudes. So the philosophic schools are many ..."

Interesting as these bits of history are, the main thing is the issue being debated, and the passage just quoted is clear enough on that: the issue is the subject and his conversion. Foundations then has emerged as a theme in 1957; so has the subject. It remains to add the theme of historical differentiation

and to import these themes more fully into theology.
This will be achieved in the work of 1959.

To go forward, however, to 1959 and the plateau I
judge that year to represent, we need to go back to
1954 and an article I have omitted, "Theology and
Understanding".[105]   Historically, this is very
significant for Lonergan's development. It shows
the full measure of his debt to Aquinas in theological
method, but also introduces the factors that
will take him eventually so far beyond Aquinas.
Two streams are meeting, but not yet in turmoil and
still less unified. As for Aquinas, then, Lonergan's
concern here is to rescue him from the "conclusions-
theology" where some were bent on locating him. The
rescue operation is performed by the same means used
in "The Assumption and Theology", namely, a concept
of theology as understanding to be found in the
Thomist works. The syllogism, says Lonergan, has
two functions: it is "an instrument for exhibiting
the grounds of a judgment on the conclusion ... But
it is also an instrument of developing understanding"[106]
and this latter aspect in St. Thomas is lost by those
who read him as a conclusions-theologian. As for
foundational ideas, Thomist wisdom plays its regular
role for ultimate validation on the human side, and
we need not go through that again. Objectively the
whole depends on God's word: "From revelation comes
the premises ... and on the truth of the premises
rests the truth ... of their conclusions".[107]

So far we do not seem to have advanced much beyond
"The Assumption and Theology". But that changes
in the latter part of the article, where there
appears in thematic form a whole new world which
had lain outside the Thomist horizon and will occupy
Lonergan now for the next eighteen years.   Still,
the breakthrough is not trumpeted but introduced
modestly enough as follows:

> "If Aristotelian and scholastic notions
> of science seem to me to be adequate for
> a formulation of the nature of speculat-
> ive theology [notice the qualification:
> 'speculative' theology] both in itself
> and in its relations to revelation, to
> philosophy, and to the teaching authority
> of the church, still I should avoid the
> appearance of making exaggerated claims

and so I should acknowledge the
existence of contemporary methodological
issues that cannot be dispatched in so
expeditious a fashion".[108]

These issues are four in number: the patterns of
human experience;[109] the relations between speculative and positive theology;[110] those between speculative theology and the empirical human sciences;[111]
and, fourthly, the way the issues of historical interpretation "are complicated by the self-knowledge of
the interpreter", presenting us with "all the complexity of the critical problem". But here, as in Insight,
one has to conceive the critical problem "not as the
easy question whether we know but as the real issue
of what precisely occurs when we are knowing".[112]

We come at last to De intellectu et methodo, a course
offered to doctorate students in theology and philosophy at the Gregorian University, Rome, in the
spring semester of 1959. It was reported rather
fully in notes taken by students, to whom we can
never be sufficiently grateful, for this course represents, as far as I know, the first documented thematizing of foundations as the problem occurs in theology.[113] It is still far enough from the 1972 position
of Method, but does mark a clear and significant
stage on the way.

We will be concerned with the first part of the notes,
on the notion of the question,[114] and especially with
the sixth and last section of this part, the one with
the lion's share:[115] "de problematibus fundamenti -
historicitatis - separationis".[116] Let us run
quickly through the approach. The first four sections deal mainly with the conditions for the existence
of a question,[117] the historical series of questions,[118]
the ordering of the answers,[119] and the series of such
orderings.[120] Examples are drawn mainly from trinitarian theology, and the problem to be tackled in the
last section already appears in the example of divine
missions; this notion is first in the ordering we
call the via analytica (St. Paul's notion of mission)
but last in the ordering we call the via synthetica
(no doubt a reference to St. Thomas in his Summa Theologiae; see pages 8-10 of the notes). The fifth
section[121] is on the criteria of any new ordering.
Obviously owing something to the lectures of 1957,
it declares the impossibility of transforming

scholasticism into a system like that of mathematical logic, but remarks that the attempt would nevertheless be very useful, for it would show clearly the futility of the eternally disputed scholastic questions and the need of a new ordering of theology; it might suggest also the need to raise the problem of method. Lonergan's mind is naturally on method throughout the course.

Section six, then, is on our threefold problem, which I translate as the problem of foundations, of historicity, of estrangement.[122] As for their meaning, Lonergan will presently explain them as the problem of <u>transition</u> from one ordering of doctrine or theology to another, the problem of <u>continuity</u> throughout the orderings, and the problem of the ever greater <u>systematizing</u> of an ordering, which means we are taken farther and farther from our sources. And he will add that they are not really three problems, but one problem of method with three aspects.[123] Still, he will set them forth singly,[124] and propose a solution in the same way.[125]

It is revealing that at this time Lonergan sees the problem of foundations as one of transitions. It means that for him theology is still "classical" in regard to its sources, whose foundations are not called in question - what happens afterwards, that creates the problem. It is, indeed, a wider problem than that of theology. The whole history of philosophy and theology is a series of orderings and of transitions from one ordering to another. Further, there are various views on what we call "perennial philosophy" or "solid Catholic doctrine" (that is, teaching which extends over time, and presumably has achieved transitions without loss of continuity); so, faced with opposing views, we cannot avoid the task of choosing. But what will be the criterion of our choice? Thus do we come to the problem of foundations. It can be seen in particular when one studies development in a single author, say, Aquinas (no doubt Lonergan has in mind here the theology of grace studied in his own doctoral dissertation). Logically one cannot account for the differences; one would have to postulate many Aquinases. Lonergan would prefer to ask what the foundation was for Aquinas as he moved from one position to another. More generally, the problem is seen in the church's transition from one ordering of its doctrine to another while nevertheless the dogmatic teaching remains permanent. "Quomodo fiet iste transitus et quibusdam criteriis eligetur nova ordinatio?".[126]

The problem of estrangement is illustrated by the familiar example of the homoousios, introduced into church doctrine by the Council of Nicea in 325 and rejected as alien to tradition by the Arians and semi-Arians. St. Athanasius did not deny the fact - the term was unbiblical, and hence alien to previous ways of talking - nor did he defend it as an ideal. But bitter constraint and sad occasion dear made him defend it for the sake of the church's faith in the Son of God.[127] As for historicity, it is sufficiently illustrated by the example already seen and now repeated: divine missions as conceived by St. Paul are not the same as divine missions as conceived by St. Thomas Aquinas. There is then a leap, and the problem of foundations is to justify that leap.[128]

How are we to justify it? Pages 16-25 struggle with the answer. We do not justify it by the external form of the words we use; one may surely think of the "fundamentalists" here, for whom words do serve as foundations. And not through manipulation of concepts and judgments (one thinks now of the "conceptualists" - adversaries in the verbum articles), for that works only within a given system. Lonergan had already rejected deduction as a means of transition[129] and returns to it again[130] to declare it helpless when questions arise that the system cannot account for - precisely the situation when there is a leap from one system to another.

Lonergan's own solution does not surprise us. It is to go behind the words, behind the concepts and judgments, in his habitual appeal to intelligence itself and its threefold formation through understanding, science, and wisdom. Wisdom is the key term, as it has been since the verbum articles, being given a critical role in the selection of the first terms and principles, and in judgment on them and all their consequents. How, for example, can one judge among the various concepts of being? not by means of some prior formula, for we are talking of the first term, but only by wisdom. And there are many ways of ordering the virtual totality of theology; shall we retain the old? or do we need a new? wisdom will decide.[131]

What is different, however, in this work of 1959, and significantly different, as we may judge with our excellent hindsight, is the searching dialectic to which Lonergan submits the notion of wisdom.[132] This critical examination can be read now as a kind of last effort to make do with the old before moving to the new. I sketch as briefly as I can the series of objections raised here against wisdom as foundation. (1) We are not born wise, or made wise necessarily by nature; so how can we even move toward wisdom? such a step would itself require us to be wise already. (2) Wisdom is not in fact a first; it presupposes understanding and science. (3) It is useless to appeal to the wisdom of authority, for the unwise will interpret authority unwisely. (4) Likewise useless to postulate a gradual progress through love of wisdom to wisdom itself; for, being unwise, how can we know we are really seeking true wisdom? (5) In any case, the danger of invoking wisdom is to endow with the virtue of wisdom the opinion of everyone, and thus promote relativism.

The objections, I would say, are predominantly of the "vicious circle" type, and would therefore be valid only within the confines of a logical system. Since for Lonergan the mind has resources that easily free one from the logical ghetto, his answer will not surprise us any more than his general position did. He calls then on already established ideas. There is the intrinsic principle of the mind's dynamism (as contrasted with extrinsic terms). There is the notion of being which already contains all knowledge in anticipation - the natural notion, of course, to be distinguished from the reflected one. There is the possibility of some progress through application of the principle of contradiction to the Porphyrean tree. An analogy here, I suggest, is the game of "20 questions" - how rapidly one can zero in on a given "x" by means of a well ordered set of questions. The reader will think: of course; but where do the questions, and the answers, come from? That is where Lonergan's next point applies: there is also the possibility of adding mastery over particular regions of being, as one grows to adult status and continues to develop. Or, briefly, to invoke an old scholastic phrase, "sapientia non stat in indivisibili".[133] Lonergan then goes on to answer the objections one by one, in a manner that would hardly suggest, except to the hindsight I mentioned, that wisdom will eventually give way to a modern adaptation.

Solutions to the other two problems are much shorter. Lonergan adduces his own work on the twofold way of analysis and synthesis,[134] and on the duality of human consciousness, as showing how two quite different thought-patterns can develop, with their consequent estrangement.[135] As for the problem of historicity, it is insoluble on the basis of a conceptualism that knows only how to manage concepts and judgments; but, if one goes behind the concepts to their fertile source in insight, one can discover the possibility also of development of understanding, of different historical conceptions of the same reality; and thus the problem of historicity can be brought to heel.[136]

The foregoing sketch will serve, I hope, to give us an idea of the way Lonergan saw the problem of foundations and its solution in 1959. But, to keep all this in perspective, we have to remember that the over-riding concern in this work, as it is in all his work at that time, is for method. The remainder of De intellectu et methodo, then, studies our ways of knowing, to develop and apply to theology five precepts of method.[137] To be noted is a strong insistence still on systematics.[138] Historical theology, in fact, is seen simply as systematic theology in fieri.[139] It is not that history is disregarded; there is reference to the lack of historical consciousness in St. Thomas,[140] followed by a long study of the historical factor today;[141] but it remains rather extrinsic to what Lonergan would consider - I think we may fairly say it in this way - "real" theology, namely, systematic understanding of revealed truth.

* * * * * * * * * * *

With this Gregorian University course of 1959 we have, I think, reached a definite plateau in Lonergan's search for foundations. In one way or another the question has been on his mind through two decades. Early reflection, however, simply carried the search back to the stable operation of the human mind, and did not explore that mind in any depth. Study of Thomist cognitional theory brought the critical problem to the fore; it was then conceived as the problem of knowing that we know, and a solution was found in terms of intellectual light and its known proportion to knowledge of the universe. Independent thinking in Insight changed the terms of the problem; it is seen now as a problem of discrimination, of distinguishing and relating two quite different types of knowing; the traditional form of the problem is dealt with firmly but briefly - negatively, in noting that negation of knowledge is self-destructive; positively, in appropriation of the real ground of knowing in the dynamism of human consciousness. When foundations become a theme in the Boston College lectures of 1957 Lonergan can easily apply the results of the previous ten years, and we may say that the search for cognitional foundations is concluded. Meanwhile, however, the existential subject has been coming more and more to the centre of attention. Furthermore, direct engagement in the actual problems of church theology, especially of trinitarian doctrine, has brought historical differentiations of thinking into sharper focus. This latter aspect is predominant in the 1959 search for the foundations of theology. The starting point, however, remains given; that is not the problem - rather it is the development of doctrine, and development in patterns of thought quite alien to those of the starting point, that must be justified. Here too the foundations that Insight, building on the verbum articles, is able to provide are found to be adequate.

A long further climb remains before we reach Method in Theology[142] and the further work of the 1970's. I cannot undertake that journey here, but I do wish to look ahead and offer some comparative reflections. In 1959, I have said, two streams were meeting; one deriving from St. Thomas, and one from the seven centuries following St. Thomas (a rough characterization). It seems fair to say that Lonergan was slower than most contemporaries to move beyond the Thomist context; it seems equally fair to say that, by the same token, he assimilated St. Thomas more thoroughly and built on him more solidly than many of his contemporaries. At any rate there is a definite shift, from this point of view, between 1959 and 1972. There is a simple index of that:

the Thomist wisdom, which was such a dominant category for many years, has all but disappeared in Method. Not perhaps in the functions wisdom served, but in the terminology and in the perspective from which problems are approached.[143] Even in Insight its functions were being taken over by the "universal viewpoint", and that too has yielded in Method to a transcendental method reaching its full human potential in dialectic, transformed then by conversions that are mainly the work of God, in order to take possession of new foundations for another formulation of the truths we live by, the whole being complemented now by an explicit principle of feedback to help us keep in perspective the old and simpler problem of bringing the past forward into our present and preaching to Torontonians and Bostonians in 1982 rather than to Corinthians in 52.

But, if we agree on the novelty of Method, we may find it profitable to return to earlier work for traces of continuity. First of all, it is the human subject that is the locus of study from the beginning, and very early the subject in his or her reality. Next, it is the appropriation of that reality, sketchily in 1940, more extensively in the Thomist context of 1946-47, more directly in the self-appropriation of Insight, that is the positive way to foundations. Thirdly, from the early years it is the subjective conditions of ignorance, bias, underdevelopment, lack of self-appropriation, etc., etc., that impede reasonable judgment and responsible decision and leave us without secure foundations. This continuity is almost labelled in the statement of Method: "the basic idea of the method we are trying to develop takes its stand on discovering what human authenticity is and showing how to appeal to it".[144] Here is a position strikingly similar to that of 1947: we know we know by knowing what we are; and to that of Insight: "Prior to all writing of history, prior to all interpretation of other minds, there is the self-scrutiny of the historian, the self-knowledge of the interpreter".[145] The form is the same, the locus of study is the same, but the material content broadens and deepens.[146]

Even in such a question as the relation of theology to its sources, I would ask whether there is not an overlooked continuity between earlier and later work. I am thinking of what seems an almost exclusive concern in earlier writings with bringing the past forward into the present, and the difficulty we have in relating that to Method's concern with interior foundations, and indeed in relating inner and outer word within Method itself. But has not the outer word of received doctrine the same foundations in principle as the inner word of God's gift of his love? If we look to interiority for the added foundation we need to formulate our doctrine today, shall we not look to interiority also to account for the transitions from one formulation to another in the past, and even to account for the original formulations of the sources themselves? I mean that, whether it be question of evangelist, or prophet, or apostle, or Jesus himself in his human thinking, the foundations we would assign from the viewpoint of Method would be found in interiority - that of evangelist, or prophet, or apostle, or Jesus. The need, obviously, becomes a need for an analogy of interiority.

But, to return to the other side of the ledger, that of development, what Lonergan had to overcome along the way was the influence of those to whom he owed the greatest debt, Aristotle and Aquinas; and I suppose the very magnitude of his debt in the more fundamental questions made the task of overcoming their influence in lesser matters all the more difficult. That is the price of tradition and discipleship. Further, what he had to add were the new dimensions of the subject and his objective history that modern philosophy, science, scholarship had brought to light. He did this piecemeal at first. Some examples: history became a theme in its own right in the Thomas More Institute lecture of 1960; meaning in its many forms began to be thematized in lectures of 1962 (at Regis College and Thomas More Institute); mediation in the Gonzaga University institute of 1963; and foundations as a fourth-level function in the Georgetown University institute of 1964 (so our scanty sources indicate). From this point of view Method appears as a final organization of elements he had been collecting for many years.

That last sentence brings me to my concluding remark, which is a reflection on the whole business of a thinker's development, and an attempt to provide a model for seeing it as a unity over time and not just the unity of some final organization. The problem is real enough. Anyone with a bent for comprehensive

thinking has presumably begun in early life and
continues in later years "to see life steadily and
see it whole". But in our world of growth and
development, where results are often tentative, where
there are blind alleys, sidetracks, slowdowns and
pauses, there is likewise bound to be, early and
late, continuing change; with Newman we have to
say that to live is to change, and to have lived
long is to have changed often. So how conceive
the life of a comprehensive thinker, who presumably
thinks more integrally and changes more profoundly
than the rest of us? The model I suggest is provided
by Insight under the general notion of emergent probability: "If the non-systematic exists on the level
of physics, then on that level there are coincidental
manifolds that can be systematized by a higher chemical level without violating any physical law. If
the non-systematic exists on the level of chemistry,
then on that level there are coincidental manifolds
that can be systematized by a higher biological
level ...", and so on through the psychic to the
level of insight, reflection, and deliberation.[147]
I am suggesting, then, that the data collected from
the years prior to thematization stand to the thematization somewhat as a coincidental manifold does
to the higher integration. I do now, however,
sufficiently understand the intricacies of emergent
probability to determine whether we have in such a
case a real instance of emergence, or a true conceptual analogy, or merely a useful image.

I would further suggest that, if the image/analogy/
instance has any value where thematization has occurred,
as in foundations, it has value also where thematization
has not occurred, as in the question of feedback. One
can collect data on this from many of Lonergan's writings. For example, there is the wheel of progress in
Insight: "... one thinks of the course of social
change as a succession of insights, courses of action,
changed situations, and fresh insights".[148] There is
the statement of Method: " ... research tabulates
the data from the past ... communications produces
data in the present";[149] this is spelled out a bit
on a later page: "Execution generates feedback ...
policy making and planning become ongoing processes
... continuously revised".[150] Most of all, there is
the ever present input of the Spirit. And, to add
practise to statements, there is the imperious example
of Lonergan's own massive engagement with modern science,

modern philosophy, and modern scholarship, generating an equally massive feedback into his method (and, eventually, one hopes, into theology and its related disciplines). But this has not been thematized, either by Lonergan himself or, as far as I know, by anyone else; it remains at the moment a coincidental manifold. One consequence of this is that the statements and still more the practise go unnoticed, and it becomes possible for reviewers to say, no doubt quite honestly, that Lonergan's orientation is to the past, with little concern for input from present experience. Such a view would hardly be possible if the data I have indicated were thematized.

Preface

1. The intent of the preface is to give an intimation of the future communal academic heuristics towards which the spiralling of foundations through eight specialties turns subjects. See n.85 of the preface.

2. "Rakka eda ni / Kaeru to mireba / Kocho Kana". The haiku is quoted from L. van der Post, A Portrait of Japan, (photographs by Bert Glinn), William Morrow & Co., Inc., New York, 1968, 107.

3. See Lonergan, Method in Theology, Darton, Longman & Todd, London, 1972, 258-62, 273-76, 302-05; McShane, "Features of Generalized Empirical Method", Creativity and Method, ed. M. Lamb, Marquette University Press, Milwaukee, 1981, 545.

4. See Lonergan, Philosophy of God and Theology, Darton, Longman & Todd, London, 1973; "The Natural Desire to see God", Collection, Herder and Herder, New York, 1967, 84-95. I will take the liberty of abbreviating the references, particularly to Lonergan's works, as the volume proceeds.

5. "In constructing a ship or a philosophy one has to go the whole way", Lonergan, Insight, Darton, Longman & Todd, London, 1957, xiii.

6. Of six projected volumes of Florida Conference papers, two were published. Lonergan wrote replies to the first three volumes.

7. James Joyce, Ulysses, 129.

8. In particular see McShane, "An Improbable Christian Vision and the Economic Rhythms of the Second Million Years", Lonergan's Challenge to the University and the Economy, University Press of America, Washington, 1980, 92-111; "Authentic Subjectivity and International Growth: Foundations", The Shaping of the Foundations, UPA, 1976, 119-140.

9. Lonergan, De Deo Trino II, Pars Systematica, Gregorian University Press, Rome, 1964, 196-204.

Preface

10. <u>Method in Theology</u>, 93-99.

11. E. Voegelin, <u>The Ecumenic Age</u>, Luisiana State University Press, 1974, 289.

12. <u>Africa: A Subjective View</u>, Longmans and Ghana U.P., 1964, 80.

13. <u>Africa in Eclipse</u>, London, Victor Gollancz, 1971, 19.

14. <u>Ibid</u>., 299-300.

15. <u>Insight</u>, xxviii.

16. <u>Method in Theology</u>, 253.

17. <u>Insight</u>, 558-60.

18. See <u>Method in Theology</u>, 19, n.5.

19. A theoretic of call requires a transposition of western and eastern spiritualities of discernment coupled with contemporary reaches into personality dynamics.

20. Harold Bloom, <u>Yeats</u>, Oxford University Press, 1970, 5-6.

21. Quoted in Richard Ellman, <u>Yeats: The Man and the Masks</u>, Dutton, N.Y., 1948, 5.

22. Bloom, <u>op. cit</u>., 10.

23. See F. E. Crowe, <u>Method in Theology: An Organon for our Time</u>, Marquette University Press, Milwaukee, 1980.

24.

25. <u>Insight</u>, 393.

26. F. E. Crowe, "The Exigent Mind: Bernard Lonergan's Intellectualism", <u>Spirit as Inquiry</u>, Herder and Herder, N.Y., 1964, 27.

27. Lonergan, "Dimensions of Meaning", <u>Collection</u>, 267.

Preface

28. *Insight*, 468.

29. It seems to me that there is a "terror of biography" that is analogous to what Eliade calls the "terror of history" (The Myth of the Eternal Return, Routledge and Keegan Paul, London, 1955, 139-162), giving rise to "a precocious weariness, a fear of movement or spontaneity" (ibid., 155), cloaked easily in steady rhythms of some conventions of encounter, morality, recreation and research, cutting off a dialectic refinement of feelings (Method in Theology, 32-34, 66, 245). But I would add my conviction that growth into theoretic conversion is a key contemporary academic issue, in particular that theoretic conversion that can be mediated by the most elementary science, physics: I would consider this mediation to be a central message of Insight. See also notes 31, 60 below.

30. "Significant improvement in the mental health of many persons might be achieved by the provision of the optimum concentration of substances normally present in the human body". Linus Pauling, "Orthomolecular Psychiatry", Orthomolecular Psychiatry, edited by D. Hawkins and L. Pauling, W. H. Freeman & Co., San Francisco, 1973, 11.

31. A praxis of friendship requires not only a full metaxic context (see Insight, 731 n. Special categories have a context from De Deo Trino II, Pars Systematica, on the historical reality of divine missions) but refinements of general categories inclusive of odyssic differentiations and tensions of interpersonal resonances. A start might be made by thus contextualizing and complexifying Lonergan's "Finality, Love, Marriage", (Collection, 16-53).

32. Lonergan's general and special categories point towards a massive transposition of the contemporary descriptive thesis regarding "history as revelation". The immediate issue, however, is the particular fact that such realities as

Preface

> electrons and the understandings of them in these last centuries are part of history. They, like the mysteries of Christ, can lead us "ad amorem invisibilium".

33. Roland McHugh, Irish Academic Press, 1981.

34. Op. cit., 57.

35. Ibid., 59.

36. Walter Benjamin, Illuminations, edited with an introduction by Hannah Arendt, translated by Harry Zohn, New York, 1968, 258.

37. Insight, 572.

38. Verbum: Word and Idea in Aquinas, ed. D. Burrell, University of Notre Dame Press, 1967, ix.

39. Method in Theology, 88 n.34.

40. Insight, 484, 522, 571. The sting refers both to the shift in expression and to the related shift in statistics.

41. Method in Theology, 14.

42. Ibid.

43. Insight, 391.

44. Method in Theology, 260.

45. Insight, 186.

46. De Deo Trino I, 274.

47. Gaston Bachelard, The Poetics of Space, Beacon Press, Boston, 1969, 61.

48. Method in Theology, 133.

49. See McShane, The Shaping of the Foundations, 140. The transposition and differentiations of the

Preface

        task of implementation is a further complex question.

50. In Ioan., cap. 1, lect. 1.

51. John Fraser, The Chinese, Portrait of a People, Collins, Toronto, 1980, 17.

52. Insight, 647.

53. I think here of the foundations person's need of post-modern general categories of "the normality of suffering" (Eliade, op. cit., n. 29 above, 95-102) and the realities of basic sin, to contextualize the special categories of absolutely supernatural justice (De Verbo Incarnato, theses 14-17). Such general categories are needed for the transposition not only of the language to which Lawrence draws attention, but also of the languages of Christian asceticism.

54. R. Poole, Towards Deep Subjectivity, Harper Torchbooks, New York, 1972, 16.

55. Kraus and Chesterton died in the same week, at the same age, 1936. An obituary essay on Kraus by Aurel Kolnai speaks of them as "the two magicians of common sense" (quoted in "Karl Kraus and the struggle against the modern gnostics" by Bela Menczer, The Dublin Review, 1950, Vol. 224, 37).

56. Erich Heller, "Karl Kraus: Satirist in the Modern World", The Disinherited Mind, Bowes and Bowes, London, 1975, 243.

57. Karl Kraus, Die letzten Tage der Menscheit, Teil 1, 2. Deutscher Taschenbuch Verlag, Munchen, 1975. Unfortunately, little of Kraus is available in English. See the essays cited in notes 55, 56.

58. Heller, op. cit., n.56, 243.

59. Method in Theology, 99.

Preface

60. Integral presence, to self and others, is a remote possibility in this late modern period. An abundance of technical language constitutes an absence (<u>Method in Theology</u>, 73) even of professors in classrooms. The retreat from differentiation of sexual intercourse (<u>Method in Theology</u>, 58-9), a pinnacle of presence in modern media, is haunted by fragmentations and isolations of consciousness. The "series of zones from the ego or <u>moi intime</u> to the outer rind of the persona" (<u>Insight</u>, 470) are veneered by roles of spoken avoidance (see p.88 above with Lawrence's chapter as context). Jaspers' "<u>Existenz</u> encountering <u>Existenz</u>", (see n.73, chapter one) ceases to be a comprehensible topic. Integral mutual presence, biography meeting biography by speaking and listening and acting with scholarly delicacy within history, stands deeply elusive, not just in journalism or politics or theology, but even in marriage.

61. The context is <u>Method in Theology</u>, 47-52.

62. See p.16 below.

63. Peter Drucker, <u>Management</u>, Harper and Row, New York, 1974, <u>17.</u>

64. From a lecture Lonergan delivered at Hobart and Williams Colleges, October 10, 1974, entitled "Self-Transcendence: Intellectual, Moral, Religious".

65. Richard Tanner Pascale and Anthony G. Athos, <u>The Art of Japanese Management</u>, Penguin, 1983, <u>90 ff., 110 ff.</u>

66. Ibid., 202 <u>et passim.</u>

67. McShane, <u>Wealth of Self and Wealth of Nations</u>, University Press of America, Washington, <u>1978,</u> chs. 2 and 6.

68. See Lonergan, "Dialectic of Authority", <u>Boston College Studies in Philosophy</u>, Vol. 3, <u>1974,</u> <u>26-30.</u>

Preface

69. T. J. Peters and R. H. Waterman Jn., Harper and Row pb., New York, 1982, 39.

70. Ibid., 318.

71. From an unpublished typescript of Lonergan on economics. More fully, P. McShane, "Lonergan and the Actual Context of Economics", Creativity and Method, ed. M. Lamb, 557-58.

72. See notes 86, 89 and 90 of chapter one.

73. Lonergan, "Dimensions of Meaning", Collection, 256.

74. See e.g., McShane, The Shaping of the Foundations, ch. 2 on musicology's needs and Lonergan's Challenge to the University and the Economy, ch. 4, on the ferment towards functional specialization in literary studies.

75. See n. 93 of chapter one.

76. Hellmut Stoffer, "Die moderne Ansätze zu einer Logik der Denkformen", Zeit. f. phil. Forschuung 10, 1956, 442-466, 601-621. Fr. Crowe describes Lonergan's notes on logic below, 126-27.

77. Susanne Langer, Feeling and Form, Scribner, New York, 1953, index under logic, non-discoursive. Lonergan's comments are in the lectures referred to in n.93 of chapter one.

78. Collection, 1-14.

79. Insight, 576.

80. On this topic, see Judson Chambers Webb, Mechanism, Mentalism and Metamathematics, Reidel Publishing Co., Holland, 1980.

81. William Kneale and Martha Kneale, The Development of Logic, Clarendon Press, Oxford, 1978, 739.

Preface

82. F. Lawrence, "Method in Theology as Hermeneutical", *Creativity and Method*, 82.

83. *Ibid.*, 83.

84. M. Proust, *Remembrance of Times Past*, Random House, New York, Vol. 2, 1042.

85. *Ibid.*, 2, 874. I would enlarge the meaning of "memory" here beyond Proust. Enlist St. Thomas' meaning of *memoria* (see *Verbum: Word and Idea in Aquinas*, 92-94). The incarnate subject can move to remember, re-member, the *intentio entis et valoris* that subjects are and might be, can remember differentiatedly the eightfold spiral of *anamnesis* and *prolepsis*. Add the pointers of notes 29, 31, 60 above. At this stage, perhaps, the compendious meaning of the title word "presently" has been noticed. A psychological presence in history is envisaged that presents, aims, with a transposed differentiated *prudentia*, towards the movement of history in its relevation of presences and presents (see *Method in Theology*, the index, under *gift*).

86. Hermann Hesse, *Wandering*, translated by James Wright, Farrar, Straus and Giroux, New York, 1972, 89.

1. "Above the *min* and the *jen* there rises the King, distinguished as the *i jen*, the One Man ... The King ruled over all 'below Heaven', *tien-hsia*". E. Voegelin, *The Ecumenic Age*, Luisiana State University Press, 1974, 289. I was originally led to the topic by an invitation to speak at the Boston Conference of 1982, under the general title, "Mind and the Mystery of Christ".

2. James Clavell, *Tai-Pan*, Dell, New York, 1966, 194.

3. *Praxisweltanschauung*: See McShane, *Lonergan's Challenge to the University and the Economy*, University Press of America, Washington, D.C., 1980, 93 ff. Add the perspective below, 41 ff.

4. *Method in Theology*, 288-89, 352. Relevant here also is a transposition of his unpublished *De Ente Supernaturale*.

5. *Ibid.*, 292.

6. *Ibid.*, 288, 153 n.1; *Insight*, 462 ff.

7. Lonergan, "Dialectic of Authority", *Boston College Studies in Philosophy*, Vol. 3, 1974, 27.

8. F. E. Crowe, "The Exigent Mind: Bernard Lonergan's Intellectualism", *Spirit as Inquiry*, Herder and Herder, New York, 1964, 27.

9. For a survey of recent Christology see B. Cooke, "Horizons on Christology in the Seventies", *Horizons* 6, 1979, 193-227; I do not think that much of it belongs in the third stage of meaning. Relevant here is F. E. Crowe, "Christologies: how up-to-date are yours?". *Theological Studies* 29, 1968.

10. See McShane, "Features of Generalized Empirical Method and the Actual Context of Economics", *Creativity and Method*, ed. M. Lamb, Marquette University Press, 1981.

11. Mao Tse-tung, "The Relationship between China and other countries", China and the Three Worlds, ed. King C. Chen, Sharpe, New York, 1979, 365-67. My references to Mao Tse-tung are not an indication of approval of his reign. The disastrous results of his policies are well documented.

12. E. Voegelin, op. cit., n.1, 240. The discussion there relates to a potential of distortion within Pauline Theology.

13. To the view of Insight one must add the perspective reached in Lonergan's Grace and Freedom.

14. Finnegans Wake, 294, "Sarga, or The Path of outgoing". Sarga is Sanskrit for "process of world creation or emanation".

15. For a discussion of this academic care see McShane, Lonergan's Challenge to the University and the Economy, ch. 1.

16. Davies Ltd., London, 1926.

17. E. Voegelin, "Reason: The Classic Experience", Southern Review, July, 1974, 248-50.

18. Mao Tse-tung, op. cit., n.11, 306.

19. Ibid., 308.

20. See the concluding page of McShane, Wealth of Self and Wealth of Nations, University Press of America, Washington, D.C., 1981.

21. Lonergan, De Deo Trino I, II, Gregorian University Press, Rome, 1964 (and De Verbo Incarnato).

22. Cited in King C. Chen, ed., China and the Three Worlds, Sharpe, New York, 1979, 3.

23. The Ecumenic Age, Louisiana State University Press, 1974.

24. I refer not only to the great leap forward of his Latin Treatises (including De Constitutione

Christi, 1961) but his reflections on method expressed in various unpublished notes which brought him to his discovery at that period of the strategy of functional specialization. These unpublished typescripts and manuscripts are enormously rich in suggestions regarding the direction to be taken in the functional specialties of oratio recta.

25. The context is an understanding of "joss", fate or luck. See St. Thomas, Summa Theologica, Ia. q.116, and add Insight, 664; Collection, 54-67. See also the Preface ns. 32 and 53.

26. Cited in Isak Dinesen, Dageurrotypes and Other Essays, Heinemann, London, 1979, 18.

27. See E. Fromm, The Anatomy of Human Destructiveness, Faucett Crest, New York, 1973, 31.

28. E. Husserl, The Crisis of European Sciences and Transcendental Phenomenology, Northwestern University Press, 1970.

29. Conversations with Eric Voegelin, Thomas More Institute Papers, Montreal, 1976, 110.

30. The Question as Commitment, A Symposium, Thomas More Institute Papers, Montreal, 1977, 118.

31. Op. cit., n.17, 251.

32. The Ecumenic Age, 193; 195: "The strain of infantilism in the public unconscious of our time".

33. In an interview during a conference on "Merging Horizons" at York University, Toronto, November, 1978.

34. Method in Theology, 40.

35. K. Horney, The Neurotic Personality of Our Time, Norbon, New York, 1937.

36. D. Riesman, The Lonely Crowd, Yale, 1961.

37. L. van der Post, Jung and the Story of Our Time, The Hogart Press, London, 1976, 268 ff.

38. Victorino Tejera, Modes of Greek Thought, Appleton-Century-Crafts, New York, 1971, 2.

39. See n.33 above.

40. C. G. Jung, Memories, Dreams, Reflections, recorded and edited by Aniela Jaffe, trans. R. & C. Winston, Vintage Books, New York, 1965. A doctor who wished to become an analyst, who had "no problems", turned out to have a latent psychosis . "His emphatic normality reflected a personality which would not have been developed but simply shattered by a confrontation with the unconscious" (p.40).

41. Ibid., 144: "I am speaking of those who cannot tolerate the loss of myth and who can neither find a way to a merely exterior world, to a world as seen by science, nor rest satisfied with an intellectual juggling with words, which has nothing whatever to do with wisdom. These victims of the psychic dichotomy of our time are merely optional neurotics".

42. Flaubert, Bouvard and Pecuchet, trans. T. Earp and G. Stonier, New Directions, New York, 1954, 194.

43. Pound/Joyce: The Letters of Ezra Pound to James Joyce, with Pound's Essays on Joyce, Edited and with a Commentary by Forrest Read, Faber and Faber, London, 1967, 194.

44. James Joyce, Ulysses, 175.

45. J. Jacobi, The Psychology of Jung, Routledge and Kegan Poul, London, 1962, 112.

46. Lonergan, "The Subject", A Second Collection, Darton, Longman & Todd, London, 1974, 73.

47. Conversations with Eric Voegelin, Thomas More Institute Papers, Montreal, 1976, 19.

49. Fichte's Sun-Clear Statement was printed in the

English translation of A. E. Kroger, in the *Journal of Speculative Philosophy*, Vol.II, 1868.

50. What is meant by "modernity" will emerge gradually.

51. George Marek, *Beethoven, Biography of a Genius*, Kimber, London, 1970, 602.

52. See E. G. Schachter, "On Memory and Childhood Amnesia", *Psychiatry* 10, 1947, 1-26.

53. "Reason: The Classic Experience", *Southern Review*, 1974, 251.

54. Bell, London, 1965, 190.

55. Colin Trudge, *The Famine Business*, London, 1975.

56. *Verbum: Word and Idea in Aquinas*, 25-26, n.122.

57. R. Wellek, "Aesthetics and Criticism", *Philosophy of Kant and Our Modern World*, ed. C. Hendel, Liberal Arts Press, New York, 1957.

58. F. Lawrence, "Political Theology and 'The Longer Cycle of Decline'", *Lonergan Workshop*, Vol. I, ed. F. Lawrence, Scholars Press, 1978, 240.

59. A. Toynbee, *Mankind and Mother Earth*, Oxford University Press, 1976.

60. K. Jaspers, *The Origin and Goal of History*, London, 1953.

61. McShane, "An Improbable Christian Vision and the Economic Rhythms of the Second Million Years", ch.6 of *Lonergan's Challenge to the University and the Economy*, University Press of America, 1980.

62. Jaspers, *op. cit.*, ch. 1.

63. Jaspers, *op. cit.*, 97.

64. Toynbee, *op. cit.*, 178.

65. The full foundational relatively invariant heuristics (see *Insight*, 392-94) will contain a sublation of *De Constitutione Christi* into a perpsective on *De Constitutione Mundi* (see the suggestions of *Insight*, 734, 742-43). The fullness I am intimating here for foundations should give rise to probing questions regarding a future systematics. As I have suggested already (Preface, xviii), systematics may be foundationally envisaged as a genetico-dialectic understanding of understandings controlled by foundational categories in a way analogous to the manner in which a heuristic of psychic development controls the understanding of a dog from egg through puppyhood. It may be useful also to reflect on earlier comments regarding the sublation of the development of logics into a new methodological systematic understanding of systems (Preface, xx-xxi). Such a systematics represents the full transposition of the functional specialties interpretation and history.

66. E. Voegelin, *The Ecumenic Age*, 68; see also 7, 27-28, 173.

67. *Ibid.*, 192.

68. See n.134, and the related text.

69. James Joyce, *Ulysses*, 129.

70. Later we will touch on the nature of authority as distinct from naked power. The relevant text on the two times of the temporal subject is *De Deo Trino II*, 196-204.

71. "Generalized empirical method operates on a combination of both the data of sense and the data of consciousness: it does not treat of objects without taking into account the corresponding operations of the subject; it does not treat of the subject's operations without taking into account the corresponding objects", Lonergan, "Religious Experience", *Trinification of the World*, eds. T. Dunne and J.-M. Laporte, Regis College Press, 1978, 84-96.

72. On the types of genuineness cf. <u>Insight</u>, 475. The view there is ontogenetic, the present effort is towards some phylogenetic indications. Chardin's nöosphere is now related to a post-modern third stage of meaning.

73. See Jaspers' "Reply" in A. Schilpp (ed.) <u>The Philosophy of Karl Jaspers</u>, Library of Living Philosophers, New York.

74. E. Voegelin, "Reason: The Classic Experience", 240.

75. A. Eichner, <u>A Guide to Post-Keynesian Economics</u>, ed. A. Eichner, Sharpe, New York, 1979, vii.

76. N. Kaldor, "The Irrelevance of Equilibrium Economics", <u>Economic Journal</u>, 82, 1972, 1240-41.

77. Leon Walras, <u>Elements of Pure Economics</u>, trans. W. Jaffe, Irwin, Illinois, 1954.

78. See W. Jaffe, "A. N. Isnard, Progenitor of the Walrasian General Equilibrium Model", <u>History of Political Economy</u>, I, 1970.

79. J. R. Hicks, "Mr. Keynes and the 'Classics': A Suggested Interpretation", <u>Econometrica</u>, 5, 1937, 147-59.

80. W. Breit & R. Ransom, <u>The Academic Scribblers: American Economists in Collusion</u>, Holt Reinhardt and Winston, New York, 1971.

81. C. Juglar, <u>Les crises commerciales et leur retour periodique en France, en Angleterre et aux Etas Unis</u>, 1862, 1889.

82. See H. Smith, "Marx and the Trade Cycle", <u>The Review of Economic Studies</u> (iv), 1936-37, 202.

83. W. Mitchell, <u>Business Cycles: The Problem and its Setting</u>, National Bureau of Economic Research, New York, 1927.

84. J. Schumpeter, <u>Business Cycles, A Theoretical</u>,

Historical and Statistical Analysis of the Capitalist Process, 2 Vols., McGraw Hill, New York, 1939.

85. M. Kalecki, Selected Essays on the Dynamics of the Capitalist Economy, 1933-79, Cambridge University Press, 1971.

86. A. Lowe, "A Structural Model of Production", Social Research, 1952, 135-76; On Economic Knowledge, Harper & Row, New York, 1965; The Path of Economic Growth, Cambridge University Press, 1976.

87. See e.g., J. Robinson, Economic Heresies: Some Old-Fashioned Questions in Economic Theory, Basic Books, New York, 1973.

88. See the works cited in ns. 10 and 15.

89. See The Path of Economic Growth and On Economic Knowledge: the under under Control.

90. See McShane, Wealth of Self and Wealth of Nations, ch.10.

91. The title of a book by Eugen Loebl, which evolved during eleven years in a Czech prison. Random House, New York, 1976.

92. Driving a car steadily in first gear is to us manifestly not a success. Driving for profit against the rhythms of economic progress may eventually become manifest as pathological.

93. Lonergan in a lecture on art during an Institute on Education, 1959 (an edition of these lectures is in process of publication by John and James Quinn in Toronto).

94. David Lewin, "Behind the Beyond", a Response to E. T. Cone, Perspectives of New Music 7, 1969, 61.

95. Ernest Krenek, "Some Current Terms", Perspectives of New Music 4, 1966, 84.

96. A. P. Merriam, "Ethnomusicology Revisited", Ethnomusicology 13, 1969, 228.

97. A. P. Merriam, The Anthropology of Music, Northwestern University Press, 1964, 18.

98. Pierre Boulez, "Sonate, Que une veux-tu?", Perspectives of New Music (1), 1963, 32.

99. The concrete probabilities of conversations of the third stage of meaning are an underlying concern throughout the present volume. Michael Vertin's chapter specifies core chasms in methodological dialogue: "Empiricism, idealism and realism name three totally different horizons with no common identical objects" (Method in Theology, 239), and these genera invite extension and subdivision.

101. Margaret Masterman, "The Nature of a Paradigm", Criticism and the Growth of Knowledge, eds. Lakatos and Musgrave, Cambridge University Press, 1970, 61.

102. Gerald Graff, "Fear and Trembling at Yale", The American Scholar, 1977, 467.

103. P. De Man, Blindness and Insight, Oxford University Press, 1971, 39.

104. E. Auerback, Mimesis: The Representation of Reality in Western Literature, trans. W. R. Trask, Princeton University Press, 1953, 482.

106. G. Flaubert, Madame Bovary, trans. Alan Russell, Penguin Classic, 1977, 196.

107. Ibid., 103.

108. Ibid., 210.

109. Ibid., 236.

110. Ibid., 329.

111. See McShane, The Shaping of the Foundations, University Press of America, 1977, 117.

112. "Reason: The Classic Experience", 251.

113. Ibid.

114. A. Maslow, Towards a Psychology of Being, New York, 1968, 204.

115. A. R. Aresteh, Final Integration in the Adult Personality, Leiden, 1965, 18.

116. A remark of W. B. Years quoted in Richard Ellman, Yeats: The Man and the Masks, Dutton, New York, 1948, 5.

117. A slogan of the Great Leap Forward period in China: see below, at n.229.

118. James Joyce, Ulysses, 70.

119. Henry McAleavy, The Modern History of China, Prager, New York, 1968, 116.

120. Quoted in Harry Schwartz, China, Atheneum, New York, 1965, 145.

121. Lonergan, De Deo Trino II, 108.

122. McShane, The Shaping of the Foundations; also the work cited in n.15.

123. See the article cited in n.126 below.

124. Lonergan, "Finality, Love, Marriage", Collection, Darton, Longman and Todd, 1967, 21.

125. Ibid., 48.

126. McShane, "Features of Generalized Empirical Method," Method and Creativity: Studies in Honor of Bernard Lonergan, ed. M. Lamb, Marquette University Press, Milwaukee, 1981.

127. McShane, Lonergan's Challenge to the University and the Economy, 93-97.

128. A. Toynbee, Mankind and Mother Earth, 32.

129. E. Voegelin, The Ecumenic Age, 173.

130. Ibid., 272.

131. August Boeckh (1785-1867), quoted in Method in Theology, 210.

132. Method in Theology, 14.

133. The Ecumenic Age, 309.

134. Leo Strauss, Liberalism: Ancient and Modern, Basic Books, New York, 1968, 3.

135. Lonergan: see n.93.

136. Lonergan, Philosophy of God and Theology, 39.

137. W. Johnston, The Inner Eye of Love, Harper and Row, New York, 1978.

138. A book by an anonymous Carthusian, Longmans, London, 1955, 59.

139. See Susanne Langer, Feeling and Form, Scribners, 1953, ch. 12. The staggered differentiations of consciousness in history allow a contemporary presence of such a dance: see L. van der Post, The Lost World of the Kalahari, Morrow & Co., New York, 1958, 264 ff., on Bushman dancing.

140. Quoted in Herbert Read, The Art of Sculpting, Princeton University Press, 1977, 74.

141. See Lonergan, Verbum, Word and Idea in Aquinas, 147-49, 184, 188-89.

142. S. Langer, Feeling and Form, Scribners, 1953, ix.

143. Ibid., 201.

144. Quoted in Jan Murray, Dance Now, Penguin Books, 1979, 112.

145. Ibid.

146. M. Eliade, The Sacred and the Profane. The Nature

of Religion, Harper, New York, 1961, 212.

147. Marcia Siegel, Watching the Dance Go By, Houghton Mifflin, Boston, 1977, 312.

148. M. Eliade, op. cit., 212.

149. Peter Brook, The Empty Space, Penguin Books.

150. Ibid., 63.

151. Ibid., 53.

152. Ibid., 64.

153. Don McDonagh, The Rise and Fall and Rise of Modern Dance, Mentor, New York, 1970.

154. Lonergan, Donald Mather Lectures, 1975, "Sacrilization and Secularization".

155. Op. cit., n.153, 100-12.

156. HCE or Finnegan. To those of my readers who find my use of Joyce puzzling I recommend a short essay by Thornton Wilder, "Joyce and the Modern Novel", American Characteristics and Other Essays, edited by Donal Gallup, Harper and Row, New York, 1979, 172-180. His final paragraph is a relevant addition to the present context: "The terrible thing is to live in our twentieth century with nineteenth century mentality. To be "out of phase" - that's what is blighting. That's what starves and frightens and shipwrecks so many souls. The realizations of new dimensions and new obligations pour in on us from the world of science, but we would rather retreat into the accustomed and the soothing. Joyce and Pound and Eliot have advanced into the new territory; they have shown us how understanding can reduce fear. The difficulties they present to readers are the exact counterparts of the difficulties we experience in living at this time, and their triumphs are notification and guide to us as to where we may find clarification and strength", 180.

157. Patrick White, The Aunt's Story.

158. R. W. Flint (ed.) Marinetti: Selected Writings, Farrar, Straus and Giroux, New York, 1972, at Introduction, 6-7.

159. On the heuristics of such fragmentations see Insight, 193-94, 456.

160. I am thinking of Molly's speech at the end of Ulysses.

161. St. Thomas' consideration, "whether a bath cheers you up", (Ia, IIae, q.38, a.5) requires the updating of modern psychology, including the contributions of M. Eliade and G. Durand.

162. R. D. Laing discusses a successful regression of a woman to apparent pre-natality in "Metanoia: Some Experiences at Kingsley Hall, London", Going Crazy, ed. H. M. Ruitenbeek, Bantam, 1972, 11-12.

163. From T. S. Eliot, "The Dry Salvage", Four Quartets.

164. The three tensions are related to the three lunacies to be discussed shortly in relation to the problems of mysticism and atheism, aesthetics and commonsense eclecticism, power and Everyman's distress.

165. Cf. "Features of Generalized Method", where I discuss seven bridges. "The image of the Bridge and the narrow gate - suggest the idea of a dangerous passage" (Eliade, op. cit., 181). The discussion of tensions here relates to some of the bridges and enlarges on that previous reflection.

166. Insight, 653-54.

167. Ibid., 686; De Deo Trino I, Thesis 5a.

168. For the relation of this tension to the mystery of God see E. & M. Morelli, Lonergan on Being, 1981, concluding question.

169. Most recently R. Doran, Psychic Conversion and Theological Foundations, University Press Of America, 1981.

170. See McShane, Wealth of Self and Wealth of Nations, Epilogue.

171. McShane, The Shaping of the Foundations, 113, n.120.

172. Ibid., 89-94.

173. Ibid., 86.

174. Insight, 741-42.

175. E. Voegelin, "Reason: The Classic Experience".

176. E. Voegelin, The Ecumenic Age, 299.

177. Ibid., 125.

178. Ibid., 115.

179. While the dynamics of atheism are a central concern of Fr. Doran in his investigation of the psyche, there is the more evident relevance of Vertin's analysis of position and counterpositions to discussions of the corresponding dynamics of mind. Chapter nineteen of Insight was tiresomely discussed at the Florida Conference of 1970. I would say that the real issue is much earlier in in the book, and one is invited to close that issue on p.388.

180. Insight, 185.

181. Ibid., 191 ff.

182. Method in Theology, 101-03.

183. On this see Doran, "Christ and the Psyche", Trinification of the World, 139.

184. Recall Peter Brook's challenge. The specification would transpose the history of Western Drama, giving a quite novel meaning to the statement "Remove Euripides and the modern Theatre ceases to exist" (D. C. Stuart, The Development of Dramatic Art, New York, 1928, 100). Perhaps

the third stage of meaning will call forth a Yes drama to which the words of the Japanese poet might be transferred. "I always think that it would certainly be a great thing if the No drama could be properly introduced into the West. The result would be no small protest against the Western stage. It would mean a revelation", (Yone Noguchi, *The Spirit of Japanese Poetry*, London, 1914).

185. Quoted in the Introduction to Beckett in *Masters of Modern Drama*, eds. H. M. Block and R. G. Shedd, Random House, New York, 1972.

186. *Method in Theology*, 351.

187. *Ibid.*, 273.

188. *Ibid.*, 237.

189. *Insight*, 417.

190. *Ibid.*, 542.

191. *Ibid.*

192. *Ibid.*, 417.

193. *Ibid.*

194. *Ibid.*, 244.

195. Hu Shih, *Development of the Logical Method in Ancient China*, Shanghai, 1922, 69-70.

196. Lonergan, "Dialectic of Authority", *Boston College Studies in Philosophy*, Vol. 3, 1974, 7.

197. *Ibid.*

198. *Insight*, 226 ff.

199. *Ibid.*, 238, 633, 690.

200. See Lonergan, *De Intellectu et Methodo*, (unpublished notes, 1959).

201. Contexts of functional specialist discussion of this topic are indicated above at n.65.

202. Lonergan, "Theology and Praxis", Proceedings of the American Catholic Theological Association, 1977.

203. A background, in English, on the sensibilities of the Incarnate Person is found in Lonergan, "Christ as Subject", Collection.

204. Method in Theology, 351. As I have noted already (see n.65 above) the adequate systematic context is massive and remote from contemporary theology.

205. Technically, McShane; "The Hypothesis of Intelligible Emanations in God", Theological Studies, 1962: Pastorally, McShane; Music That Is Soundless, University Press of America, 1980.

206. 'Wrap', not 'constitutes'. The issue is complex: see Insight, 734; De Constitutione Christi, 1961, 51-82; De Deo Trino II, 217-22.

207. De Verbo Incarnato, 1964, 323.

208. De Deo Trino II, 234.

209. De Deo Trino II, 240-44: "Denique tandem cum ad tantum opus in toto mundo per se vel per alios efficiendum mittantur ipsae divinae personae, non brevi quodam vocabulo terminus missionum assignatur, sed maximi operis stadia successiva distinguendo", 244. Recall n.65 above.

210. De Deo Trino II, 249-59.

211. Ibid., 234.

212. De Verbo Incarnato, 324.

213. De Deo Trino I, 295.

214. On the vision of Christ and the evolution of his human knowledge see F. E. Crowe, "Eschaton in the Mind and Heart of Jesus", The Eschaton: A Community of Love, Villanova University Press, 1974.

Lonergan deals with the topic in Thesis 12 of
De Verbo Incarnato; the treatment in 1964 is
more extensive: 1961, 333-61; 1964, 332-417.

215. Mao Tse-tung, Selected Readings, Foreign Language Press, Peking, 1971, "Reform our Studies", 206-07.

216. See n.1.

217. Method in Theology, 27.

218. Ibid., 250.

219. Conversations with Eric Voegelin, 19.

220. Insight. 215.

221. I have considered R. E. Whitson, The Coming Convergence of World Religions, Newman Press, New York, 1971, in a related context in The Shaping of the Foundations, 135 ff.

222. See Mao Tse-tung, Selected Readings, 85 ff., and 432 ff.

223. Yung Ping Chen, Chinese Political Thought, Martinus Nyhoff, The Hague, 1966, 109.

224. Mao Tse-tung, Selected Readings, 109 ff.

225. Insight, 232.

226. Recall the text at n.40, p.5 above.

227. Insight, 235.

228. Mao Tse-tung, Selected Readings, 465.

229. See Joan Robinson, "China, 1963: The Communes", Collected Economic Papers, Vol. 3, Oxford, 1965, 192-206, reprinted in China in Revolution, ed. V. Simone, Fawcett, New York, 1968, 340-53.

230. Insight, 234.

231. Mao Tse-tung, Selected Readings, 308.

232. Ibid.

233. Lonergan, "Natural Right and Historical Mind-edness", conclusion. In this article Lonergan discusses the three plateaus of minding.

234. William Cobbett, Rural Rides, ed. Asa Briggs, Everyman's Library, New York, 1973 (2 vols.). Among the various biographies of Cobbett Chesterton's short William Cobbett stands out as inspired.

235. See The Economy of Cities, Vintage Books, N.Y. 1970.

236. Quoted in Isabel and David Crook, "An on-the-spot investigation of a People's Commune", China in Revolution, ed. V. Simone, Fawcett, N.Y., 1968, 362.

237. Insight, 234.

238. I would recall Insight 498, on knowledge of forms.

239. William Cobbett, Rural Rides (Vol. 2), Everyman's Library, New York, 1973, 104. I am indebted here to a Master's thesis in history by my wife Fiona: William Cobbett's Ideal England, (Dalhousie University, Halifax, 1981).

239a. James Clavell, Shogun, Dell Publications, New York, 1975, 528-29.

240. Joan Robinson, China in Revolution, 345-46.

241. Jean Chesnaux, China: The People's Republic 1949-1976, Pantheon, New York, 1979, 102-03.

242. See McShane, "Features of Generalized Empirical Method": The Bridge of Bones.

243. Hu Shih, Development of the Logical Method in Ancient China, Shanghai, 1922, 72.

244. Quoted in op. cit., n.236, 354.

245. Ibid.

246. The key issue in Doctrines is intellectual conversion. See Method in Theology, 318 "only

intellectual conversion can ...". See also McShane, "The Core Psychological Present of the Contemporary Theologian", *Trinification of the World*, eds. T. A. Dunne and J.-M. Laporte, Regis College Press, Toronto, 1978, 84-96.

247. E. Voegelin, *The Question as Commitment,* 20.

248. The itch in its full psychic openness is a central topic in ch. 2; the asking is a focus of Lawrence's attention in the conclusion of ch. 4.

249. F. E. Crowe, *The Doctrine of the Most Holy Trinity*, Regis College, 1965, 190-91.

250. *De Deo Trino II*, q.III.

251. The context is the 18th place, *Insight*, 661-63.

252. *De Deo Trino II*, 196.

253. *Insight*, 650.

254. Recall n.32 of the Preface, p.142 above.

255. F. E. Crowe, *op. cit.*, n.249, 190.

256. *Summa Theologica*, III q.8, a.3.

257. Recall n.65 above.

258. *De Deo Trino II*, *Assertum* XIV, *Assertum* XVIII.

259. *Ibid.*, *Quaestio* XXVI, *Assertum* XVIII.

260. *De Deo Trino I*, 276.

261. *Ibid.*, Thesis 5a; II, 104-07.

262. *De Deo Trino II*, 244 l. 2.

263. *De Deo Trino I*, 274.

264. *De Verbo Incarnato*, Theses 15-17.

265. Not presenting "the past as worse than it really

was", Method in Theology, 251.

266. De Constitutione Christi, 124-48.

267. De Deo Trino II, 255.

268. Ibid., 249-56.

269. Ibid., 244-48.

270. Ibid., 256 ll. 1-6.

271. I would note that a present addition to, or reach of, the functional specialty Systematics can become a relatively invariant component of foundations. See n.65 above.

272. The "messianic secret", a refrain of St. Mark.

273. De Deo Trino II, 200.

274. Ibid., 200, 202.

275. Ibid.

276. John 12, 32. In a relevant context: De Deo Trino II, 254.

277. Luke 22, 62.

278. Insight, 700.

279. Mao Tse-tung, one of 37 poems quoted in Jerome Ch-en, Mao and the Chinese Revolution, Oxford University Press, New York, 1965, 344.

1. B. Lonergan, Method in Theology, 237-44.

2. Lewis Mumford, The Transformations of Man, Harper Torchbooks, New York, 1956, 137-68.

3. On cosmological, anthropological, and soteriological self-understanding, see Eric Voegelin's Order and History, 4 volumes, Louisiana State University Press, Baton Rouge, 1956-74. The term, mechanomorphic, is Matthew Lamb's. See his History, Method and Theology, Scholars Press, 1978.

4. Robert Doran, Psychic Conversion and Theological Foundations, Scholars Press, 1981.

5. See Robert Doran, "Theological Grounds for a World-Cultural Humanity", in Creativity and Method: Essays in Honor of Bernard Lonergan, ed. Matthew Lamb, Marquette University Press, Milwaukee, 1981, 105-22.

6. Robert Doran, Subject and Psyche: Ricoeur, Jung, and the Search for Foundations, University Press of America, Washington, 1977.

7. R. Doran, "Psychic Conversion", The Thomist, 1977, 200-236.

8. R. Doran, "Subject, Psyche, and Theology's Foundations", Journal of Religion, 1977, 267-87.

9. Lonergan, Method in Theology, 30-34.

10. Ibid., 64-9.

11. Ira Progoff, The Symbolic and the Real, McGraw-Hill, New York, 1973; The Practice of Process Meditation, Dialogue House Library, New York, 1980.

12. Lonergan, Method in Theology, 241-3.

13. Ibid., 238-40.

14. Doran, Subject and Psyche, 118.

15. Lonergan, Insight, 472-9.

16. R. Doran, "Christ and the Psyche", in *Trinification of the Word*, eds. J.-M. Laporte and T. A. Dunne, Regis College Press, Toronto, 1978, 112-43.

17. C. G. Jung, *Aion: Researches into the Phenomenology of the Self*, 2nd Ed., Princeton University Press, Princeton, 1968.

18. C. G. Jung, *Memories, Dreams, Reflections*, Vintage Press, New York, 1961, 217-20.

19. B. Lonergan, *De Verbo Incarnato*, 1964, 552-93.

20. Peter Homans, *Jung in Context: Modernity and the Making of a Psychology*, University of Chicago Press, Chicago, 1979.

21. R. Doran, "The Theologian's Psyche: Notes toward a Reconstruction of Depth Psychology", *Lonergan Workshop I*, ed., Frederick Lawrence, Scholars Press, 1978, 93-141.

22. R. Doran, "Aesthetics and the Opposites", *Thought*, 1977, 117-33.

23. R. Doran, "Aesthetic Subjectivity and Generalized Empirical Method", *The Thomist*, 1979, 257-78.

24. R. Doran, "Dramatic Artistry in the Third Stage of Meaning", *Lonergan Workshop II*, ed. Frederick Lawrence, Scholars Press, 1981, 147-99.

25. R. Doran, "Metaphysics, Psychology, and Praxis", to be published in *Lonergan Workshop III*.

26. R. Doran, "Primary Process and the 'Spiritual Unconscious'", to be published in *Lonergan Workshop IV*.

27. Eric Voegelin, *The New Science of Politics*, University of Chicago Press, Chicago, 1952, 186.

28. R. Doran, "Jungian Psychology and Lonergan's Foundations: A Methodological Proposal", *Supplement to the Journal of the American Academy*

of Religion, 1979, 23-25.

29. R. Doran, "Jungian Psychology and Christian Spirituality", Review for Religious, July, 1979, 497-510; September, 1979, 742-52; November, 1979, 857-66.

30. Karl Rahner, "Thomas Aquinas on the Incomprehensibility of God", in Celebrating the Medieval Heritage: A Colloquy on the Thought of Aquinas and Bonaventure, Journal of Religion, (Supplement), 1978, ed. David Tracy, S107-S125.

31. R. Doran, "Psyche, Evil, and Grace", Communio, 1979, 192-211.

32. See n.20 above.

Vertin

1. Ph.D. dissertation, Department of Philosophy, University of Toronto, 1973.

2. My own little study, an M.A. research paper done in 1967 in the Department of Philosophy, University of Toronto, was entitled, Critical Realism: Cognitional Approach and Ontological Achievement, according to Bernard Lonergan.

3. Etudes sur la psychologie des mystiques, I, Beyaert, Bruges, 1924, and II, L'Edition Universelle, Bruxelles, 1937.

4. Le point de départ de la métaphysique: Leçons sur le developpement historique et théorique du problème de la connaissance (henceforth PD), 5 vols. The first edition of the first volume appeared as early as 1922, while a revised edition of the fifth appeared, posthumously, as late as 1949. (For the details of each volume's publication-history, se "Bibliographie du Pere J. Marechal", Melanges Joseph Marechal, I, L'Edition Universelle, Bruxelles, 1950, 47-65).

5. The first four volumes of PD provide an interpretive thematization of the history of philosophy. Marechal, proceeding in a manner not unlike that of Aristotle in the first book of his Metaphysics or Gilson in his Unity of Philosophical Experience, claims that the history of philosophy, when studied as a whole, illustrates the ultimate inevitability of the basic position-set that on independent grounds he maintains to be the correct one. The fifth volume then presents the argument for that basic position-set in more strictly systematic terms.

6. Lonergan, Method, 238. The rejection of the principle that knowing is like looking is of course one of the more prominent features of Lonergan's work in general, beginning well prior to 1972.

7. Ibid., et passim. The earliest instance that I know of where Lonergan uses the expression "intellectual conversion" is in Intelligence and Reality, the stencilled notes for lectures

at the Thomas More Institute, Montreal, 1950-51, 14, 16, 17. Cf. De methodo theologiae, the stencilled notes for lectures at the Gregorian University, Rome, 1962, 3. (Both of these sets of notes are available at the Lonergan Centre, Regis College, Toronto).

8. See e.g., Insight, chs. 9 - 10.

9. PD, V, 404.

10. PHI 352Y (1972-77), PHI 330Y (1977-78), and PHI 331Y (1979-81), at St. Michael's College in the University of Toronto.

11. Philosophy Courses, 1980-81, St. Michael's College in the University of Toronto, Toronto, 1980, 40.

12. See, e.g., Method, 20-21; et passim in Lonergan's later works

13. I think it safe to say that these courses have been very well received. They have had memberships of about 15 students, on the average, usually with delightfully diverse academic backgrounds and personal interests. Titles of some of the major second-term essays, on which a large part of the final grade depends, have been these: "Skinner and Rogers: Contrasting Foundations in the Development of Modern Psychology"; "The Nature of the Real in the Poetry of Wallace Stevens"; "Diverse Understandings of the Self-Knowledge of Jesus Christ"; "The Presentation of 'the Real' in Financial Accounting: A Cognitional Evaluation of the 'Current Value" vs. 'Historical Cost' Accounting Controversy"; "Discontinuous Knowing: Some Epistemic Notions in Quantum Mechanics"; "Methodological Presuppositions and the Concept of Form in the Novel: A Brief Comparison of Henry James, D.H. Lawrence, and Virginia Woolf"; "The Explicit and Implicit Philosophy of Sociological Theory"; "Differing Epistemological Criteria within the Canadian Labour Movement"; "Methodological Presuppositions of the Progressivist and Traditionalist Educational Movements"; "The Meaning of Ballet"; "Karl Rahner and Giles Milhaven on 'Natural

Law'"; "The Possibility of Objective News Journalism"; "Towards an Appreciation of Architecture: An Essay in Methodology"; "The Phenomenology of Humor"; "Analytic and Primal Therapy: The Methodological Underpinnings of Two Different Psychotherapeutical Approaches"; and "Television and the Knowing Subject: A Comparison of 'Sesame Street' and 'Misterrogers' Neighborhood'".

14. The papers in this group that have been published are the following: "'Immateriality', 'Self-Possession', Phenomenology, and Metaphysics", Proceedings of the American Catholic Philosophical Association, 52, 1978, 52-60; "The Doctrine of Infallibility and the Demands of Epistemology", The Thomist, 43, 1979, 637-52; and "Marechal, Lonergan, and the Phenomenology of Knowing", in Matthew Lamb, ed., Creativity and Method: Studies in Honor of Bernard Lonergan, Marquette University Press, Milwaukee, 1981, 411-22.

15. Although the present paper obviously is heavily influenced by Lonergan's writings, its primary concern is not to study them but rather to advance further, even if only minimally, along the path on which Lonergan himself originally set out. Consequently, the numerous references to those writings that I shall make in my footnotes are generally intended to illuminate my own contentions rather than to claim agreement with his. Nonetheless, I shall eventually claim that my most important contentions here are already intimated in Lonergan's writings in some way, (see pp.83-86).

16. Just as a functionally-specialized theology aims immediately at conceptually thematizing and expressing the concrete religious living that it both presupposes and ultimately is measured by, so - on my understanding - functionally-specialized operations in general aim immediately at conceptually articulating and spelling out the concrete performances (and contents) that those operations both

presuppose and ultimately are measured by. (See, e.g., Method, 135, 138-40).

17. I use the word "philosophical" in the "newer" sense wherein it refers to the structure (1) not merely of objects but also, and more fundamentally, of the conscious subject and, moreover, (2) of the conscious subject not just as intellectual but also as moral and religious. (See, e.g., Lonergan, Philosophy of God, and Theology, Darton, Longman & Todd, London, 1973, 13. Cf. Method, 337-40. Also see below, n.32).

18. See Method, 128-32, 235-93. Putting the point in slightly different terms, we may say that fourth-level functional specialties regard pure models, ideal-types that are utterly general, "upper blades" that categorially are wholly indeterminate. (Cf. Insight, 312-13, 461, 522-23, 577-78, 580-81, 586-87).

19. See Method, 128-30, 235-66. Differences may be complementary or genetic or dialectical. With complementary differences, the differing elements are mutually compatible and mutually completing. With genetic differences, the later elements subsume and transform the earlier. With dialectical differences, the differing elements are radically and unalterably incompatible. (See, e.g., Method, 236-37). Though the body of this paper stands within Dialectic, the conclusion extends into Foundations. (See pp.80-83).

20. The distinction between cognitional and decisional operations is less prominent in Lonergan's later writings than the distinctions among intellectual, moral, and religious levels of operations. (See, e.g., Method, 120-22, 316-17, 340; Philosophy of God, 38, 52-55. Cf. below n.32). In these later writings Lonergan ordinarily is more concerned to compare and contrast the entire sequence of (states and) operations on one of these levels with the entire sequence on another, and less concerned to treat in detail the

cognitional as distinct from the decisional operations on the latter two levels.

21. It remains, of course, that the phenomenology prefigures the epistemology and the metaphysics. (See, e.g., Method, 20-21; cf., 25, 83, 261, 297, 316).

22. Although I enthusiastically support the women's movement, in this particular paper I do not use such expressions as "her/his", in order to avoid further complicating a text that already has its share of neologisms and difficult constructions.

23. The sequence of steps in one's originating or genetic work and the sequence in one's pedagogical or expository work are, of course, not necessarily the same. (See, e.g., Method, 345-46). On another point, I might note that by "basic" phenomenological suppositions I mean those that set the essential lines of a phenomenological theory but do not necessarily develop it in all significant details.

24. Technically speaking, "intellectual conversion" comprises phenomenological, epistemological, and metaphysical stances. (See, e.g., Method, 238). In this paper I am expressly concerned only with the first of these components (and the varieties of its absence), the one that is fundamental. (Cf. above, n.21).

25. What is at issue here is the collectivity not of every single basic phenomenological supposition ever made but rather of the principal classes of such suppositions, classes distinguished in terms both of (1) what the suppositions regard and (2) how they regard it.

26. This claim regarding both the variety of questions and the diversity of responses to each, a claim that I say is suggested and illustrated by the study of history, is not established (or, for that matter, disestablished) by the study of history. For it is a philosophical claim, not an empirical one; and, like every philosophical claim, the

evidence to which it makes appeal is ultimately personal. (cf. pp.80-1). Note that throughout this paper I am using the word "cognitional" (and its cognates) in the sense of "elementary cognitional" and not "compound cognitional", i.e., in the sense wherein it denotes any cognitional act or content and not only the unitary syntheses of elementary cognitional acts or contents. (see Method, 12). Again, to speak of "levels" and "dimensions" is, of course, to use spatial metaphors for what is not fundamentally spatial at all.

27. My aim in choosing these particular labels for the five levels in question was to get terms that would be both (1) sufficiently narrow to focus attention on the cognitional (and not also decisional) acts (and not merely contents) that distinguish those levels and (2) sufficiently broad to avoid seeming to exclude non-Lonerganian accounts of the structures of those acts. (cf., e.g., Method, 9).

28. Derivatively, the characteristic sensory-level contents include remembered and imagined colors, sounds, odors, tastes, etc., as well. (Cf., e.g., Method, 181-206).

29. On intelligibility as subdistinguished in this way, cf., e.g., Insight, 245-50. Further subdistinctions of intelligibility, not required for the purposes of the present paper but crucial in a more detailed account, are the following: in terms of viewpoint, descriptive intelligibility and explanatory intelligibility; and in terms of realm, positive intelligibility and hermeneutic intelligibility, and, again, secular intelligibility and transcendent intelligibility. These further subdistinctions, in turn, require corresponding additional subdistinctions of factuality, value, and holiness.

30. Cf., e.g., Insight, 245-50.

31. Cf., e.g., Method, 34-38.

32. I should like to add three points, by way of amplification. First, some of Lonergan's

writings since Method in Theology, though not that book itself, provide a precedent for my speaking of a level of operations, bound up with religious experience, that is distinct from the fourth level and beyond it. (See, e.g., Philosophy of God, 38, 52-55. Cf. Method, 101-24). Second, in speaking of "holiness" as a cognitional content on this, the fifth level, I am referring not to the "content without a known object" that is religious experience itself (Philosophy of God, 38) but rather to an aspect of categorially determinate things and properties that is grasped in the light of religious experience. (See, e.g., Method, 115-17). Thirdly, the prior point manifests my understanding that religious experience, though indeed a (radically fulfilling but categorially indeterminate) content in relation to the pure structure of the subject, is a constitutive element of the augmented structure via which the subject knows (and decides with regard to) categorially determinate contents. (Cf. Method, 105-117; Philosophy of God, 38-39, 50-52).

33. Thus the characteristic contents of any given cognitional level are both (1) the intentional-dimension contents, namely, colors, sounds, odors, tastes, etc., or intelligibility, or factuality, or value, or holiness, and (2) the conscious-dimension contents, namely, the primitively self-present acts by which those respective intentional-dimension contents are made cognitionally present. Presumably these conscious-dimension contents can in turn become intentional-dimension contents of the subject's reflective cognitional acts. Again, note that by speaking of consciousness simply as "utterly primitive" cognitional self-presence I am leaving open the question of its precise structure. That is, by "consciousness" I do not necessarily mean - as Lonergan ordinarily does mean - "wholly non-reflective cognitional self-presence". (See., e.g., Insight, 320-38; Method, 7-20).

34. These terms are mine. I have found the terms that are already in common usage ("empiricist",

"rationalist", "realist", "idealist", etc.) to be multiple in their accepted phenomenological senses, laden with epistemological and/or metaphysical overtones, and insufficient in any case for my purposes; and thus I have decided, though not without a certain reluctance, to introduce my own. Again, in order to keep this paper within its assigned limits, I shall refrain throughout from referring to specific historical figures whose work clearly illustrates, in my view, certain of the basic phenomenological suppositions about cognitional intentionality and/or consciousness. (I make an exception in the case of Lonergan. See above, n.15). Nonetheless, the well-informed reader will no doubt be able to discern examples of several of these basic phenomenological suppositions as explicit or at least implicit in the writings of Plato, Aristotle, Aquinas, Hume, Kant, Hegel, etc., not to mention other important figures in the history of philosophy and other disciplines.

35. It is, of course, highly unlikely that any theorist would simultaneously make absentialist suppositions about all five levels of cognitional intentionality!

36. Note that no fewer than four different reductionist suppositions about any given level of cognitional intentionality are theoretically possible. Note also that no theorist could simultaneously make reductionist suppositions about all five levels of cognitional intentionality, save at the price of inconsistency.

37. The word "beyond" here does not necessarily have more than just phenomenological import. That is, what is phenomenologically "beyond" may, on occasion, be metaphysically "within". The point is simply that from the phenomenological standpoint the subject-as-knower is receptive, not productive, of its cognitional contents.

38. Thus, if one grants that immediacy and receptivity are paradigmatically the characteristics of visual cognition, one may express the general

form of immediate-receptionist suppositions as "knowing is looking". To give an example, I would claim that the immediate-receptionist supposition about ideational intentionality is one key phenomenological element of the basic philosophical position-set that Lonergan labels "naive realism". (See, e.g., Method, 263-65).

39. Thus one may express the general form of pure-productionist suppositions as "knowing is making". To give an example, I would claim that the pure-productionist supposition about ideational intentionality is one key phenomenological element of those basic philosophical position-sets that Lonergan labels "idealism". (See, e.g., Method, 238-39, 264-65).

40. Cf., e.g., Lonergan, Verbum: Word and Idea in Aquinas, University of Notre Dame Press, Notre Dame, 1967, ch. IV, esp., 165-68; and Collection, 160-63.

41. See above, n.37.

42. These media themselves may in turn become contents that are received, if and when the subject-as-knower engages in cognitional activity that is reflective.

43. To give an example, I would claim that the mediate-receptionist suppositions about ideational and judicative intentionality are key phenomenological elements of the basic philosophical position-set that Lonergan labels "critical realism". (See, e.g., Method, 238-40, 263-65). Note that since mediately receptive cognitional acts presuppose the contents on the prior cognitional level, a theorist cannot make the mediate-receptionist supposition about sensory intentionality.

44. See above p.72.

45. These terms are mine. (Cf. above, n.34).

46. Recall that the sense in which I use the word "consciousness" is broader than the

sense in which Lonergan customarily uses it. (See above, n.33).

47. Recall the absentialist suppositions about cognitional intentionality, above, p.73.

48. For my own stand on the relative methodical priority of cognitional intentionality and cognitional consciousness, see below, p.81-3.

49. Lonergan calls this notion of cognitional self-presence the "<u>conscientia-perceptio</u>" notion. (See <u>De constitutione Christi ontologica et psychologica</u>, Pontificia Universitas Gregoriana, Romae, 1956, 130-34. Cf. <u>Collection</u>, 175-87).

50. I would call this view, in which - with cognitional self-presence correlative with reflection - all reflection is more or less complete and all cognitional self-presence thus is more or less full, the "strong version" of the "<u>conscientia-perceptio</u>" notion of cognitional self-presence.

51. Note that unless a theorist makes explicit the particular grounds upon which it is based his absentialist supposition about a given level of cognitional consciousness implies the absence only of <u>utterly primitive</u> cognitional self-presence, not necessarily of <u>all</u> cognitional self-presence, on that level.

52. Thus, in this case and in all others as well, reductionist suppositions about cognitional consciousness are correlative with the corresponding reductionist suppositions about cognitional intentionality.

53. The scope and limits of possibility for reductionist suppositions about cognitional consciousness are the same as those for reductionist suppositions about cognitional intentionality. (See above, n.36).

54. Alternatively, I would call this view, in which - with cognitional self-presence correlative with reflection - reflection can be partial and not just more or less complete

and cognitional self-presence thus can be primitive and not just more or less full, the "weak version" of the <u>conscientia-perceptio</u>" notion of cognitional self-presence. (Cf. above, nn.49-50).

55. In Lonergan's terms advanced reflective cognitional self-presence is "self-knowledge". (See, e.g., <u>Insight</u>, 319-28; <u>Collection</u>, 224-27).

56. It is this notion of primitive cognitional self-presence that Lonergan calls the "<u>conscientia-experientia</u>" notion. (See <u>De constitutione Christi</u>, 130-34; cf. <u>Collection</u>, 175-87). In Lonergan's usual terms, primitive cognitional self-presence, conceived as non-reflective, is "consciousness". (See, e.g., <u>Insight</u>, 320-28; <u>Collection</u> 224-27; <u>Method</u>, 7-20).

57. The reader will recall that I envisage both parts of this twofold claim as philosophical rather than empirical in character, although suggested and illustrated by the study of history. (See above, n.26).

58. Except that there can be no mediate-receptionist supposition about sensory intentionality. (See above, n.43).

59. This definition makes dialectical differences among integral sets a matter of degree. Two integral sets may differ dialectically in as many as ten suppositions or as few as one.

60. For example, a theorist could not consistently make the absentialist supposition about ideational intentionality and the ideational reductionist supposition about some other level of cognitional intentionality. (Also, see above, nn.36, 43, 51, 52, 53).

61. By my reckoning, the total number of intentionally-consistent integral sets that are theoretically possible is well over a million.

62. Moreover, the number of theoretically <u>possible</u> integral sets considerably exceeds the number

of theoretically probable ones. Though not impossible, it is highly improbable, for example, that a theorist would simultaneously make the pure-productionist supposition about ideational intentionality and the mediate-receptionist supposition about judicative intentionality, or, again, the immediate-receptionist supposition about ideational consciousness and the internal-presentialist supposition about judicative consciousness.

63. This claim, seemingly presumptuous at first glance, merely reflects the nature of the enterprise that I have undertaken here. (Cf. above, nn.26, 57).

64. Cf., e.g., Insight, xviii-xix; Method, xii.

65. Recall above, n.19.

66. To the best of my knowledge, these conclusions match the conclusions to which Lonergan comes on as many of these issues as he explicitly addresses.

67. Cf., e.g., Insight, 323-24; Method, 9-10, 15-20. My terminology here in regard to the fourth and fifth levels, slightly different from that of Lonergan, reflects my effort to distinguish and internally to differentiate the cognitional processes on those levels more fully than he does. (Recall above, nn.20, 32).

68. For a fuller elaboration of this point, see Lonergan, De constitutione Christi, 130-34; Collection 175-87; and Michael Vertin, "Marechal, Lonergan, and the Phenomenology of Knowing", esp., 419-22.

69. Among other things, this implies that, as a matter of fact, the second appendix of my doctoral dissertation is methodologically more basic than the body! (Recall above, 67-68).

70. This exaggeration of the immediacy and/or receptivity of human knowing overestimates

the passivity and underestimates the spontaneity of the knowing subject.

71. This exaggeration of the constructivity of human knowing overestimates the spontaneity and underestimates the passivity of the knowing subject.

72. Such an advance-commitment not only would have undermined the philosophical (and thus ultimately personal) character of my work, but it would even have contravened Lonergan's own frequent advice against substituting "fidelity to the Lonergan school" for personal effort. I am reminded, in this connection, of his parting remark to those attending the Lonergan Workshop at Boston College in 1974: "Good-bye, and be good non-disciples!".

73. The references to Lonergan's writings that I have made in the footnotes of this paper provide some indication of the texts to which I would make appeal. (Cf. above, n.15).

74. See, e.g., Method, 21, 249; cf. Insight, 387-89.

75. Lonergan in his writings clearly envisages cognitional acts as possessing a distinct conscious as well as an intentional dimension, and as going forward on four or even five distinct levels. He cannot but presuppose that the correct structural account of these two dimensions and five levels first recognizes their occurrence and distinction. And he regularly argues that achieving the correct structural account comes about through displacing mistaken ones. (See, e.g., Insight, 271-78, 319-28, et passim; and Method, 6-25, et passim. Also see above, n.32). Nonetheless, when speaking explicitly of "intellectual conversion" and the "positional" cognitional phenomenology that expresses its fundamental component, Lonergan ordinarily does not expressly mention knowledge of the conscious as distinct from the intentional dimension of one's knowing, or knowledge of its fourth and fifth as distinct

from its first three levels. He does not expressly distinguish one's recognition of the occurrence and distinction of the dimensions and levels from one's recognition of their structure. And in seeking to articulate the general form of mistaken structural accounts, he highlights the "ocular" myth, which I would argue to be the more important but not unique general form, while he does not note the "volitional" myth, which I would argue to be a distinct though less important general form. (See, e.g., Method, 238-43, 249-53. Also see above n.20).

76. What I have said about Lonergan's remarks on "intellectual conversion", I would apply - mutatis mutandis - to this remarks on the variety of its absence. (See above, n.75).

77. I must indicate at this point my recognition and acceptance of Lonergan's claim that one's affective states have a certain causal influence upon one's cognitional (and, a fortiori, decisional) acts. (See, e.g., Method, 37-40, 115-19, 240-43, 289). I would also accept this claim's implication that an essential part of a fully adequate phenomenology of knowing is a phenomenology of affectivity, something from which I have prescinded in the present paper. Finally, I underline for the reader an implication of the claim that human cognition goes forward on five levels, namely, that to know any thing or property fully is to grasp not just its sensible or conscious features, intelligibility, and factuality, but also its value and holiness.

78. Then, with a great gain in clarity and precision, "cognitional" conversion could be subdistinguished into its ten moments: "sensible-intentional" and "sensible-conscious", ideational-intentional" and "ideational-conscious", "judicative-intentional" and "judicative-conscious", "evaluative-intentional", and "evaluative conscious", and "fiducial-intentional" and fiducial-conscious".

1. Lonergan, *An Essay in Circulation Analysis*, unpublished typescript, 65.

2. *Method in Theology*, 48.

3. Lonergan, "Finality, Love, Marriage", in *Collection*, Darton, Longman, Todd, London, 1967, 38.

4. *Ibid.*, 24.

5. *Ibid.*, 38-39.

6. "The Role of a Catholic University in the Modern World", *ibid.*, 115.

7. "Dimensions of Meaning", *ibid.*, 262.

8. *Ibid.*, 263.

9. *Ibid.*, 263.

10. *Ibid.*, 261.

11. The hypothesis of the "three waves of modernity" comes from Leo Strauss. In my eight years of teaching Perspectives in Western Culture and New Horizons of the Social Sciences, year-long courses which cover many of the key texts in political science, law, economics, sociology of the period under question (16th to 20th centuries), I have come across no evidence whatsoever that would make Strauss's interpretation controversial. See Lawrence, "Political Theology and 'the Longer Cycle of Decline'", *Lonergan Workshop I*, Scholars' Press, 223-255; "The Horizon of Political Theology", *Trinification of the World: A Festschrift in Honor of Frederick E. Crowe*. Eds. T. A. Dunne & J.-M. Laporte, Regis College, Toronto, 46-71: both published 1978.

12. A. Bloom, "Commerce and 'Culture'", *This World* 2, 1983, 5-20.

13. "Finality, Love, Marriage", *Collection*, 39.

14. A. Bloom, op. cit., 5-6
15. "Finality, Love, Marriage", Collection, 38.
16. Method in Theology, 50.
17. "Existenz and Aggiornamento", Collection, 249.
18. Method in Theology, 50.
19. Ibid., 155.
20. Ibid., 224.
21. Acts 28:26. This is neither to deny nor to underplay the importance of doing with Lonergan what Lonergan did with Thomas Aquinas, or indeed of doing with any other authors what he did. I am simply underscoring what I now feel may be a sine qua non (as well as perhaps the ass's bridge) for doing this with Lonergan.
22. Frederick E. Crowe, "Lonergan's Early Use of Analogy", Method. Journal in Lonergan Studies I, 1983, 41.
23. In the spelling out of J. B. Metz' ideas about the narrative appropriation of the dangerous memory of Jesus Christ, who suffered, died, rose again, I have been greatly helped by the work of Rowan Williams. This strikes me as a pastoral articulation of the point of Lonergan's systematic theses on the redemption in De Verbo Incarnato.
24. Lonergan, "Mission and Spirit", Experience of the Spirit, eds. P. Huizing, W. Bassett, Seabury, New York, 1974/76, 77.
25. Ibid., 34.
26. "Reality, Myth, Symbol, Boston University Studies in Philosophy & Religion I, 1980, 33.
27. Ibid., 34.
28. "Mission and Spirit", op. cit., 77.
29. Ibid., 77.
30. See McShane, Music This Is Soundless: An Introduction to God for the Graduate, University Press of America, 1977, 1-2.

1. Gratia Operans: A Study of the Speculative Development in the Writings of St. Thomas Aquinas, Gregorian University, Rome, 1940, 338 pages. Breakdown in communications with Rome prevented the award of the doctorate until the academic year 1946-47.

2. "St. Thomas' Thought on Gratia Operans", Theological Studies 2, 1941, 289-324; 3, 1942, 69-88, 375-402, 533-578. The book form: Grace and Freedom. Operative Grace in the Thought of St. Thomas Aquinas, ed. J. Patout Burns, Darton, Longman & Todd, London, and Herder and Herder, New York, 1971. My references will be to the book.

3. David Tracy, The Achievement of Bernard Lonergan, Herder and Herder, New York, 1970, 39-44.

4. On this continent, at Regis College, Toronto; Concordia University, Montreal; University of Santa Clara, Santa Clara. Overseas, at Dublin, Naples, Manila, Sydney and Melbourne. There are 47 introductory pages, divided as follows: Preface, 1-2; Introduction, 2-9; "The Form of the Development" (ch.1), 10-47. But it has become customary to refer to the whole as the Introduction. My references will be to the pages of the typescript.

5. Gratia Operans, 1940, 10. Hence, the title of ch.1, "The Form of the Development" - clarified also by contrast with the title of ch.2, "The Data of Inquiry".

6. Ibid., 6

7. Ibid., 32

8. "The Form of Inference", first published in Thought 18, 1943, 277-292; then as ch.1 in Collection: Papers by Bernard Lonergan, S.J., ed. Frederick E. Crowe, Herder and Herder, New York, 1967, 1-15. My references will be to Collection.

9. Ibid., 14.

10. Ibid., 15.

11. Ibid., 15. In "Finality, Love, Marriage", Theological Studies 4, 1943, 477-510, published the same year therefore as "The Form of Inference", there is a long paragraph discussing and applying various types of implication; see Collection, 28, n.34.

12. Bernard J. F. Lonergan, Method in Theology, Darton, Longman & Todd, London, and Herder and Herder, New York, 1972, 292.

13. Ibid., 242.

14. Ibid., 338. See also Lonergan's Philosophy of God, and Theology, Darton, Longman & Todd, London, and Westminister, Philadelphia, 1973, 12: " ... proof ... presupposes the erection of a system ... but the system itself ... has its presuppositions. It presupposes a horizon".

15. "The Form of Inference, Collection, 15.

16. In "The Assumption and Theology", 76, n.17 (see n.48 infra): "it is not an implication as such but the affirmation of an implication that is true or false, certain or probable".

17. "The Concept of Verbum in the Writings of St. Thomas Aquinas", Theological Studies 7, 1946, 349-392; 8, 1947, 35-79, 404-444; 10, 1949, 3-40, 359-393. The articles were published in book form, with an Introduction added by Lonergan, some twenty years later: Verbum. Word and Idea in Aquinas, ed. D. B. Burrell, University of Notre Dame Press, Notre Dame, 1967. My references will be to the book.

18. Verbum. Word and Idea in Aquinas, 215.

19. Ibid., 34.

20. Ibid., 47-95.

21. Ibid., 48.
22. Ibid., 59.
23. Ibid., 60.
24. Ibid., 6.
25. Ibid., 60.
26. Ibid., 64-65.
27. Ibid., 65.
28. Ibid., 56, 67, 70.
29. Ibid., 66-75.
30. Ibid., 68.
31. Ibid., 74.
32. Ibid., 75.
33. Ibid., 75. More on the relation of ontology and epistemology, ibid., 87. See also "Insight: Preface to a Discussion", Collection, 160, on ontological cause and cognitional reason (this was a paper read to The American Catholic Philosophical Association at its 1958 meeting).
34. Verbum: Word and Idea in Aquinas, 75-88.
35. Ibid., 80.
36. Ibid., 80.
37. Ibid., 79, 83.
38. Ibid., 83.
39. Ibid., 85.
40. Ibid., 74.
41. Ibid., 7.

42. Ibid., 87.

43. Ibid., 88.

44. Ibid., 88.

45. Insight: A Study of Human Understanding, Longmans, Green & Co., London and Philosophical Library, New York, 1957, 370.

46. See n.143 infra. A point to be kept in mind, in relation to Lonergan's continual insistence on human development, is the slow growth of wisdom; see, for example, "The Natural Desire to See God", Collection, 89: "wisdom is the cumulative product of a long series of acts of understanding" (this was a paper read to The Jesuit Philosophical Association at its 1949 meeting).

47. See Collection, 85.

48. "The Assumption and Theology", first published in Vers le dogme de L'Assomption, Fides, Montreal, 1948, 411-424; then as ch.4 in Collection, 68-83. My references will be to Collection.

49. Collection, 76.

50. Ibid., 72.

51. Ibid., 73.

52. Ibid., 75.

53. Ibid., 82.

54. First published in The Modern Schoolman 27, 1949-50, 124-38, and then as ch.6 in Collection, 96-113; my references are to the latter.

55. Collection, 97.

56. Ibid., 97.

57. Ibid., 108.

58. Ibid., 111.

59. Ibid., 107.

60. "Syllogism ... is ... an instrument for exhibiting the grounds of a judgment on the conclusion", quoted

61. The published form of 1957 differs from the typescript of 1953 mainly in having a new Preface and revisions to the mathematical and scientific examples of the first five chapters. The 1953 typescript is available at some of the Lonergan Centers of Research (n.4, supra).

62. *Insight*, 399-400.

63. Ibid., 672. Lonergan does not, in "The Form of Inference", use the term, syllogism, for arguments of the form, "If A, then B; but A; therefore B". Nor does he do so, as far as I know, in *Insight*.

64. *Insight*, xvii.

65. Ibid., xvii.

66. Ibid., 253. Robert M. Doran, *Psychic Conversion and Theological Foundations*, Scholars Press, 1981, 59, refers to "what *Insight* calls the polymorphism of human consciousness and identifies as the root of the foundational dilemma".

67. *Insight*, xxviii.

68. Ibid., 279.

69. Ibid., 281.

70. Ibid., 284.

71. Ibid., 285.

72. Ibid., 285-87.

73. Ibid., 286-87.

74. Ibid., 284.

75. Ibid., 285.

76. Ibid., 549. In the notes on Mathematical Logic (n.27, infra) Lonergan tells us: "The criterion of truth is analyzed ... in 'Insight', Chap. X as a virtually unconditioned", III/2.

77. Insight, 329-32.

78. Ibid., 329.

79. Ibid., 332.

80. The rest of ch.11 speaks passim of this foundation as not subject to revision (see especially Section 7, "Description and Explanation", 332-35, and Section 8, "The Impossibility of Revision", 335-36). Section 6 would stand to these Sections as the reflection that appropriates foundations does to the reflection that appropriates the security of the foundations.

81. Compare, s.v., Subject, the Index of Insight with that of Understanding and Being: An Introduction and Companion to Insight, eds. Elizabeth A. Morelli and Mark D. Morelli, The Edwin Mellen Press, New York and Toronto, 1980. Though the latter book edits lectures of 1958, covers the same ground as Insight, and is less than half the size, the references to the subject in its Index are far more numerous. I recall a remark of Philip McShane, when he had worked on the Index to Method, to the effect that an index reveals mercilessly the horizons of the indexer.

82. Insight, 550.

83. Ibid., 551.

84. Ibid., xxix.

85. Ibid., 181.

86. Ibid., 293.

87. Ibid., 396.

88. Ibid., 397.

89. Ibid., 407.

90. De methodo theologiae was a course given at the Gregorian University in the spring of 1962; a good part of it is available, in notes taken by students (60 pages, legal-size), at the various Lonergan Centers; the same ground was covered in an Institute on the Method of Theology, in the summer of 1962 at Regis College, Toronto. - For my little history of "wisdom" I refer the reader again to n.143 infra.

91. Insight, 332.

92. Ibid., 551.

93. R. Doran, op. cit., (supra n.66) remarks, 214, n.33 (to his ch. 2): "In Insight, Lonergan does not use the term, foundations, in this context [that of chs. 11-13], but refers to cognitional theory as the basis for metaphysics, ethics, and theology". On the matter of revisions of Insight, users of the first edition may have noticed that line 24, page 341, should have "inflexibility" rather than "flexibility" for the Kantian categories.

94. A sheaf of 22 pages is available at the various Lonergan Centers, under the title, "Mathematical Logic. Notes for Lectures at Boston College, July, 1957". They are numbered by lectures; thus "III/2 means page 2 of lecture 3. For some help in relating mathematicians' interests to those of Insight, see Philip McShane, "The Foundations of Mathematics", ch. 2 of Lonergan's Challenge to the University and the Economy. Understanding and Being (n.24 supra) has some remarks on the foundations of science, 235-238.

95. III/2.

96. III/3. On the meaning of "provisional" here, see Insight, 306-07.

97. IV/5.

98. V/1.

99. V/1.

100. Available at the various Lonergan Centers under the title, "Existentialism. Notes on Lectures at Boston College, July, 1957". But there have been different "editions"; for my references I use that of the Thomas More Institute, Montreal, 1957, but I have numbered the pages consecutively (1-28).

101. "Existentialism. Notes on Lectures at Boston College, July, 1957", 27.

102. Ibid., 20.

103. Ibid., 28.

104. See The New Scholasticism 32, 1958, 97.

105. First published in Gregorianum 35, 1954, 630-48, and then as ch.8, 121-41, in Collection; my references are to the latter.

106. Collection, 125.

107. Ibid., 131.

108. Ibid., 135.

109. Ibid., 135.

110. Ibid., 137.

111. Ibid., 139.

112. Ibid., 141.

113. There are 72 pages of notes, legal-size and single-spaced, available again at the Lonergan Centres. According to my sources, our chief benefactors are Francesco Rossi de Gasperis and P. Joseph Cahill, both students of the course.

114. *De intellectu et methodo*, 1-25.

115. *Ibid.*, 11-25.

116. *Ibid.*, 1.

117. *Ibid.*, 1-4.

118. *Ibid.*, 4-5.

119. *Ibid.*, 5-8.

120. *Ibid.*, 8-10.

121. *Ibid.*, 10-11.

122. As reported in the notes, Lonergan uses both "separatio" and "chasma/chaos" (this in reference to Luke 16:26) where I translate "estrangement". In the lectures of 1957 on Existentialism he spoke of the "existential gap" between one's horizon on oneself and what one really is (p.22 of the notes). The context is different but the idea of gap is the same. For our context, see the statement of *Method*, 276: "Scholarship builds an impenetrable wall between systematic theology and its historical religious sources".

123. *De intellectu et methodo*, 16.

124. *Ibid.*, 11-16.

125. *Ibid.*, 16-25.

126. *Ibid.*, 11-12. There is an extremely interesting account of the way the same truth may be understood in greater or less degree, in *Divinarum personarum conceptio analogica*, Gregorian University Press, Rome, 1957, 17-19, where Lonergan takes us through four stages of understanding scripture. I have to omit that account here, but it cannot be stated too emphatically that his whole search for foundations was conducted in a continual engagement with actual theology, in this case, the theology of the Trinity.

127. *De intellectu et methodo*, 12-14.

128. *Ibid.*, 14-16.

129. *Ibid.*, 12.

130. *Ibid.*, 17-18.

131. *Ibid.*, 17. Lonergan's students will recall his affection for the Thomist phrase, "<u>sapientis est ordinare</u>".

132. *Ibid.*, 18-20.

133. *Ibid.*, 20.

134. On which see "Theology and Understanding", <u>Collection</u>, 127-130, and <u>Divinarum personarum conceptio analogica</u>, 20-28.

135. *De intellectu et methodo*, 22-24.

136. *Ibid.*, 24-25.

137. *Ibid.*, 26-72.

138. See ibid., 40-43, 50-52, on the precept "<u>Intelligere systematice</u>".

139. *Ibid.*, 63.

140. *Ibid.*, 54.

141. *Ibid.*, 55 ff.

142. On the question of foundations, a distinct stage is marked by the lecture of 1967, "Theology in Its New Context". It was first published in <u>Theology of Renewal</u>, v.I, ed. L. K. Shook, Herder and Herder; New York, Montreal, Palm, 1968, 34-46. It is included in <u>A Second Collection: Papers by Bernard J. F. Lonergan, S.J.</u>, eds. William J.F. Ryan and B.J. Tyrrell, Darton, Longman & Todd, London, 1974; Westminster, Philadelphia, 1975, 55-67.

143. There is no reference to wisdom in the Index to A Second Collection. There is one in Philosophy of God and Theology, and it is to wisdom as Heraclitus saw it. There is one in Method, and it is to the wisdom literature of the Bible. The traditional use of the word returns however, in "Christology Today: Methodological Reflections", Le Christ Hier, Aujourd'hui et Demain, eds. Raymond Laflamme and Michel Gervais, Les Presses de l'Universite Laval, Quebec, 1976, 45-65; see 49: "Sound judgment ... has to move us to the comprehensive reasonableness named wisdom". But to trace this history would really be to write the second part of this article, the later stages of Lonergan's search for foundations; if I cannot do that now, perhaps I may mention two ideas to investigate on the way; dialectic is obviously one, and the other is involved in dialectic: it is the role of community, for, as Lonergan keeps saying, science is no longer a "habit" in someone's mind, it is in the keeping of the community - and so in its own way is wisdom.

144. Method in Theology, 254,

145. Insight, xxix.

146. The similarity here of Insight and Method suggests the possibility of a fruitful analogy of the idea of the "self-justifying". There is self-justifying knowledge (Insight), self-justifying love (Method), and one may add the "self-justifying joy" of the artistic experience (Insight, 184-85); this last needs its own investigation which I have not been able to undertake.

147. Insight, 205; and see the Index, s.v., Coincidental m.

148. Ibid., 223.

149. Method in Theology, 135.

150. Ibid., 366.